The Dark Mirror

The Dark Mirror

Psychiatry and Film Noir

Marlisa Santos

LEXINGTON BOOKS
A division of
ROWMAN & LITTLEFIELD PUBLISHERS, INC.
Lanham • Boulder • New York • Toronto • Plymouth, UK

Published by Lexington Books
A division of Rowman & Littlefield Publishers, Inc.
A wholly owned subsidiary of The Rowman & Littlefield Publishing Group, Inc.
4501 Forbes Boulevard, Suite 200, Lanham, Maryland 20706
http://www.lexingtonbooks.com

Estover Road, Plymouth PL6 7PY, United Kingdom

British Library Cataloguing in Publication Information Available

Library of Congress Cataloging-in-Publication Data

Santos, Marlisa, 1970–
The dark mirror : psychiatry and film noir / Marlisa Santos.
p. cm.
Includes bibliographical references and index.
ISBN 978-0-7391-3665-2 (cloth : alk. paper)
1. Film noir—History and criticism. 2. Psychiatry in motion pictures. 3. Mental illness in motion pictures. I. Title.
PN1995.9.F54S36 2010
791.43'6561—dc22 2010014179

The paper used in this publication meets the minimum requirements of American National Standard for Information Sciences—Permanence of Paper for Printed Library Materials, ANSI/NISO Z39.48-1992.

Printed in the United States of America

To Randy

&

To my mother

Neither is afraid of the dark.

Contents

Acknowledgments

Writers know that a book takes on a life of its own, spreading its Medusa tentacles far and wide. Here are some people whose lives and efforts have touched this book.

First thanks go to "Dark Marc" Dolezal (www.noirfilm.com), certainly for providing an outlet and support for aficionados and fans of *film noir*, but also for providing access, through his "Danger and Despair Knitting Circle," to obscure *noir* films seminal to this book that I might never have otherwise seen.

Much sincere appreciation goes to Dr. Don Rosenblum, dean of the Farquhar College of Arts and Sciences at Nova Southeastern University. He has been consistently supportive of my research efforts and specifically supportive of this project as I juggled various work responsibilities. Many thanks also go to Division of Humanities staff (Dotty Hayes, Denia Fonseca, and especially Santa Alimonte) and colleagues (Andrea Shaw and Shanti Bruce) for their encouragement and support.

The assistance of Dorinda Hartmann, of the Wisconsin Center for Film and Theater Research, was instrumental in securing the images for the book, as was the help of Buddy and Ron from Photofest. I am also indebted to James Yanchak, for his typesetting, and to Rick Beardsley for his generosity in sparing James for this assistance.

Finally, and most importantly, I must thank my family (my mother, Myrna Santos, and my brother, Radleigh Santos) for their love and encouragement. And to my husband, Randy Burling, for innumerable large and small acts of aid, kindness, and devotion throughout the years of this process. Like me, he has thrived on a steady diet of *noir*, even as it has been recycled into leftovers and snacks. Without him, this book would not have been possible.

Introduction

Spellbound, Psychoanalysis, and *Noir*

"Have you ever been psychoanalyzed?"—Dr. Lilith Ritter
"I saw one in a murder movie once."—Stan Carlisle

—*Nightmare Alley* (1947)

Discussing the role of psychological themes and motifs in *film noir* seems almost too obvious. Indeed, it is hard to stumble across a *noir* that does not deal with issues of introspection, alienation, internal conflict, and tortured impulses. But one begins to wonder, when viewing the catalogue of the *noir* series, why *noir* is peppered with offhand remarks, if not overt plots, that deal explicitly with psychiatry or psychoanalysis. For instance, we can easily recall the following remark in *Gilda* (1946) by Gilda (Rita Hayworth) to Johnny Farrell (Glenn Ford): "Any psychiatrist would tell you that your thought associations are very revealing." Or in *This Gun for Hire* (1942), when Raven (Alan Ladd) comments, "Every night I dream. I read somewhere about a . . . about a kind of doctor. A psych-something. You tell your dream, you don't have to dream it anymore."

The subject matter of these films is not psychoanalysis, but the language of psychiatry permeates the storylines of these and countless other *noirs* in subtle ways. Beyond the subtexts of psychoanalysis that surface in the narratives of *noir*, it is striking to notice how many actual plots of *noir* center around psychiatrists, psychoanalysis, asylums, and insanity. It is no accident that the onset of *noir* in the U.S. roughly coincides with the popularization of psychoanalysis in American culture; this popularization suits the *noir* atmosphere, especially in the contradictory, yet thrilling nature of psychoanalysis: the ability of a "science of the mind" to eliminate the mysteries of the human psyche and the simultaneous nature of this science to expose the depths of unknowability of the human psyche. I would argue that this ultimate contradiction turns out to be the driving force of the elusive *noir* sensibility.

Though *The Interpretation of Dreams* was first published in 1899, psychoanalysis was not even popular in the early part of the twentieth century in Europe, let alone in the United States. In 1911-1912, the membership roll of the Vienna Psychoanalytic Society was only 34, and that was the largest membership in the world; eight years later, in 1920, only ten people attended the annual meeting of the fledgling American Psychoanalytic Society in New York.[1] However, this was soon about to change. The years following both world wars would have a profound effect on the public interest in psychoanalysis. According to Reuben Fine, the popularity was easy to understand: "Unlike the academic psychologies, here was a psychology that did have something to say about the breakthrough of mankind's most primitive and irrational urges, which had just caused such havoc in the civilized world."[2] The years leading up to and following World War II were particularly crucial to the popularization of psychoanalysis in the U.S., as a great number of European psychoanalysts fled fascism and Nazism as American émigrés. And the second World War also popularized psychoanalysis because of the use that war physicians made of psychoanalytic techniques to treat combat neuroses. Indeed, this was not an effect lost on the general populace, as is evidenced by the following from a 1947 *Life* magazine article on psychoanalysis: "In part [the demand for psychiatrists] reflects the alarming prevalence of mental and emotional disorders in the population today; in part, it merely reflects the increase in popular knowledge and acceptance of psychiatry, and especially psychoanalysis, as a cure. During the war millions of service personnel had direct contact with psychiatry for the first time and large numbers of them received more or less elaborate psychiatric treatment."[3] Such popularized interpretations of psychoanalysis in newspapers and magazines of the 1940s show varying degrees of accuracy in their representation, but it is clear that in some form, psychoanalysis and the prevalence of mental illness was becoming more and more culturally recognizable by larger groups of American people.

It is during this period of the growing popularity of psychoanalysis in American culture, combined with the second World War and its aftermath, that *film noir* is born. The war and the popularity of psychoanalysis provide its parentage. Consider the following questions posed by Keith Sward, a psychiatrist who wrote an article for *The Screen Writer* in 1948: "[W]hy are so many of the 'psychiatrics' straight murder thrillers? (*Shock, Spellbound, The Locket, Rage in Heaven, Dark Mirror, Possessed, Fear in the*

Night, and *Secret Beyond the Door.*) Is Hollywood cashing in on a current fashion in the pulp field?. . . As the pulp writers have been handling their material for some time, detectives have become psychologically minded; the brain has been displacing the gun."[4] It is worth noting that all the films Sward lists are now considered *noirs*, though at the time, they were still seen as "straight murder thrillers." *Film noir* bears much resemblance to earlier crime dramas and police procedurals, but its mood, devices, and outcomes clearly took a new and darker turn. The characteristic about *films noir* that transcends some of the less universal features, such as black-and-white photography with moody lighting, crime in plots, and non-linear narrative devices, is the mood of cynicism and despair that permeates all films in the *noir* cycle. Arthur Lyons rightly points out that the thematic thread that unites all *noirs* is "that the universe of the protagonist, either internal or external, is out of control."[5] The chaotic war and post-war mood in America merge with the psychoanalytic boom to produce the curious and disturbing result of *noir* in film. According to J.P. Telotte, the lack of geographical scars of the war on the American landscape forced an imaginative compensation that borrows from newsreel and documentary footage, leaving *noir* to emphasize "that those stark images were part of our own, not some distant, foreign culture, and repressing them, returning them to the depths where we might have preferred they remain, or simply containing them within the bounds of conventional generic narrative would be more difficult than vanquishing some foreign enemy."[6] It is these depths that are so strikingly probed in *noir,* depths that mirror the post-war collective unconscious. The idea of a precarious containment of dark and destructive impulses, and thus, a certain cynicism, is a common *noir* thread, and is also at the heart of psychoanalysis. Even Borde and Chaumeton, in the earliest study of *noir*, note that "there's a certain cynicism in the views of Freud that accords well with the moral décor of the series. Psychiatry no longer believes in traditionally defined good or evil. It knows that criminal behavior patterns often hide self-destructive reactions or guilt complexes, while moral conscience (the superego) is linked to the instincts it represses by means of an entire network of complicity."[7] The very philosophies at the heart of psychoanalysis, then, are also at the very heart of *noir*: human motivations and behavior tend to shades of gray, not black and white, and while it is worth pursuing their sources, such pursuit can be dangerous or even futile.[8]

This is not to say that the impact of psychoanalysis on film began with *noir*. Indeed, the birth of film itself coincides with the birth of psychoanalysis, and the two are linked throughout their histories.[9] But after 1939, according to Borde and Chaumeton, numerous Hollywood producers' names were found on the subscriber list of *The Psychological*

Review and the general popularity of psychoanalysis found a ready home in Hollywood.[10] I would argue that the onset of film *noir* is one of the most direct by-products of this popularity and conveys the fascination with psychoanalysis in a way that not only displays, but also internalizes it. The most basic ideas of psychoanalysis, those that deal with the subconscious mind, for instance, provide the very foundation of not just the plot, but the very ethos of *noir*. Narrative structures and devices of *noir* construct its cinematic universe as full of uncertainty and doubt; character struggles reflect this unstable universe, and the lack of plot resolution in many *noir*s leaves a final emphasis to the viewer in this regard. Thus the elusiveness of meaning in *noir* almost makes the films themselves, if seen as living, breathing creatures, as less than sane, if reason and orderliness of mind make one sane. Patrick Fuery theorizes likewise, as he describes the viewer's relationship to a filmic text that resists interpretation: "The sense, and presence, of resistance is one of the fundamental aspects of psychoanalysis; for Freud it was part of the very constitution and operation of the unconscious. Resistance is what enables the unconscious to exist, and what makes psychoanalysis necessary. By its very existence the unconscious resists meaning and interpretation, almost as if this was part of its primary function."[11] *Film noir* texts resist meaning, in both their construction and interpretation, and thus become "mad" minds that need to be healed. But of course, such healing is not possible, and viewers are drawn into the madness only to feel more unstable—or perhaps to feel that the instability they feel in the upheaval of their daily lives is more "normal" than they might have thought. Thus, as Richard Maltby argues, "the telling of the story is a form of psychotherapy, and the place of the analyst is taken not only by a character in the story but also by the audience."[12] *Noir* characters also bear this theory out—for instance, that of the *noir* detective, which often manifest themselves as psychiatrists in various films. By this kind of interpretation, the ubiquitous detectives—usually seedy ones—in *noir* can conversely be seen as psychiatrists, as they chase down meanings in dark and dangerous places, acting for the benefit of others while risking harm to themselves.

Probing the complex relationship between *noir* and psychoanalysis reveals several manifestations in the films. The subsequent chapters broadly define the more obvious of these manifestations, beginning with one of the most easily noticed: the *noir* psychiatrists. Here the myriad depictions of the psychiatrist figure in *noir* are discussed—some nefarious, as in such films as *Strange Illusion* (1945, Edgar Ulmer), *Nightmare Alley* (1947, Edmund Goulding), and *I, the Jury* (1953, Harry Essex); some helpful, as in such films as *The Dark Past* (1948, Rudolph Maté), *The Sleeping Tiger* (1954, Joseph Losey), and *Shadow on the Wall* (1950,

Pat Jackson); and even some as impersonators, as in *Hollow Triumph* (1948, Steve Sekely). The way that female psychiatrists are depicted is unique with respect to the general assumptions about female characters and femmes fatales in *noir*. The second chapter moves beyond the figure of the doctor to the depiction of the types of psychiatric treatments in *noir*. The two main sub-categories of this chapter are the use of hypnotism, with or without drug therapy (often called narcosynthesis), and the depiction of asylums or mental sanitariums. The former is well-represented in such films as *Possessed* (1947, Curtis Bernhardt) and *Nightmare* (1956, Maxwell Shane), while the latter shows itself in such films as *Behind Locked Doors* (1948, Budd Boetticher) and *The Snake Pit* (1948, Anatole Litvak). An important theme studied in this chapter is the idea of hypnotism and/or sodium pentothal causing a loss of control in the individual—that post-war "medical advances" to further the treatment of mental illness may actually have more to be feared from than the disease.

The third chapter focuses on one of the most ubiquitous mental illnesses depicted in *noir*: memory loss. A good portion of this chapter is devoted to the experience of the amnesiac war veteran, as illustrated in such films as *Crack-Up* (1946, Irving Reis), *High Wall* (1947, Curtis Bernhardt), and *Somewhere in the Night* (1946, Joseph Mankiewicz). The analysis of such films is informed by research regarding the therapy experiences of actual World War II veterans and the way that the popularization of psychiatry during the later 1940s and 1950s in the U.S. was spawned by reports of such experiences. This chapter will also deal with amnesiac characters that are not veterans, in such films as *Man in the Dark* (1953, Lew Landers), *Street of Chance* (1942, Jack Hively), and *Dial 1119* (1950, Gerald Mayer). The phenomenon of amnesia is important to the general idea of *film noir*, as it encapsulates the ultimate experience of alienation in *noir*: having a phantom "other" self that has lived (and perhaps killed) under one's own identity, but without one's own consciousness.

Other kinds of mental illness in *film noir*, such as the homicidal or sadistic psychopath, kleptomania, sexual neurosis, paranoia, and psychosomatic illnesses, are discussed in the fourth chapter. Films like *The Big Combo* (1955, Joseph Lewis), *Rage in Heaven* (1941, W.S. Van Dyke), *The Dark Mirror* (1946, Robert Siodmak), *Secret Beyond the Door* (1948, Fritz Lang), and *Leave Her to Heaven* (1945, John Stahl) are key in this analysis, as it is clear that the depiction of mental illness in *noir* illuminates the idea of mental maladjustment as a "normal" condition within the *noir* world. Finally, the fifth chapter, entitled, "The *Gaslight* Phenomenon: Inducing Insanity in *Noir*," concerns itself with an intriguing facet of *noir*: plots involving one or more characters who try to convince another character that he or she is insane. Films that fall into this category include *Dark Waters* (1944, André de Toth), *My Name is Julia Ross* (1945, Joseph Lewis), *Shock* (1946, Alfred Werker), *Sleep My Love* (1948, Douglas Sirk) and *The Second Woman* (1951, James Kern). This phenomenon sheds light on the nightmarish persecution often found in *noir*, as characters are made to question their own mental faculties and confront the fears of loss of control, even perhaps as their own identities are called into question.

Spellbound: A Case Study of Psychiatric *Noir*

Though many of the above films deal with more than one aspect of psychoanalysis in *noir*, one film in particular, Alfred Hitchcock's *Spellbound* (1945), embodies more of the above features than other films and provides an intriguing model for the analysis of the other films later in this study. In *Spellbound*, we see the depictions of benevolent female psychiatrist, malevolent (and murderous) male psychiatrist, impersonated psychiatrist, amnesiac war veteran, post-war sanitarium, and dream therapy, all in one *noir* that turns on itself in numerous ways. Many have commented on the film's failure to accurately depict psychoanalysis—this issue exists for most, if not all, of the films that are discussed in this study. However, the accuracy of the depiction by scientific psychoanalytic standards is less important than the way that the psychoanalysis, inaccurate or not, functions in these *noir*s and is represented to the popular imagination. Much has been discussed about Hitchcock's contentious relationship with David O. Selznick, a passionate disciple of psychoanalysis. Hitchcock viewed psychoanalysis with amused skepticism, and even though it becomes a focus of the film, it is not immune to Hitch's dark humor. In *Spellbound*, psychoanalysis ultimately saves the day, but not before providing an array of suspect characters that succeed in their endeavors often despite, not because of, their efforts.[13] Reportedly, Hitchcock responded to the objections of May Romm, Selznick's psychoanalytic advisor to the film, "But May, it's only a movie." Hitchcock also revealed his ambivalence—or more accurately, contempt—of psychoanalysis in the interviews with François Truffaut.[14] Hitchcock was likely suspicious of the popularity of psychoanalysis, seeing it as not solving societal problems, but rather "adding one more snare to the ensemble of illusions by which human beings trick each other and are gulled in turn."[15] This certainly seems to be the case in *Spellbound*, where the inhabitants of Green Manors Sanitarium are alternately comical and frightening—doctors and patients alike—in their misapprehensions about the world.

The psychiatrist figures of psychoanalysis in *Spellbound* are portrayed as a wide range of caricatures, from the lecherous Dr. Fleurot (John

Emery) to the smitten Dr. Peterson (Ingrid Bergman) to the doddering Freud clone Dr. Brulov (Michael Chekhov), and finally to the evil Dr. Murchison (Leo G. Carroll), who exploits his psychological expertise to frame John Ballantine (Gregory Peck). Fleurot, Peterson, and Murchison are all inhabitants of Green Manors; scenes that feature them interacting, with or without other psychiatrists, emphasize that they are anything but mature professionals, but rather pre-adolescent children. Fleurot either makes leering advances on Peterson or waxes philosophic about her inability to show emotion. As the only "girl" psychiatrist in the asylum schoolyard with "boys," Peterson uses wit and intelligence to hold her own, but it is difficult when incidents such as lateness to dinner is met with jeers and jokes, prompting her to describe the dinner table as a "kindergarten." According to Andrew Britton, Green Manors can be seen as "a monstrous, perverted family, characterised at once by sexual repression, a claustrophobic lack of privacy, and a pervasive immaturity and childishness."[16] Only limited psychiatric treatments are seen in *Spellbound* to take place at the asylum; these are confined to the beginning of the film. Strict objectivity is emphasized in the psychoanalytic technique used by Peterson as she treats Miss Carmichael (Rhonda Fleming) and Mr. Garmes (Norman Lloyd). These two patients form counterpoint "double" figures to Peterson and Ballantine: the "nymphomaniac" Carmichael represents the opposite of Peterson's apparent sexual repression, and the self-destructive Garmes, who is sure he has murdered his father, parallels the guilt-complex-driven Ballantine.[17] Aside from the brief psychoanalysis sessions between Peterson and these two patients, there is no other evidence of the kinds of treatments that go on, only the presence of moderately bullish orderlies and an open recreation room in which the patients interact and play cards. The function of Green Manors is clearly not to show treatments for mental illness but rather to highlight the sanitarium as an environment not of healing, but of power and competition.

The megalomaniacal (and murderous) psychiatrist in *noir* is typified by Dr. Murchison. Murchison appears to be benevolent when the film begins, resigned to the fact that a new, younger doctor is about to arrive to replace him as the head of Green Manors. However, the audience senses that all may not be well, as Murchison's mental breakdown is alluded to as being a direct precursor to his "retirement." Murchison could not accept what he viewed as the usurpation of his position as chief physician at Green Manors, and so he murders Dr. Edwardes, his successor—however, he hardly suspects that Ballantine, the man who was with Edwardes when he is killed on the ski slopes, will turn up, claiming to be Edwardes. Murchison maintains his benevolent façade while looking for opportunities to implicate the unstable Ballantine as the murderer.

Murchison is one of many father figures to Peterson, and eventually one that she must "kill" in order to become whole herself, not to mention in order to restore wholeness to her patient, Ballantine. Her analysis of Ballantine's dream, explored in greater detail below, is the solution to the murderous puzzle, and though Peterson has no evidence outside of Ballantine's dream that Murchison is Edwardes' murderer, her confrontation leads Murchison to first threaten her, and ultimately to kill himself. Psychiatrists like Murchison who are often depicted in *noir* represent the darkest side of psychiatry: individuals who seek to use their knowledge of the human psyche (and how to manipulate it) in order to take advantage of others.

Dr. Peterson and Dr. Brulov are depicted as benevolent psychiatrists, but still clear "types" in *noir*: Peterson as the female angelic "savior" psychiatrist who plays detective in order to rescue her patient (and lover), and Brulov as the grandfatherly Freudian with his beard, German accent, and wise advice. Peterson appears, at least in the fictional world of the film, to be a competent psychiatrist, but still relies on the advice of her mentor, Brulov, especially when she realizes that she has fallen in love with her patient. The objective rationalism that she displays in the film is threatened by her romantic feelings for Ballantine, as she begins to ascribe ethereal explanations for his behavior, invoking obscure moralism that would seem to have no place in a film about psychoanalysis. Much is made in *Spellbound* of the mysterious morality that Ballantine must possess in order to make him incapable of murder. The love-struck Dr. Peterson naively proclaims that she "couldn't feel this way toward a man who was bad, who had committed murder. [She] couldn't feel this pain for someone who was evil." However, Brulov points out that there is no real surety in psychologically evaluating the nebulous idea of "moral character" to which humans stubbornly cling. Though the film's opening titles provide an oversimplifying explanation of psychoanalysis that defines it as having an almost moral power, as it drives "the devils of unreason from the human soul," morality is not really a relevant concept when psychoanalytically assessing the unconscious mind. Beyond attaching to psychoanalysis a moral power (and duty), *Spellbound* reveals psychiatry to be a process of inquiry and a solution to mystery. Psychiatrists in *noir* are often portrayed as detectives, as only one other kind of detective form in *noir*, like the tortured private eye or disturbed policeman. In an interesting role-reversal of this type of portrayal in *Spellbound*, a real detective, the hotel sleuth that Peterson meets when she is trying to find Ballantine, refers to himself smugly as "a kind of psychologist" who sums up Peterson's story as one of many "cases" he has seen before. The interchanging roles of psychiatrist and detective are telling when considering the function of the psychiatrist in *noir*: often one who solves mysteries—first of the human mind, but often leading to solutions of crime that result from the mysteries of the psyche. This is the scenario in *Spellbound*, as Peterson seeks to solve the mystery of Ballantine's amnesia and true identity, a solution that in turn reveals the truth about the murder of Dr. Edwardes.

The amnesiac ex-veteran Ballantine is another stock character type in *noir*, vacillating between sensitive lost soul and violent misogynist as he struggles to discover his true identity. He has lost his entire memory of a self and life before arriving at Green Manors impersonating Edwardes. He has unwittingly assumed Edwardes' identity and only over the course of a few days begins to realize that not only is he not Edwardes, but also that he has no idea who he really is. As will be evident in other *noir* stories of amnesiac veterans, this situation is metonymic of the scarred war veteran's reintegration into civilian post-war society, a society that is often as alien to him as the disorientation of amnesia. Amnesia in *Spellbound* is described in psychoanalytic fashion by Ballantine as "a trick of the mind for remaining sane. You put a horrible thing behind a closed door." This "horrible thing" in amnesiac *noirs* is literally the murder or actions committed during the protagonists' blackouts, but symbolically all the "horrible things" that they have witnessed as a result of the war or, in the case of *Spellbound*, that relate to a childhood trauma. Ballantine had initially sought Dr. Edwardes for help in dealing with his "nerve shock" after a wartime plane crash. Though Ballantine is a doctor himself and able to recognize his own mental pathology, what he is incapable of consciously realizing is the effect that the childhood guilt trauma of accidentally killing his brother has had on his adult life. In response to Ballantine's definition of amnesia, Peterson replies, "We have to open that door," to which he responds, "I know what's behind that door: murder." In this and other amnesiac *films noir*, the antihero simultaneously fears and desires the knowledge of the phantom "other"—it could just as easily confirm him to be a criminal as an innocent man.

For Ballantine, the nothingness that stares back at him when he tries to recall his "true" identity is just as frightening as confronting the possibility that the "other" who inhabits this nothingness might well be a murderer. In an existential crisis, Ballantine finds the creation of a new, blank life that is not liberating, but terrifying. He explains the experience to Dr. Peterson in the following way: "I have no memory. It's like looking into a mirror and seeing nothing but the mirror. And yet the image is there, I know it's there. I exist, I'm there." Royal Brown points out the castration image imbued in this scene,[18] a castration that additionally signifies a loss of body linked to wartime amputation—instead of a missing limb, Ballantine has a missing memory that likewise subjects him to a loss of power. The integrity of Ballantine's very self is at stake, the value of which is determined by his guilt or innocence. But Ballantine is deeply afraid to recall too much and gets violently frustrated at Peterson for trying to unlock the secrets of his mind. It seems as though he would be glad to start a new life with her if he could indefinitely elude the police, a destructive form of denial.

The ways that Ballantine's childhood and wartime traumas come to light in the course of his analysis confirm their connection to his amnesia-provoked existential crisis. For example, in an effort to pinpoint where Ballantine had had contact with Edwardes, Peterson prods him to walk up to a train ticket-seller and ask for a ticket to the same destination that he must have heard Edwardes ask for before his death. Ballantine, overcome by psychic stress, nearly faints after coming up with "Rome" as his destination. The city of Rome connects with his wartime experiences, the plane crash that caused the burn on his hand being one of the few clues to the life of his phantom "other," and the subsequent trauma that occasioned his seeking help from Edwardes. The mythological implications of the use of Rome as the city of choice, when any European city could have sufficed, are telling. The legendary founders of Rome, Romulus and Remus were twin brothers, one of whom killed the other because of disputes regarding the site upon which their city would be built. Therefore, the doubling of selves, and the subsequent killing of one of them, is akin to the mental struggles that Ballantine experiences. Rome is at the beginning of a chain that connects these events, a chain of experience overtaken by Ballantine's shadowy double, and ending with Edwardes' murder and Ballantine's amnesia. The "truth," then, of Ballantine's character as it relates to Edwardes' death is shown to be inextricably linked to his wartime trauma and his inability to reabsorb into law-abiding, "normal" society. This is a feature seen over and over again in *noir*s that feature amnesia-stricken veterans. Later, when Ballantine and Dr. Peterson return to Gabriel Valley, he recalls the similarity between his inadvertent role in his brother's death and the death of Edwardes that he was powerless to prevent, thereby ushering in a flood of memory that re-introduces his amnesiac self to his phantom "other."

It would seem that, at least in his own consciousness, the mystery of the missing self is solved, but as Ballantine points out, there are areas, which he quickly dismisses, that are still "fuzzy" in his memory. Peterson's persistence unearths what will become the most important "evidence" of the "case": Ballantine's dream in which Murchison is exposed to be the actual murderer of Edwardes. The surreality of Salvador Dali's dream design accords with the style of many dream sequences in *noir*, albeit more artistically; dream sequences that appear in films prior to the *noir* sequence tended toward the linear and realistic. Scenes like Dali's emphasize the surreal nature of dreaming, from the oversized objects in peculiar situations to the convoluted sequence of events, to the symbolic emphasis of these objects. In its expression of the convolution and symbolism of actual human dreaming, Dali's dream reinforces "the fact that in *film noir* putative reality and the world of dreams are crucially interwoven, indivisible in light of the internal progressions—those darkly luminous spirals and zigzags—that underlie the external grid of a man's life."[19] The intersection of this "external grid" with the dark mazes of the unconscious mind is the central problem of the amnesiac *noir* antihero, in that at the point of intersection, he finds what appears to be a blank "other" self, which may not be blank at all and may be a criminal manifestation of his hitherto "innocent," if tarnished, self.

Though the resolution of the drama centers on Peterson's final analysis of Ballantine's dream, her approach is one that deviates from the process of typical psychiatry in that, according to Jerrold R. Brandell, it "appears to minimize, if not completely discount, the analyst's intuitive discernment in favor of a more detached, positivistic decoding method. The patient's dream in *Spellbound* has become an intellectual conundrum that can be separated from the analytic process altogether, and whose true meaning is arrived at through deduction."[20] Granted, numerous deviations from "correct" psychoanalytic technique are general in *noir*, but the fact that the psychiatrist becomes a "decoding" detective is a significant, not random, deviation, as mentioned above. Peterson's deconstruction of the dream makes her into a bloodhound, tracking Ballantine's movements in order to reconstruct his absent memory, but gives little attention to his psyche as a whole, as she focuses on the traumatic event that, according to the plot, caused the entire psychological breakdown.[21]

But in true *noir* fashion, Peterson's detective pursuits offer no clean resolution, regardless of how the narrative tries to force the audience in that direction. When Ballantine likens regaining his memory of skiing with Edwardes, and then of his traumatic childhood involvement in his brother's death, to "looking into a picture book, an old one, seeing the familiar pictures one at a time," it is clear that the book is still a few pages short. As Christopher Morris argues, Ballantine's flashback "cannot, after all, prove his brother's death was accidental, since there is never a way viewers can read motive from this boy's or anyone's face; we can only take John at his word that his feelings for his brother were wholly benign as he started to slide. The parallel between the deaths of John's brother and Edwardes now raises the issue of whether Edwardes' fall was accompanied by any aggressive wish on John's part."[22] The viewer is left with a vague sense of disturbance, as Peterson assures Ballantine that it wasn't his fault, and must take for granted that Ballantine's motives were pure and the deaths accidental. There is also never a point at which Ballantine shows that his entire memory is regained. This feature once again highlights the lack of certainty attached to psychological analysis and the application of any idea of sure "truth" to the human mind. This is shown clearly when, almost as if to prove wrong the power of the mind to heal itself, the police arrive to arrest Ballantine with the evidence of a bullet lodged in Edwardes' back, a fact that seemingly refutes at least part of Ballantine's regained memory of the event. Edwardes sailed over the edge of the snowy cliff not by accident, but because he was shot in the back; certainly Ballantine cannot remember shooting him, but who can trust him, a former amnesiac and murder suspect? The fact that Ballantine's story does not end with the regaining of most of his memory emphasizes not so much the psychological subtleties of healing an amnesiac, but rather the lack of any "system," whether legal or psychoanalytic, that can completely explain the inner workings of the human mind and find ultimate "truth." And certainly all such "systems" become suspect in the post-war *noir* world. Thus, Ballantine becomes less of a restored mind than a "third self"—the product of the unity of his blank self and his phantom "other" that results in a combination ultimately changed from the person he was before the accident. He cannot step neatly back into his original self because he has been altered, and the traumas that were submerged finally came to the surface. Such an inevitable, and often inexplicable, change is emblematic of the self changed by the harshness of the wartime and post-war world. While we would like to have things make sense in such a world, our best efforts are usually futile; if the world seems rational, it is only because of our own delusions or happy accident.

Peterson's neat analysis of the dream that implicates Murchison is supposed to provide an ending resolution, but has its flaws as well; all of these instabilities in the narrative make the final scene in the film even more odd and disturbing. The "fairy tale" ending can lead one to agree with Brill that "the illness of John Ballantine has its primary significance not as a medical syndrome but as a story element similar to the curse of the evil sorcerer in *Sleeping Beauty.* It is an enchantment to be overcome by a heroic kiss."[23] Alternately logical or illogical, *Spellbound*'s depiction of psychiatry in its *noir* atmosphere shows the dependence of one concept on the other. The film asserts resolution, but is filled with doubt—these arise from Ballantine's psyche but are meant to provoke an unstable mood in the viewer about the world at large. Freedman intriguingly connects Hitchcock's state of mind with "the despairing Freud of the late metaphysical writings: the Freud that is, for whom the vicissitudes of the psyche and hence of culture itself are governed by the indominability of the death-drive, the inevitability of repetition-compulsion, the interminability of analysis, and the impossibility of cure."[24] And so it is for *film noir* itself, as the ensuing chapters will show.

Notes

1. Reuben Fine, *A History of Psychoanalysis* (New York: Columbia University Press, 1979), 88.
2. Fine, *History*, 89.
3. Francis Sill Wickware, "Psychoanalysis," *Life* 3 (Feb. 1947): 98.
4. Keith Sward, "Boy and Girl Meet Neurosis," *The Screen Writer* 4, no.3 (Sept. 1948): 24.
5. Arthur Lyons, *Death on the Cheap: The Lost B Movies of Film Noir* (New York, Da Capo Press, 2000), 9.
6. J.P. Telotte, "Voices from the Deep: *Film Noir* as Psychodrama," in *Film noir Reader 4*, ed. Alain Silver and James Ursini (New York: Limelight Editions, 2004), 145-46.
7. Raymond Borde and Etienne Chaumeton, *A Panorama of American Film noir: 1941-1953*, trans. Paul Hammond (San Francisco: City Lights Books, 2002), 19-20.
8. Frank Krutnik sums this idea up well: "On the one hand, the depiction of psychoanalysis as a rationalist 'science' has its aim the eradication of disorder and deviance. On the other hand, psychoanalysis serves the function of bringing out a complex and patently destabilising undercurrent of excessive and disordered desires which elude easy rationalisation" (53).
9. For an overview of psychiatry in film in general, see Rabkin and Schneider. Interestingly, the subject has been widely discussed by psychiatrists themselves; see, for instance, Fearing, Gabbard, and Kubie. Many humorous pieces have also appeared; Holland is one example.
10. Borde and Chaumeton, 18.
11. Patrick Fuery, *Madness and Cinema: Psychoanalysis, Spectatorship, and Culture* (New York: Palgrave Macmillan, 2004) 44.
12. Richard Maltby, "The Politics of the Maladjusted Text" in *The Movie Book of Film Noir*, ed. Ian Cameron (London: Studio Vista, 1992), 47.
13. In *The Hitchcock Romance: Love and Irony in Hitchcock's Films*, Lesley Brill points out that Hitchcock's approach is "less belittling" than "poking fun at psychologists who fancy themselves to be dealing in new goods . . . but his amusement is good-natured and the figures he caricatures are portrayed as naïve, not vicious" (239).
14. See François Truffaut, *Hitchcock*, rev. ed., trans. Helen G. Scott (New York: Simon and Schuster, 1984).

15. Jonathan Freedman, "From *Spellbound* to *Vertigo*: Alfred Hitchcock and Therapeutic Culture in America" in *Hitchcock's America*, ed. Jonathan Freedman and Richard Millington (New York: Oxford University Press, 1999), 79.
16. Andrew Britton, "Hitchcock's *Spellbound*: Text and Counter-Text." *Cineaction!* 3/4 (Winter 1986): 72-83.
17. See Brown and Boyd for discussions of the tension created in the viewer by such doubling.
18. Royal S. Brown, "Hitchcock's *Spellbound*: Jung Versus Freud." *Film/Psychology Review* 4 (Winter-Spring 1980): 35-58.
19. Nicholas Christopher, *Somewhere in the Night: Film Noir and the American City* (New York: The Free Press, 1997), 222.
20. Jerrold R Brandell, "Eighty Years of Dream Sequences: A Cinematic Journey Down Freud's 'Royal Road.'" *American Imago* 61, no.1 (2004): 59-76.
21. Britton points out one weighty inconsistency in the dream analysis, the fact that "if the proprietor of the casino is simply Dr. Murchison, there is no reason whatsoever, apart from considerations of narrative-suspense, why he should be masked in the dream, since Ballantyne [sic] has scarcely come in contact with him, and there is no necessity for his identity to be repressed" (80).
22. Christopher D. Morris, *The Hanging Figure: On Suspense and the Films of Alfred Hitchcock* (Westport, CT: Praeger, 2002), 146.
23. Brill, 259.
24. Freedman, 80.

Chapter One

Noir Psychiatrists

The Good, the Bad, and the Bogus

> "I read somewhere about a kind of doctor, a psych-something. You tell your dream, you don't have to dream it anymore."
>
> —Raven, *This Gun for Hire* (1942)

Though it may not be readily apparent, the figure of the psychiatrist in *film noir* appears nearly as often as other stock *noir* characters, such as the femme fatale or the private eye. If this seems hard to believe, consider the prevalence of minor psychiatrist characters who appear briefly in cocktail party and hospital scenes, and then the more prominent psychiatrist characters, who appear in leading roles in such films as *Nightmare Alley* and *The Dark Past*. Lutz Koepnick points out the link between the figure of the psychiatrist or psychoanalyst in films directed by German exiles after 1939, from whom *noir* was a prolific result. These characters not only serve as narrative signposts and flashback catalysts, but also articulate "Hollywood's preoccupation throughout the 1940s with the subject of repression and displacement, paranoia and pathological doubling."[1] In the intensely psychological world in which *noir* takes place, it is not surprising that when the psychiatrist appears, he or she has the capacity for doing alternately the most good or the most harm. If danger may lay in wait at any moment, there is little more dangerous than someone who can use one's innermost secrets and fears as the means for doing damage. Nicholas Christopher argues that many *noirs* "revolve around sophisticated urban psychiatrists as central characters, often villains, who manipulate the hero's mental labyrinth in exactly the way more pedestrian villains like gangster overlords or corrupt politicians manipulate the workings of the greater urban labyrinth to achieve their ends."[2] The temptation to assume this kind of power is compelling; though there are clear depictions in *noir* of both beneficent and nefarious psychiatrists, there are also psychiatrist impersonators—and these emerge, not surprisingly, motivated at best for self-preservation and at worst for unabashed greed. As Glen O. Gabbard and Krin Gabbard argue, "Just as psychiatrists were out of place in Frank Capra-land, they were welcome and even necessary in the more complex world of *film noir*."[3]

Mary Ann Doane astutely notes that Hollywood films in the 1940s and 1950s made loose, if any, distinctions among psychoanalyst, psychiatrist, and psychologist characters.[4] I will also take some liberty in analyzing this character type and point out that though there are varying degrees of medical expertise portrayed, most of these characters are put forth as MDs rather than the more modern occupations of therapist or counselor. But these figures are more than simply doctors: they also embody, to varying degrees, equal measures of priest, fortuneteller/oracle, and private detective, as they strive to make sense of a wayward patient's mind, using tools that are alternately inspired by faith, mystery, and science. The psychiatrist figure in noir thus embodies all the hopes and fears regarding human potentiality and despair, and systems that are used in society to address them. Often, the noir psychiatrist is portrayed (and is treated by other characters) as a quack or a huckster; just as often, he or she is elevated to the status of divine soothsayer, brilliant scientist, or savvy detective. Much of these conflicting depictions are a result of the societal ambivalence toward psychiatry and the hopes (though usually clouded by suspicion) that accompany its prospects. The kindly psychiatrist as *noir* detective is evident in *The Dark Past* (1949), in which Dr. Andrew Collins (Lee J. Cobb) responds to the criminal who holds him and his house guests hostage by psychoanalyzing him as a way of saving their lives—including that of the criminal himself, Al Walker (William Holden). Collins happens to be a police psychiatrist, a role that blurs the lines even further between detective and doctor. In the film's opening sequence, through the context of recommending a young offender for treatment at a psychiatric hospital, Collins explains that "people behave badly sometimes—doesn't mean they're bad." He likens psychiatric illness to a wounded foot by saying that "an inside hurt that's been festering for years" should mean as much as any illness for which one would need to seek medical attention. These comments early in the film, before the flashback that will comprise the majority of the screen time, both frame the position of the psychiatrist as spiritual advisor (hate the sin, not the sinner) and frame psychiatric illness as a medical infirmity, thereby legitimizing it.

To illustrate his point about the importance of treating psychological illness, Collins tells the story of Al Walker, an escaped convict who takes over Collins' lake house with his gang as he is trying to make his escape via boat pickup. Walker is a tough character, not afraid to slap around Collins' guests, and even shoot one who questions him. He mockingly responds to Collins' inquiries by saying, "a psychiatrist—we had one in the pen' . . . know what I think? Anyone who goes in for that stuff's a little barmy himself." But Walker cannot help but be fascinated by Collins' chess set and books on criminal insanity. Collins is portrayed as an ideal psychiatrist, at once paternal, respectful, and didactic. He is a curious scientist, with keen enough insight to realize that a breakthrough for this unstable criminal may also mean his own survival. His efforts to distract Walker may be just as equally seen as an effort to educate and in effect, treat him. Collins tries to demystify the profession of psychiatry for Walker by explaining, with the aid of a drawing of a brain on a pad, that the mind is like an iceberg, with the conscious mind visible and aware and the unconscious mind real but hidden. He points out that the conscious is "afraid" of the unconscious, so much so that it builds a wall, called a "sensor band," to separate itself. Collins' job thus becomes necessary when the "sensor band" fails to do its job and thoughts and ideas creep across the boundary. The interesting implication here, outside of the introduction of the "sensor band" concept, which seems to be a filmic invention, is that the conscious and unconscious minds need to be separate for protective purposes in the first place, rather than a goal of integration. The barrier that is created and apparently necessary protects the "order" of the thinking, conscious mind from the "chaos" of the mysterious, unconscious mind; however, such barrier failure is implied to be all too common, given the existence of psychiatry. Furthermore, this implication extends to the world of *noir* itself, which acknowledges that a normal world seems to exist, but life keeps crossing the barrier into the abnormal.

Aside from the "sensor band" reference, Collins displays key traits of a textbook psychiatrist, including the viewpoint of mental illness as just another kind of sickness, the belief that the affected person must want to be helped in order to be effectively treated, and common treatment tactics, such as free-association, the use of symbolism to unlock the unconscious, and most importantly, dream analysis. Nicholas Christopher points out that in a number of *film noir*s, including *The Dark Past* and *Spellbound*, dreams are used "not as mere stylistic devices but as vehicles for the essential purposes of advancing plot and revealing character."[5] The entire film rests on the eventual dream analysis of Walker by Collins, an analysis that will reveal the source of Walker's psychosomatic ailment of paralyzed fingers. He has convinced himself that this paralysis came from his being "in a wreck." The "wreck," as it turns out, is one of his own mental making: the childhood trauma of doting mother, abusive father, and eventually his own involvement in his father's death. This is a prime example of what Collins had described as the unconscious being comprised of "things pushed down" during childhood. Walker does not want to listen to Collins' suggestion that his mind might be causing the paralysis, and it is only through Walker's cousin, Betty (Nina Foch), who is another member of his gang, that Collins learns that Walker has recurring nightmares. A desire to be free of the nightmares is what eventually leads Walker to open up to Collins, even though he still thinks of Collins as "a gypsy fortune-teller," probing depths that are still mysterious to him.

The comparison between psychiatrist and fortune-teller is revealing, as both have seemingly uncanny insights into the mysterious and utilize the interpretation of symbols to shed light on reality. Collins's analysis of Walker's dream is just this way, as his probing questions reveal that the umbrella in Walker's dream is actually a table, the bars are policemen's legs, and the rain is beer and blood dripping down around him and through the table-top. Only at the end can Walker bring himself to accept that the man in the dream is his father, and he had a direct role in his death by bringing the police to the saloon. Collins eventually succeeds in making Walker realize the roots of his criminal behavior: "Any man you're after becomes your father . . . every time you kill a man, you're killing your father all over again." And as a consequence, Walker becomes a better human being, but a worse criminal; ironically, though he can move his fingers again, he can no longer kill another man again. When he tries to shoot his way out of Collins' house, there is a striking shot of his father's face superimposed over that of the policeman. Though Collins is posited as the restorer of order at the end of the film, his last words in voice-over still undercut the supposed order that his story illustrates: "There with very little difference in the basic human equation goes any one of us or our kids. Which one ends up as Al Walker and which one gets to come out a decent member of society may very largely be up to us." Though Collins implies that nurture, rather than nature, determines our fate as either upstanding citizen or disturbed criminal, and is therefore controllable, there is also the undertone in these words that suggests that the line is so fine between these two that any misstep on our part may condemn our children to a life of insanity or crime.

A similar rehabilitative relationship between psychiatrist and criminal is seen in *The Sleeping Tiger* (Joseph Losey, 1954). After well-intentioned (and Army-trained) Dr. Clive Esmond (Alexander Knox) gets a gun away from would-be attacker Frank Clemmons (Dirk Bogarde), he invites him to stay at his home and be treated for psychiatric illness. What Clemmons (and the viewer) cannot know at this point is that he is walking into a dysfunctional household in which Esmond's wife, Glenda (Alexis Smith), is just as much, if not more, disturbed than Clemmons himself. We will see that Esmond is not the ideal husband, as he will frequently ignore Glenda in favor of his work, but he persistently believes throughout the film that Clemmons is worth helping, despite much evidence to the contrary. This persistence begins with his assertion at the opening of the film that it is one thing to practice psychology in the prison ward, but another to have a patient with criminal tendencies in the "ideal circumstances" of a peaceful and generous home. Outside of the eventual irony of Esmond's belief that his home is ideal, he truly believes that because of Clemmon's youth and intelligence, he can be saved, despite his recidivist record of violence and robbery. What makes him especially interesting to Esmond is the fact that Clemmons comes from a "good family"—perhaps much like his own.

During his residence at Esmond's house, Clemmons spends half his time in sessions with the doctor and half his time with Glenda, with whom he develops a dangerous flirtation from the moment they meet. Scenes of Esmond probing Clemmons about his childhood are cut with horseback riding scenes of Clemmons and Glenda, implying that Clemmons is receiving two different kinds of "therapy." His relationship with Glenda seems anything but therapeutic, though, as it is antagonistic and even violent, while sexualized. Glenda vacillates between being attracted to Clemmons and wanting him to keep away from her, and while Esmond is trying to open Clemmons up to realizing that events in his past have affected his present behavior, she is dismissive of this interpretation: "Lots of people come from broken homes. I did. I came from two homes a thousand miles apart, and I was a stranger in both of them. My mother hated me, literally . . . but I made a life for myself, just the same." Glenda fancies herself well-adjusted, but her mental instability that emerges as the film progresses seems to reinforce her husband's contention in his books that "childhood is what counts." Clemmons, by contrast, believes that "people are born the way they are" and is skeptical about any treatment being able to help him. He also believes that Glenda is of the same sort as he; while she looks "like nothing can shake" her, she's "empty," "hungry," and "a tight wire." "It wouldn't take very much to break you," he says.

While the desperate and tortured characters of Glenda and Clemmons seem right at home in *noir*, the character of Esmond is depicted as out of that element—benevolent, but naïve and dim, as he stubbornly keeps believing in Clemmons, or at least in the idea of saving him. The *noir* psychiatrist is thus seen here as well-meaning but essentially ineffectual, when faced with both the pathologies of Clemmons and his own wife. The fact that Clemmons is not only reticent but also lies during his analysis reinforces the inherent weakness of a "science" that depends on the self-disclosure of those who may be least reliable to do so. Clemmons first claims that his mother died, that he and his father got along well, "like brothers," and that he also got along well with his stepmother. After Esmond later tells Clemmons that he knows his mother did not die, but rather ran away, Clemmons admits the truth that he actually hated both his father, who drove away his mother, and his stepmother, who he describes as "ice on the outside and rotten on the inside." This is ironically a description that closely matches Glenda as well, as it becomes increasingly clear that her cool composed exterior as a doctor's wife masks turbulent and perverse tendencies that ultimately become self-destructive. That Clemmons is drawn to her seems no mystery after this revelation.

Though Esmond appears to be breaking through Clemmons' reserve and making some progress with his treatment, this does not prevent Clemmons from meeting up with an old crime partner and robbing a jewelry store. When the police arrive to question Clemmons, Esmond vouches for his whereabouts and combined with a lack of concrete evidence and Clemmons maintaining that he "wouldn't do anything like that" to the doctor, he remains free. Almost in an attempt to prove himself right in believing in the rehabilitation of Clemmons, Esmond goes out of his way to protect him thereafter, by first bribing the maid's fiancé Bailey (Glyn Houston) to keep quiet about Clemmons assaulting her and later giving the police an alibi for Clemmons a second time after he steals Esmond's gun to rob an office. At this point, Esmond's doggedness seems less about faith than about science, as he seems to view the complaints of other members of the household and the police as bothersome intrusions that are distracting him from the more important work at hand. Though he is warned early on by both his own assistant and the police inspector that taking Clemmons in is too dangerous, Esmond cannot seem to stop himself from pursuing the aim of curing him. He says that he "can't quit, can't let the boy down," even as he knows that Clemmons hates him, but is not sure why.

As it turns out, Esmond's persistence seems to bring results, as it is after this that Clemmons finally seems to trust him and honestly open up to him. By Esmond almost identifying with Clemmons and his crime, he therefore becomes like an accomplice to Clemmons, rather than an adversary. It is at this point that Clemmons finally reveals that his hatred of his father arises from his father turning him in to the police after he stole a bicycle, for which his father refused to give him Clemmons' own money to buy. After he is released from jail, he tells Esmond, he tried to kill his father, but his father overpowered him instead, forcing him to kneel in front of his stepmother and beating him into submission. When his father died a week later, Clemmons blamed himself for wishing his father dead. The close-ups of Clemmons' tearful anguished face, as he repeats, "wasted . . . wasted," underscore the level of breakthrough that Esmond has achieved. He assures Clemmons that the hate and guilt that he felt has made him do these other things, and he is not to be blamed for his father's death. When Esmond had tried to explain Clemmons' situation to Bailey earlier in the film, he said, "All of us are capable of anything, given the right provocation. . . . Clemmons had a childhood that drove him to the verge of killing. I'm trying to destroy his urge to hate . . . in you, in me, in the dark forest of every human personality, there's a tiger . . . a sleeping tiger." Though Glenda ridicules this sentiment and his bribe to Bailey at the time, by saying, "psychology pays off," the breakthrough session with Clemmons proves Esmond right that his instincts were on target and his efforts were not in vain.

The "sleeping tiger" explanation is fully consistent with the *noir* world, in which average human beings are pushed to extraordinary lengths given desperate circumstances. One explanation for such a world can easily be the "sleeping tiger" of the unconscious in its unpredictability and uncontrollability. And though through psychiatry, Esmond is able to curtail Clemmons' criminal behavior, the specter of psychological disturbance in his own wife remains the uncontrollable element in the film. Esmond cannot see Glenda's psyche unraveling before his eyes, and though Clemmons is the obvious catalyst for her demise, the implication is that her instability could have surfaced at any time. While Clemmons is lying to Esmond and robbing stores and offices, Glenda forms a violent and passionate relationship with him, which begins with her alternately flirting with and rebuffing him and is marked by passionate embraces that are punctuated with violence. Glenda seems conflicted by her feelings for him, and the more passionate their relationship becomes, the more she lashes out at him and undergoes drastic mood swings. At one point, when she has raised her hand to strike him, she angrily declares, "I wish I were a man!" She in fact often seems masculinized in the film, displaying a short haircut, wearing masculine riding clothes in many scenes, and wearing a turtleneck and pants rather than a dress when they go dancing. Given what Glenda early in the film describes as her acrimonious relationship with her mother, it does not go too far to assume that her desire to be a man and have the power and control that go with it, may stem from her powerlessness and anger toward her mother; being a man could likely be the only way to overcome this failing.

Moreover, Glenda's violent outbursts throughout the film indicate a suppressed masculine aggression directed at both Esmond and Clemmons that signifies her frustration at the confines of her life and her inability to free herself from them. Her often dismissive attitude toward her liberal and gentle husband's feminized impulses suggests an intriguing gender role reversal that may be in part responsible for his inability to truly recognize her psychological struggle.

However, once Clemmons' breakthrough occurs, he ignores Glenda in favor of fishing and camping with Esmond, as he has accepted him as a benevolent father figure, in contrast to his own abusive father. Glenda now becomes increasingly agitated by his inattention, and when Clemmons is not responsive to her suggestion that they run away together, she says, "You've never seen me really angry . . . I warn you . . . you don't know what I'm capable of." This statement ironically is just what Esmond maintains is the true dangerous potentiality of humanity. And Clemmons' "reformed" decision to turn himself in because he believes that he will never be free until he has paid for what he has done sends Glenda into a rage. His refusal to see her again in favor of loyalty to Esmond seems to tip her over the edge, and in revenge, she reports Esmond that Clemmons has raped her. When Esmond pretends to shoot Clemmons to see Glenda's reaction, she becomes hysterical, eventually running away and crashing her car into a billboard depicting a painting of a tiger. Esmond, who has followed her, and also crashes his car, implores bystanders, "We've got to help her." The last line of the film we hear is, "No help for her, sir." The ultimate lack of "help" in the film in this final sequence sharply jolts the audience away from the seeming progress that Esmond made with Clemmons. Her crime of infidelity trumps all of Clemmons' offenses in the denouement, but there is the undeniable question of how real or reliable is the help that the psychiatrist provides anyone else if he is incapable of helping his own wife exorcise her own demons. Earlier in the film, when Esmond wonders to Glenda whether or not he sees himself too much as god-like by "tampering" with people, Glenda responds, "if the halo fits, put it on . . . don't pretend you don't like winding people up like little toys." The bitterness in this remark not only illuminates her own resentment, but also looks forward to the powerlessness of the film's resolution. The psychiatrist has the potential to influence the behavior of others in the guise of a cure, but the opportunity to do damage is maybe even greater.

A similar dynamic of benevolent psychiatrist who is helpless in aiding his own wife is seen in Otto Preminger's *Whirlpool* (1949). There is the added attraction in this film of a nefarious quack hypnotist, David Korvo (José Ferrer), who takes advantage of wealthy women and their psychological frailties. Ann Sutton (Gene Tierney) is caught between Korvo and her husband, Dr. William Sutton (Richard Conte). From the start of the film, it is evident that there is some distance in their married relationship, as Ann wishes that she were more intelligent so that he could talk to her "about his scientific problems." Ann, however has problems of her own: narrowly escapes being arrested for shoplifting and when she returns home, seems to want to tell her husband about it, but cannot. Her husband is ironically the best person to help her face what turns out to be chronic kleptomania, but her shame prevents her from asking for his aid. The person who does come to her aid is Korvo, who happens to witness the episode in the department store and helps her escape. Korvo insinuates himself into Ann's life by pretending to be her friend and then offering to be her doctor. Once he gains her confidence, it is a small matter for her to agree for him to treat the insomnia and headaches from which she suffers. Korvo slyly manipulates her into undergoing his hypnosis by suggesting that if she does not do something to help herself, then her husband will find out about her condition. According to Korvo, her mind "is sick and threatening to get out of hand" and he entices her by offering "nine hours of peaceful, happy sleep." What she will receive, however, is the sleep of oblivion—the surrendering of her consciousness to Korvo and his nefarious schemes. As he begins the hypnosis the camera moves in for a close-up of his face, followed by a reverse shot of a shadow crossing her face—a clear visual cue of the beginning of his deep influence over her.

The mysterious Korvo, whose prey is wealthy women, is somewhat representative of the myth of seductive psychoanalyst and the intimate relationship one enters into with a person who learns one's most guarded and personal secrets. At a party early in the film, he is described by the host as someone who "reads souls, guides human destinies, with the aid of the stars and makes fortunes for other people . . . at a nominal fee." Korvo maintains that he is not a fortuneteller, nor a hypnotist, but "uses a variety of tools at [his] disposal." He performs a parlor trick of correctly psychologically assessing one of the guests, but it turns out that his information came from the guest's fiancée before the party. Korvo is set up almost as an evil doppelganger of William Sutton, one who is disguised as a helpful force in a chaotic world, but is actual the very essence of destructive power. One of Sutton's patients, Teresa Randolph (Barbara O'Neil) is in fact a former "patient" of Korvo's, and she tells Ann that while her husband helped her a great deal, Korvo is to be avoided, that he is only after Ann's money. Ann is outraged, and believes that

Korvo really can help her. An interesting juxtaposition between Sutton and Korvo occurs in the scene in which Sutton tells Ann that his upcoming trip to San Francisco, and hence separation from her, is "a great sacrifice to psychiatry." He also mentions how proud he is when people at parties say how beautiful she is. As this conversation is going on, the hypnotic suggestion for sleep placed by Korvo activates, and Ann falls asleep without even taking off her robe or slippers. Korvo's power over Ann has clearly usurped her husband's influence, even in the bedroom, implying its seductive reach. Though Sutton's claim to Ann is legal marriage, his bond with her seems to rely entirely on her physical beauty and so does not seem particularly more meaningful than Korvo's attentions.

As Korvo's hold on Ann increases, he tries to convince her that her husband is responsible for her problems, because he has her "in a torture chamber called Mrs. William Sutton." Ironically, as Janet Walker also points out, "while [Korvo] uses Ann unscrupulously and against her will, there is a sense in which his function is to help her *express* her deep wishes, bringing forward the idea of resistance to marital oppression."[6] Her struggle between her role as psychiatrist's wife and hidden identity as kleptomaniac manifests itself in her being drawn further and further into Korvo's web. The viewer's lack of conscious knowledge mirrors Ann's as, with no transition, Ann is seen opening her husband's office safe and removing patient records, after which she takes them to an unidentified house and hides them in a closet. The camera pans to reveal Teresa Randolph's portrait, and then Randolph herself lying dead on the floor. In a dizzying turn of events, Ann now finds herself arrested for the murder and her own husband in doubt as to her innocence. Her amnesia of the event ("I couldn't have done it . . . unless I'm crazy") complicates even further her already complicated mental state and in her desire to hide from her husband her minimally criminal actions of shoplifting, she is now in the position of having to defend the drastic criminal action of murder to him. Under the guise of "freeing" Ann, Korvo has further imprisoned her for his own purposes. Ann's identity crisis follows both a familiar psychoanalytic and a familiar *noir* pattern: in an effort to repress her anxieties further, she does more and more harm to herself.

The distance between Ann and Sutton grows as he doubts Ann's innocence, believing that she is lying to protect Korvo. Sutton wonders why she went "to a quack like that for doctoring," especially when he was available to her. In frustration, Ann tells him that he does not want to hear the truth, that he will not let her tell it. Ann's private suffering is at the root of her problems: her inability to communicate to her husband the resentment she felt at being treated like a child in their marriage, in the same way that she had been treated by her father. We later learn that Ann's kleptomania began because of her father's controlling actions regarding her trust fund money; similar feelings of impotence caused her to steal once again, when Sutton wanted her to be "a poor doctor's wife" and not to spend her own money. Ann tells Sutton, "You made me play-act, pretend I was healthy and happy, instead of sick and miserable."

Ann appears to be suffering from an old-fashioned form of hysteria brought on by suppression of desire. The actions of her "other" self, hidden by hypnotic amnesia, are the symbolic expression of these desires ignited by her sexual attraction to Korvo and her willingness to respond to his suggestion. The appearance of the crime that has occurred as a result of this expression ironically reveals itself to be a catalyst for possible revelation and growth in her marriage.

Though much evidence, contrived by Korvo, mounts against Ann, Sutton begins to believe in her innocence. Much like the faithful Constance Peterson in *Spellbound*, Sutton tells the lieutenant that "fingerprints and a few odd circumstances can't wipe out a woman's heart and character as if they never existed." The clear science behind the fingerprint evidence against Ann is juxtaposed not against an equal "science" of psychiatry, but rather Sutton's faith in Ann, and this begins to save her more than his psychiatric prowess. Knowledge of hypnosis also paves the way for establishing Ann's innocence, since Sutton argues that though Korvo knew he could hypnotize Ann to steal her husband's recordings of Teresa Randolph, he could not hypnotize her to murder Randolph, since people cannot be hypnotized to perform any action "against their moral convictions." The recordings are crucial evidence of Korvo's guilt, as they prove that Randolph had already been abused by Korvo and that she intended to take legal action against him, providing the most obvious reason for him wanting her dead. Korvo wryly tells the lieutenant that such recordings are "one of the latest wrinkles in psychoanalysis: wiretapping the subconscious." Though Korvo aims to discredit them by characterizing them as too personal for public scrutiny, the recordings posit Sutton as yet another detective in this case with scientific evidence in proving the killer.

Of course the real murderer is Korvo, whose alibi depends on the same hypnosis with which he framed Ann. After undergoing gallbladder surgery, he hypnotizes himself to eliminate the pain, allowing him to murder Teresa Randolph and return to the hospital. This is made plain to the viewer when, as the police seem to be closing in on him, Korvo must hypnotize himself again, since he fears their discovery of the recordings. As Korvo uses a mirror for the self-hypnosis, the power of his gaze is emphasized: the eye, and not the voice, seems to have the primary power to effect the changes in consciousness, as the camera moves in for a close-up of Korvo's pained, sweaty eyes in the mirror. Korvo's malignant gaze has mesmerized Ann to the brink of her own destruction, but despite his efforts he reveals himself to be the killer and she is exonerated. Though Sutton vows that he will cure Ann, seeming to realize his part in the resurfacing of her childhood neurosis, and Korvo is eliminated, the close call that Ann experiences, as is the case in many *noirs*, leaves the viewer with an unshakable dread. The power represented by both Sutton and Korvo underscores Ann's inability to have control over her own identity, as well as her destiny. Though Korvo is portrayed as the evil side of the mind-doctor coin, Sutton, in spite of his benevolent intentions, cannot be viewed as a savior. He fails to see Ann's personality difficulties or even her insomnia, and unwittingly is the catalyst for her resurgent kleptomania. The psychiatrist figures in *Whirlpool* bookend each other to provide an unsettling view of both the power and the helplessness of the mind and of the practitioners who endeavor to control it.

Another familial relationship involving a nefarious psychiatrist is seen in Edgar Ulmer's *Strange Illusion* (1945)—only this relationship's influence takes place from beyond the grave. In this film, the intrigue of psychoanalysis—as well as precognition—is explored by its blending with a Hamlet-inspired storyline. We are presented with a gold-digging psychopathic killer in league with an evil psychiatrist to institutionalize his prey's neurotic, but suspicious son. Paul Cartwright (Jimmy Lydon) is loyal to the memory of his judge father, and his disturbing dream of his father being usurped by a shadowy figure bearing gifts to his mother and sister opens the film. The expertly lit and foggy dream sequence features a shadowed man whom everyone else believes is Paul's father returned, but is actually a sinister double, who gloats, "It's just what I've been waiting for," as the viewer sees a train derail in the background. Add to this the mysterious circumstances of his father's death and the morbid series of letters that Paul receives from his father after his death, as if from a ghostly presence, through the family lawyer, and the psychological tone of the film is set.

In the letter that Paul receives right after he experiences the dream, his father writes, "It will be your responsibility as man of the family to protect your mother and Dorothy by being constantly vigilant of their associates" and mentions "unscrupulous imposters" of whom Paul should beware. Paul's mother discouraging him from coming home for the holidays is enough to spur him to anxious action, in spite of the advice of the family doctor, Martin Vincent (Regis Toomey), who tries to impress upon him the fact that "for healthy minds, a dream is just a dream," and not the prophecy that Paul believes. It is curious that the script races along, much like the derailed train, without stopping to question the oddly possessive (even for its time) nature of the dead father's letter to Paul. The audience is asked to accept as beneficial what seems like Judge Cartwright's dangerously paranoid obsession with the "associates" of his wife and daughter. The request is motivated more, it seems, from possessive distrust than love or protection, a distrust that the father wants perpetuated after his demise. Paul simply accepts this charge as good and right, and tells his mother—to whom he refers as "Princess"—when he returns home, "You're my responsibility now." The fact that Brett Curtis, her paramour, is a genuine threat notwithstanding, Paul's surrogate husbandhood is more than a little disturbing.

Paul's first meeting with Curtis (Warren William) occurs under a huge portrait of Paul's late father that is later removed from the living room to the study by his mother, at which point Paul remarks, "He looks so alive, it's almost as if he could speak." Paul has come to believe that he is his father's voice—and power—in the living world, but he is not the most effectual at being the dominant masculine force that can drive Curtis from the house and away from his mother. On the first evening he is at home, when shown the bracelet that Curtis has given his sister, Dorothy (Jayne Hazard), coupled with the Schumann concerto playing (both occurrences in his dream), Paul faints. A neurotic prophet, he insists to Dr. Vincent after the incident that it could not have been a coincidence, that his intuition is not convinced. Vincent replies that such "intuition" can become obsession. Ironically, through the manifestation of his own neurosis, Paul is attempting to eliminate a force in Curtis that is not only dangerous, but dangerously psychotic itself.

Meanwhile, the true nature of Curtis begins to be revealed as he visits his accomplice, opportunistic psychiatrist Dr. Muhlbach (Charles Arnt), head of the aptly-named Restview Manor sanitarium. Muhlbach is presented as one who crosses a sacred professional line in psychiatry, as we learn that he took on Curtis as a partner, instead of keeping him as a patient. Their scheme for Curtis to murder Judge Cartwright and marry his widow is being ruined due to the interference of Paul, who Curtis labels a "neurotic type." Muhlbach gleefully counters that Paul sounds like a case for "mental analysis" adding that "sometimes these cases destroy themselves." In the course of their conversation, Curtis describes Dorothy as "a complete conquest . . . a little beauty too," after which Muhlbach admonishes him to take care—"that weakness of yours will ruin all our plans." Add to this an earlier reference to Curtis' driving phobia and the viewer is surrounded by neurosis, psychosis and perversion from all angles and in multiple characters. Curtis is possessed by revenge against Judge Cartwright, as well as by a weakness for young girls, and Paul is possessed by the spirit of his father. Ulmer himself characterized the story as "about a father-son relationship," which he said interested him because of his fascination with psychoanalysis; this description highlights Ulmer's intention to drive the force of the film primarily from Paul and his father and the threat of an impending surrogate father.[7]

Despite Curtis' efforts to hurry his impending marriage to Virginia Cartwright (Sally Eilers), she stalls, sensing Paul's resistance. A family dinner is planned, including Curtis and Dr. Muhlbach, likely for Virginia in the hopes that the family can become more united. Before dinner, Dorothy expresses a desire to hear more about psychiatry from Dr. Muhlbach, saying "I'd love to be psychoanalyzed sometime" as if such an experience would be just like having one's fortune told or palm read. This sentiment reinforces the idea of psychiatry as part science and part superstition, especially since we have already seen that Muhlbach is an unscrupulous practitioner. As it turns out, Virginia's reluctance regarding Curtis and marriage is even more heightened after Paul experiences another fainting spell, this one brought on by Curtis saying "just what I've been waiting for." The context of his waiting happens to be the mundane domestic duty of carving a turkey at a family dinner, but of course symbolically, he is assuming the duty of the head of the household—now not Paul's father—by this action. Dr. Muhlbach, conveniently being on hand, recommends that Paul be admitted to his care, a prospect that, when not succumbing to a fainting spell, Paul embraces; he imagines that it would be the ideal opportunity to discover what Curtis and Muhlbach are up to. Though Muhlbach professes that he would not "consider him a patient, merely a guest" and that his care will consist of "a few heart-to-heart talks, plenty of food and rest," as soon as Paul is safely sequestered in his locked observation room with a disconnected phone, Curtis presses harder for Virginia to marry him. As we have already seen, Curtis not only desires Virginia, but also young women in general and his character is made more complex by his inability to resist them. Despite all he has to lose by such risky behavior, he ogles the teenage friends of Dorothy and Paul's girlfriend, Lydia (Mary McLeod), gropes Lydia and starts kissing her underwater in the Cartwright pool, and goes as far as to make bold advances even toward Dorothy. Curtis is not simply a gold-digging murderer, but one who cannot even see one set of his psychotic criminal intentions through before being confounded by an entirely different set of psychotic criminal intentions.

Curtis' plans are thwarted, however, by Paul's previous discoveries with Dr. Vincent that prove Curtis to be actually the suspected killer Clyde Barrington. Paul is still able to act as the hero, once he is freed by the police, at which point he leads a narrow rescue of Dorothy in the boathouse, where she had been cornered and had presumably begun to be molested by Curtis. Paul, predictably, passes out at the end of the film, but in his dream sequence, all is well: the fog clears, as he, his mother, Lydia, and Dr. Vincent can see a clear path ahead on which to walk. The film may seem to end in an entirely conventional way with a dream sequence parallel to the opening, but in fact the ending is more creative—and disturbing—than it may seem. True resolution would have been happiness and peace in real time, but instead, in true *noir* fashion, the film is resolved with yet another dream, which the audience, in keeping with the logic of the film, is being forced to assume is as—or more—truthful than objective reality. Paul's original dream "prophecy" in fact *does* come true, while many things in the real world deceive.

The role of the nefarious psychiatrist in *noir* is complicated by female portrayals of this type. Malevolent female psychiatrists are some of the most dangerous *femmes fatales* in *noir*, since they not only possess the usual physical charms and seductive intelligence, but also psychiatric knowledge and techniques that allow them additional power. Two films that show this most strikingly are *I, the Jury* (1953) and *Nightmare Alley* (1947). One of the Mickey Spillane *noirs*, *I, the Jury* has Mike Hammer (Biff Elliot) investigating (and trying to avenge) the death of a former police friend, Jack Williams. The dizzying plot and numerous characters, coupled with a bizarre Christmas frame, create a particularly disorienting experience for the viewer. Jack Williams is shot as the film begins and as he is dying, crawling and groping his way across the floor in the process, the opening titles roll, and "Hark, the Herald Angels Sing" is heard in the background. This opening sequence aptly sets the stage for the film, as Hammer gropes his way around the multiple players and motives in order to uncover Jack's killer.

Many possible suspects emerge and much seems to depend on the guests at a party that Jack had the night before he died, including Jack's girlfriend Myrna Devlin (Frances Osborne), art collector George Kalecki (Alan Reed), Kalecki protégé Hal Kines (Robert Cunningham), twins Mary and Esther Bellamy (Tani Seitz and Dran Seitz), and psychiatrist Charlotte Manning (Peggie Castle). Dr. Manning was treating some of the guests, including Myrna, who was a former thief. Hammer visits Manning, who seems oddly accustomed to receiving evening patients. Noticing her book, *Analyze Yourself*, in the apartment, he comments in voice-over that he would find out later that Manning was "no swami with a crystal ball, but the real McCoy—anything from a mental motor overhaul to a tune-up." The idea of the psychiatrist as mysterious fortuneteller is reinforced again in this film, but Manning is also recognized as a true practitioner—which almost makes her more dangerous. The viewer's first look at her is at her dressing table, as the statuesque blonde attires herself in a flowing gown to receive Hammer. As they talk, she tells him that it is a pleasure to see his mind work—"so penetrating and logical . . . after all, the mind," she says, "is what I deal with in my profession." Mike responds that he did not come there to have his head examined, but she quips that her assessment is "compliments of the management." She shares with Mike that through her treatment of Myrna, she had learned a lot about Hammer from Jack, to which he replies that she should go directly to the source if she wants to learn about him. She assures him that there is a lot, to the contrary, she could tell him about himself he wants to "give her a ring sometime." The seductive banter that goes on in this scene is framed by psychiatry, who knows what about whose mind. After Mike leaves Manning's apartment, she contemplates his half-eaten drumstick, as if it held all the evidence of the world, looking almost as if she would like to finish eating it to find out his secrets.

Much of the movie proceeds as a typical Hammer story would, with Mike searching out various seedy characters, getting into fights with some of these characters, and getting into sexual encounters with other ones. Through all this, information is hard to come by and contradictory. He continues to seek Manning out and in their second meeting, her hair is loose and she wears a negligee. They debate about whether Mike has a "suicide complex" since she claims he has "a need for trouble." Though he wants her help, and she agrees that "two minds are better than one," she also says "I'm a human being, not a magician" when he presses her for information about Kalecki, who was also one of her patients. She asks Mike if he would mind if she "played detective for a minute," to which he responds that she's moving in on "his racket." In this instance, psychiatric analysis is seen once again as both mysterious fortune-telling and detective work. For both Hammer and Manning, detecting is not a sanctioned enterprise—he is a "private dick" and she is a psychiatrist with, as we come to find out, no ethical sensibilities. Mike believes that they are working as a team, but Manning has her own agenda, using her sexuality to divert Mike's attention while finding out how much he knows.

Mike believes that the key to solving Jack's murder is finding out "what made Myrna tick," since she was an ex-jewel thief and may have double-crossed Jack if she were part of a gang again. Another visit to Manning for more insight finds her developing photos of her patients for her next book. When she shows him one photo of a man in a hypnotic stupor caused by sodium pentothal, Hammer quips, "I'm beginning to feel like this guy." As is typical in *noir*, the more Hammer discovers, the more confused he becomes. The use of sodium pentothal in psychiatric *noir*s is quite common, as is further explained later in this book. In this case, Manning explains to Mike that the drug "allows him to talk freely." We will see this effect attempted firsthand, as Manning later injects Myrna to try to discover what, if anything, she told anyone about Manning being at Jack's party. When Myrna becomes delirious and does not answer, Manning slaps her. This is the first visible crack in Manning's veneer as a psychiatrist and as a person.

When Myrna turns up dead later as a hit-and-run victim, and Mike talks further with police captain, Pat Chambers (Preston Foster), he begins to make some sense of everything, coming to the conclusion that Kines, Kalecki, the Bellamy twins and Myrna were all part of a jewel theft gang and that Jack had invited them all to a party for a confrontation. Manning is at the center of the gang too; as Mike comments, "the problem started" when Kines went to Manning for psychoanalysis and she hypnotized him, finding out about their scheme and wanting to get in on the money. Mike surmises, that now that Kalecki is dead (shot by Mike earlier in the film), Manning will be the new boss of the gang. He returns to Manning's apartment one more time to confront her and waits for her in darkness, in a scene that mirrors the confrontation scene between Fred MacMurray and Barbara Stanwyck in *Double Indemnity.* When she appears, he has his gun pointed toward her and mentions that he figured out that she had a secret entrance/exit through her darkroom—after all, "nobody disturbs a person in a darkroom." The darkroom has particular significance since it is a place of darkness, but one that brings about illumination—the development of photographs signifying the revelation of "truth." In Manning's case it means much more, as the darkroom was the vehicle through which she fulfilled her secret identity, but it also calls into question the nature of the truth that her photographs might reveal. We see the photo of the man in the pentothal stupor, witness the seeming "unsuccessful" effect of the drug on Myrna, and also see the dangerous effect of hypnosis on Kines, as Manning used the procedure to discover information for financial gain. The "dark room" represents the darkness that is Manning and her destructive power, her ability to mine the dark depths of the psychological unknown to produce her own gain.

Confronted by Hammer, Manning, returning to psychiatric form, wants to "talk this out." Hammer replies, "I've already had a long talk with myself, right through a head full of nightmares, and it's all clear now." As he talks, Manning slowly takes off her coat, undoes her hair and removes her shoes, and she soothingly tells him to "get it all out." She tries to put him at ease so that she can gain control of the situation, telling him that her mistake was falling in love with him and mourning how much they could have done together—the world could be theirs, she says. The conversation ends when she asks him to hold her tight; the embrace turns deadly as she pulls a gun out of a plant, but he shoots her first.

Manning's death is similar to that of most *noir* femmes fatales, but her role as a psychiatrist makes her power much more sinister. She is beautiful and seductive, but displays a nearly impenetrable power in her ability to discover and use information. Though she is physically portrayed as extremely feminine, her surname matches what can be seen as a masculine level of power, one that is nearly a match for that most masculine *noir* protagonist, Mike Hammer.

A similar malevolent female psychiatrist is seen in Edmund Goulding's *Nightmare Alley* (1947), though with far different, and more chilling, resolution. In *Nightmare Alley*, the world of psychiatry is juxtaposed with the world of the carnival, and the elements of faith, superstition, magic, and con-game manipulation in both worlds are presented as complementary. We meet carnival worker Stanton Carlisle (Tyrone Power) early in the film, as he expresses his love for the carnival because "it gives you sort of a superior feeling, as if you were in the know and they were on the outside lookin' in." This is the kind of power that motivates Stan throughout the film and provides foreshadowing of the elements of psychiatry used later in the film; one might imagine the same superior thrill felt by a psychiatrist, who has special and secret knowledge of others.

Also introduced early in the film is the mysterious figure of the "geek," the nature of whom is never clearly defined, only suggested as a bestial human who eats live animals. One of Stan's fellow carnival workers, Zeena (Joan Blondell) tells Stan that the geek is a "sore point" in a carnival, because while it is usually one of their biggest draws, a lot of performers will not work a show with one in it. Stan cannot understand how someone "could get so low," and Zeena sagely responds, "It can happen." Visually, the shots of carnival life early in the film are simultaneously garish and dark, which matches, as Tony Williams also points out, its shifting chiaroscuro of knowledge and mystery:

> *Nightmare Alley*'s carnival world exists on the borders of civilization. Although having rules of its own where its inhabitants look after themselves, [Lee] Garmes's cinematography presents it as a world containing traps for the unwary. These include not only the "marks" taken in by the tricks of the trade, but also its own inhabitants. Separated from the world of everyday normality, the fairground's *noir* environment reveals it as a world populated by performers who are often one step away from a threatening fate represented by poverty and destitution.[8]

This "threatening fate" is clearly realized in the relationship between Zeena and her husband, Pete (Ian Keith), who is an alcoholic. They had worked a "mentalist" act in the carnival in which Zeena would appear psychically to know details about audience members based on codes that Pete would feed her as he selected audience members with questions. Now, Pete struggles with his alcoholism, and while he realizes that if it were not for Zeena, he would be just like the geek, he simultaneously resents her for it, since it was her infidelity that was the catalyst for his drinking problem. Zeena clearly seems to feel more pity and guilt than romantic love toward Pete at this point, wanting to put him in a "cure," but lacking the money. The atmosphere of the carnival, then, is the milieu for all sorts of psychological damage, as its games and cons pretend knowledge and insight of the human mind that is anything but present in reality.

Hungry for success, Stan tries to convince Zeena to create a new her act using her code with him instead, and she is tempted by the promise of the money they could make. Meanwhile, Pete reminisces about the old act and though he is violently resistant to Stan working the code with Zeena, shows Stan what the pitch was like, reenacting his energetic spiel: "Man has sought to look behind the veil that hides him from tomorrow. And through the ages, certain men have looked into the polished crystal . . . and seen. Is it some quality of the crystal itself, or does the gazer merely use it to turn his gaze inward? Who knows? But visions come." He then begins to feign sight of a boy and dog running through rolling hills, and Stan is taken in, saying "Yes! His name was Jib! Go on . . ." Pete laughs, and says, "See how easy it is take 'em in? Every boy has a dog." This display of a typical mentalist carnival con speaks to the universality of human experience and the qualities of human nature that allow such deception to be possible—much perhaps like a faith in science or medicine (or psychoanalysis) may blind one to potential dangers. Stan is taken aback by this display, but learns a valuable lesson as well. And though the film presents Stan's gifting Pete with wood alcohol instead of moonshine as an "accident," it is obvious that a Freudian conclusion would be more than appropriate here: there are no "accidents," especially when Stan has much to gain from Pete's death.

As Stan and Zeena perfect their act, Stan juggles romantic relationships with both Zeena and Molly (Coleen Gray), another carnival worker. Molly is the one who first tells Stan about the code and also learned it watching Stan and Zeena work. Zeena calls Stan "a born mentalist" and he is clearly portrayed as having particular manipulative skill, which is evident in a scene in which a sheriff arrives to shut the carnival down. Stan is able, through sleight of hand and smooth talk, to convince the sheriff that he knows all kinds of things about him, and seems to hypnotize him, the sheriff ultimately forgetting why he came to the carnival at all and wandering away. Stan becomes increasingly enamored of his own power, adding a gospel element to the act to help the con even further. He says he learned the Bible in the orphanage where he grew up, where he was taught scripture "after they beat us black and blue." Stan is smart and cynical and is intent on using his skills for money and power, regardless of whether others are hurt. One of his first victims is Zeena, whom he repays by leaving the carnival with Molly and using the code on their own in a new act—this time in ballrooms to society clientele rather than the workers and farmers who visit the carnival.

Calling himself "The Great Stanton," Stan develops a lucrative act, but his life is changed by the appearance in the audience one evening of "consulting psychologist" Dr. Lilith Ritter (Helen Walker), who is just as independent and potentially dangerous as her name implies. Intrigued by Stan's apparent ability, Lilith questions him and allows that "psychologists admit the validity of mental telepathy under certain . . ." but he cuts her off by asking if this is "one of those joints," implying that a psychiatrist's office is no different than any other "joint" where any charlatanism might take place. When Lilith asks him if he has ever been psychoanalyzed, he replies, "I saw one in a murder movie once . . . a good mentalist could have straightened the whole thing out in five minutes." The use of the word "mentalist" throughout the film is striking, as the term almost sounds like "mental scientist" or something more legitimate than what it actually is. The mentalist bears important similarity to the psychoanalyst—both rely on knowledge of the human mind, particularly human weakness and frailty, although their motivations are ostensibly different: the psychiatrist aims to cure, while the mentalist aims to con.

However, Stan believes that their two professions are more similar than different, especially in his distrust of psychology and his belief that what Lilith does is nothing more than a different kind of con. He will later discover how true this assumption is, but at the outset, he simply seems to want to put her in her place. He wants to know "her angle," and she asks him to call her at her apartment, similar to the way that Charlotte Manning began to draw Mike Hammer into her web. After Stan leaves her office, Ritter proceeds to see a patient, Mrs. Peabody (Julia Dean), who is troubled by dreams that her daughter is still alive. Ritter records this session, noting that dreams are "one of the clues we have about the subconscious mind . . . it's the psychologist's way of looking at the patient's tongue." Lilith allies her practices with medical science as a way of legitimizing them and thereby inducing "confidence" in others. When Stan discovers her recording system, he sees a golden opportunity, and tells her, "you don't realize what you've got here . . . we could set the whole town on its ear," especially with the high-profile clients she has. She acts outraged by his suggestions and maintains that the recordings are sacred. When he asks her whether she is an actual medical doctor, she says no, but the confidentiality is the same in her patient relationships. During this scene, bars of shadow appear on the wall behind Ritter, underscoring the prospect of Stan becoming imprisoned by his association with her. As we will see, Ritter's ethics are as much a part of her "act" as is Stan's mentalist "powers."

Added to the film's backdrop of mysterious powers is the use of the tarot, of which Zeena is a practitioner. Zeena reads Stan's cards and warns him against the change in work he is thinking of, which shows his fortune as the hanged man. Earlier in the film, Stan rejected Zeena's reliance on the tarot, and ridiculed her fear of the reading that showed success for her and Stan but the hanged man for Pete. He told her that he could not believe she would fall for one of her own "bootcatchers," but this reading later in the film visibly disturbs him. We also learn later in the film that Stan is having trouble sleeping and is getting massages to help alleviate his anxiety. As a result, during the massage after the tarot reading, Stan becomes unglued by the sight of the alcohol the masseur is using, as it reminds him of Pete's death, and runs straight to Ritter for help. As much as he viewed her and her profession with a jaded eye before, he now believes that it would have to be someone like her who could help him overcome the guilt he feels over Pete's death. She soothes his fears, saying that his reaction was triggered by the smell and that his guilt feelings are "natural" because though he did not mean to cause Pete's death, he did profit by it. J.P. Telotte points out that Lilith "has her own stage patter, her probing questions and solicitous approach echoing Stan's almost word-for-word."[9] In fleeing from Zeena's tarot he falls right into Lilith's psychoanalytic clutches, never imagining that his "treatment" is a con.

Ritter and Stan do begin working together, and his "act" evolves into an almost evangelical enterprise as, beginning with a "vision" of Mrs. Peabody's dead daughter, he begins to act as a conduit for the dead, using the information from Lilith's sessions to convince his marks that he can see and speak to their dead loved ones. Others call him a miracle worker for the comfort he gives, but he calls himself a "spook worker." Mrs. Peabody's brother-in-law, Ezra Grindle (Taylor Holmes) is suspicious of his sister-in-law's devotion to Stan, especially her intention to build him the "finest tabernacle in the world" so that he can expand his spiritual pursuits; however, since Grindle happens to be one of Lilith's patients as well, Stan is able to invoke some details regarding a girl he had loved who had died, and he "fell apart like a broken doll." This is another example in *noir* of the shattering effects that knowledge gleaned from psychoanalysis can have, and though Stan is confident in his power over Grindle at this point, it is this association that causes

Stan's downfall, since Grindle asks what no one else has asked of him: to materialize his dead loved one. Stan believes he must comply in order to keep Grindle's faith, but faces resistance from Molly when he asks her to impersonate the dead sweetheart. She tells him that he is "going against God" and that God will not stand for him making "everything holy and sacred into a gag." More important than the religious implications is the implication that Stan has crossed a moral line with this prospect and has presumed too much in his desire to control others. He maintains that there is "no difference between this and mentalism—just another angle of show business." Despite his own psychological difficulties, Stan persists in the view that human emotions are essentially superficial and therefore open to any manipulation for "entertainment"—and for him, profit. It is strikingly clear here how the inherent cynicism in *noir* might be linked to the influence of psychoanalysis, as human emotion is simultaneously exposed and undermined.

The "show" put on for Grindle backfires, as Molly breaks down when Grindle begins to cry at her approach. Exposed as frauds, Stan and Molly must leave town, and Stan now badly needs the money he has made with Lilith. After he discovers that she instead has given him a package of $1 bills, he angrily returns to her apartment, only to be confronted by her gun-wielding housekeeper and Lilith pretending that he is a deranged patient. Which of course, he is, and she has the recording to prove it. She tells him that he is suffering from serious paranoia and his attempt to implicate her in the con is just "transference." The true power in their relationship is now realized, as Lilith has used her psychoanalytic knowledge to drive Stan nearly into madness, as she claims that she does not even hear the police siren that he hears approach the building. She offers to give him a sedative and drive him to the hospital where he "can have a nice, long rest." Stan's expression of disbelief throughout this scene is familiar; we have seen it, as Telotte points out, repeatedly in the film: "when Pete demonstrates his mind-reading spiel, when [Lilith] plies her fraudulent psychoanalytic patter on him, and when Stan similarly 'works' several gullible characters. This repeated expression reflects the almost mesmerizing power of discourse to control and even transform people through the 'truth' it constructs, even as it shows Stan's equal ability and vulnerability, his capacity both to control and to be controlled."[10]

Lilith actually constructs and projects insanity onto Stan who, as we have seen, is unstable to begin with. With Molly safely on a train, Stan hides from the police and cannot seem to recover. He cannot eat and begins to drink heavily, just like the geek and Pete. A close-up shot reveals Stan unshaven, about to drink, looking disturbingly like Pete, as a voice-over of the geek's screams heard at the beginning of the film complete the scene. The camera then cuts to Stan, now a hobo, pontificating under a bridge about the future and visions and his crystal ball, the bottle. And again, just like Pete did, he puts on the same act about the dog, with another hobo buying in, just as he did. Then Stan revels, "how easy it is to hook 'em," musing that this is a "stock reading, fits anybody, every boy has a dog, every boy has a beautiful grey-haired mother . . . every boy except for me." This admission highlights the fact that he too has been taken in, only not by this "stock reading," but rather by his own weakness and trust of Lilith. She accomplishes her seduction of Stan in a different way than Charlotte Manning seduces Mike Hammer. Where Manning is voluptuous and feminine, Lilith is almost masculine, as her bound hair, suits, and fedora signify. As an orphan, Stan lacked a strong father figure, and Lilith makes up for this, representing "a controlling parental fantasy image deeply embedded within his own psyche that will eventually lead to his downfall."[11]

Stan winds up at a carnival trying to sell himself as a mind-reader, but failing that, accepting a job as a geek. The boss assures him that "it's only temporary, until we can get a real geek," but it is clear that Stan is the "real geek"—what would the "real geek" look like, if not Stan? The same man who, in his early days at the carnival, wondered how a man like the geek could have sunk so low, now when asked if he can handle the job as a geek, says "Mister, I was made for it." This appears to be true since later that night, he is wild, craving alcohol, and acting as much the geek as the one we saw at the beginning of the film. What seems to be becoming the darkest of endings is mitigated by Molly's appearance; she is part of this carnival and says that she will "look after him." He hangs his head and then embraces her, in this scene darkly echoing the relationship between Zeena and Pete. The boss now realizes that he is "Stanton the Great," and when a fellow worker asks, "How can a guy get so low?" he responds, "He reached too high." Stan's hubris and fall is intimately tied with his pursuit of the knowledge of the human mind. His desire to discover the secrets of emotional motivations and weaknesses unknowingly puts his own mental stability him at risk. Lilith Ritter emerges unscathed as the consummate villain; as a doctor, she is portrayed as being smarter and even more cynical than Stan about human nature. Her skills and techniques and moreover, her cold detachment, protect her from being subsumed in the vortex of guilt and desperation in which Stan finds himself trapped.

It has been noted that often *noir* psychologists and psychiatrists, instead of shown to wield the power they might possess, are depicted as the most confused, the most unstable, the most powerless of characters. Examples of these include Dr. Wilma Tuttle (Loretta Young) in William

Dieterle's *The Accused* (1949) and Dr. Richard Wanley (Edward G. Robinson) in Fritz Lang's *The Woman in the Window* (1944). However, these types of characters tend to lean toward the professor or teacher of psychology, rather than the practitioner, suggesting that they are "less" of a doctor. Similar to Stan Carlisle, they find themselves victims of the very psychological forces and weaknesses they should be mastering. However, another character type puts forth the concept of psychiatrist identity as desirable and powerful enough to risk everything to attain. We see such an example in an early *noir*, *Fingers at the Window* (Charles Lederer, 1942). The story centers on a series of axe murders that are perpetrated by an impersonating psychiatrist, who manipulates others through hypnosis to kill for him. He and the other psychiatrist figures in the film, who show varying degrees of psychiatric skill and credibility, collectively undermine the ability of psychiatry to solve any of society's ills.

One early indication of this undermining can be found in the odd dynamic among the police, county psychiatrist, and the cadre of reporters who camp out at the police station to get the latest scoop on the axe murders. The reporters play the role of a cynical Greek chorus, as they are fully involved with the police and their actions in the case and are also well-versed in popular psychology. As police inspector Gallagher (Charles D. Brown) tries to get a suspect to talk at the beginning, the camera pans left, and we see the group of reporters right behind him listening, and even groaning when Gallagher offers him a glass of water. They comment that there are "five lunatics" already in "padded cells eating jelly omelets at the taxpayers' expense." At this point, Dr. Cromwall (Walter Kingsford), the county psychiatrist and one of the many psychiatrists we will see in the film, enters, saying, "Haven't you fellows caught on yet there's such a thing as lunacy in the world?" The jovial and somewhat comical interactions among all of them undercut the gravity of psychological illness, at the same time that they illuminate it, as Cromwall explains to them that the suspect is "in the midst of an hallucination," continuing to Gallagher, "I'm gonna show these men what schizophrenia really is." He then explains to the reporters that the suspect is talking to "his other self. . . . He's in a world apart—a world no ordinary or normal person could ever enter. Just look at him . . . [Reporters peer into room at him] He's hearing his own voice, arguing with it." Cromwall insists, "You've got to get away from the idea that you're dealing with ordinary criminals." Though it attempts some widening of understanding, there is little in this explanation that seems to aid the police or even the reporters in discovering the suspects or even the motives in these particular crimes. The following exchange highlights this frustration, as the reporters press Cromwall regarding why this is happening:

Cromwall: It's mass hysteria . . . an epidemic, like a real estate boom or a wave of suicides.
Reporter: You mean you want us to go on telling our readers that a bunch of insane men are hacking away at them willy-nilly for no reason?
Cromwall: You've got it!
Reporter: Well boys, there's nothing like psychology!

As we have seen before, the function of the psychiatrist here is less about illumination than about futility regarding understanding the human mind. In a later scene, they joke with Cromwall, saying, "Hello Doc, how's your dementia praecox catatonia?" and "I dreamt about a beautiful blonde last night, what's my psychology?" The jolly Cromwall simply laughs. It is only the cynicism of the reporters that makes this more of a *noir* than a slapstick comedy.

The criminal on the loose is the most unconventional sort, the faux psychiatrist Caesar Ferrari (Basil Rathbone), who we initially only hear but not see, as he wields the power of suggestion on his unsuspecting victims, hypnotices them to commit murder for him. Ferrari has taken on the identity of a rich, dead psychiatrist, Dr. Santelle, and he must eliminate those who knew him as his previous persona. The police are essentially searching for a phantom, as unwitting, glassy-eyed automatons systematically commit Ferrari's murders. The final victim, on whom the film focuses, is Ferrari's ex-fiancé Edwina Brown (Laraine Day) a dancer who is fortunate enough to meet out-of-work actor Oliver Duffy (Lew Ayres) who aids in her surviving Ferrari's plot. Duffy is resourceful, another of the many characters who display detecting talent in *noir* even thought they are not detectives. After he helps her escape from one of Ferrari's assassins, the police pepper Edwina with questions, wanting to know if she has ever seen or heard of the killer, and asking her to "think hard." Since everyone in this film is an amateur psychologist, Duffy interjects, "There's no reason or pattern to these crimes . . . this man was an out-and-out lunatic." Gallagher shoos him away, sending him to join the reporters with the offhand comment, "That's more of your line." Though the killer escaped from Edwina's apartment, she is the only living witness, but Dr. Cromwall can offer no more illuminating advice than the fact that she should get some sleep. More energy seems to be spent trying to orchestrate a subsequent photo shoot of Edwina and Duffy for the reporters' stories than on actually solving the case, and Dr. Cromwall can offer no substantial solutions.

Both Duffy's observations and the scenes with a mysterious accomplice point to the fact that a simple explanation of a crazed killer is not sufficient. When Gallagher shares that he has his force rounding up "criminals, morons and derelicts" before they can injure anyone, Duffy shakes his head and objects to the reporters printing that story: "There's reason back of these crimes . . . not just lunacy." He tries to tell Gallagher that there is something sinister and rational behind the crimes because there are two "lunatics" involved, but Gallagher brushes him off, convinced that he is caught up in an imaginary "mastermind theory." To prove that Duffy does not have all the answers, Gallagher tells him that every victim's name begins with B. As Duffy is puzzling this new information on his way out, Dr. Cromwall and Edwina are seen observing a man in a cell, Bixley (Charles Wagenheim), the one who tried to kill her. Cromwall calls Duffy over, wanting to see if Bixley has "any reaction" to Duffy. The attitude toward the mentally ill in the film, including Cromwall's own actions, seems almost a bridge between the later, more informed films that feature psychoanalysis and the earlier "Bedlam"-type films that viewed the mentally ill as sideshow freaks for display. Cromwall gleefully points out that Bixley is "wonderful, the most perfect example of split personality you ever saw," as he describes Bixley's penchant for writing notes on little pieces of paper and putting them in a certain order. Cromwall calls his condition "Beshchaftegundsdrang—a mania for putting things in order," which is, according to Cromwall, "a kind of paranoia that's really rare." Dr. Cromwall oddly taunts Bixley, first trying to get his attention, as if calling out to a dog or a baby, and then telling him that Duffy is his real enemy. Cromwall is depicted in this scene as hardly even a doctor, in his somewhat immature relationship with Bixley, whose confinement resembles that of an animal in a cage more than a criminal awaiting trial.

In an effort to gain more information, Duffy goes to Ridgley Clinic where, he poses as insane to get admitted. In the clinic, we see yet another example of a stereotypical psychiatrist figure, Dr. Immelman (Miles Mander), who, predictably, has a German accent, and is treating a seemingly never-ending list of patients. To look at the line of patients waiting outside the clinic, one would think that indeed an epidemic of insanity had befallen the city. Duffy tells the doctor that he wants "to go to the moon" and then goes about straightening all the items on the doctor's desk. The befuddled psychiatrist, is amazed, as he tells his nurse that he has only seen "three cases" like this one, and wants to use him in a lecture to the psychiatric society. Duffy's real object is to get a look at the clinic's patient files, which the doctor allows, even though the nurse points out that these were only open to be seen by psychiatrists. The doctor comments, "A crazy man is just as valuable to psychiatry as psychiatrists." Duffy realizes that all of the men, with names beginning with B, who are suspects in the ax murder cases have files here, and realizes that it must be a psychiatrist who is at the root of the murders. The positioning of a psychiatric doctor as the cause of the spate of violent murders, rather than a set of homicidal psychotics themselves, highlights the potential destructiveness of the psychiatric profession, an idea that also surfaces when Duffy and Edwina visit the meeting of psychiatrists to which Immelman refers. They listen to a paper by a Dr. Santelle, which describes the treatment of "dementia praecox" with use of insulin and affirms that the danger of insulin therapy "in the hands of experienced trained professionals is negligible." Insulin "therapy," involving the administration of insulin to induce temporary, successive coma states, was a precursor to the use of electroshock therapy for treating schizophrenia and paranoia. The description of the process at this point in the film, can barely be heard over the conversation between Duffy and Edwina; though it is somewhat buried, these details further suggest the dangers of psychiatric practice and its potential lack of boundary in treatment.

Duffy muses to Edwina about the injustices in the case, how doctors are "supposed to help people," but instead the killer psychiatrist "uses poor mad people's brains, their hallucinations . . . he's embarked on a little program of extermination." This "program" includes Ferrari's attempted murder of Duffy, who winds up in a hospital and again subject to Ferrari's murderous coercions, as he injects him with massive amounts of insulin. The double nature of such psychiatric "treatment" is again highlighted and somewhat justifies the cynical notions regarding psychiatry that frame the film in the beginning. Ferrari has impersonated a psychiatrist simply for motives of financial greed, but as such has various creative weapons at his disposal for ensuring his success, such as the use of insulin hypnosis on others to effect the subsequent murders needed for his protection. Duffy's characterization of the situation—that such actions by a doctor are reprehensible not only because of his charge as a physician but also because he is taking advantage of those who are not able to defend themselves—turns out to be accurate, but ironically, no one will believe him. Immelman and Cromwall, the Laurel and Hardy of psychiatry, pronounce Duffy as the psychopath, they now seem to believe that Duffy has been the source of the murders. They characterize him as a "man who used persecution psychotics to commit his crimes . . . what you would call a case of a master mind." Watching Cromwall and Immelman self-congratulatingly pronouncing judgment on Duffy, who seems to be the most well-adjusted and sane character in the film, further emphasizes the lack of credibility of psychiatry portrayal in the film. Though they eventually discovered the true method of the murders, their obviously false assessments of Duffy, coupled with the reliance that Gallagher and the police place on these assessments, attack the notion that the practice of psychiatry is ultimately helpful to the human condition. This idea is further emphasized when these portrayals are combined with the third psychiatrist portrayal in Ferrari/Santelle, who is a greedy and murderous egomaniac. And in another ironic twist, the only reason Edwina is saved from Ferrari/Santelle is the police's desire to protect Ferrari/Santelle from Duffy. The triumphant music that closes the film is an unnerving close to a story that continually reinforces the dangers posed by reliance on the psychiatric profession. *Fingers at the Window* paints psychiatry as part of the problem involved with a mass urban epidemic of psychosis and psychiatrists as bumblers and criminals who exacerbate rather than ameliorate, the condition.

Another and similar manifestation of this character type is seen in Steve Sekely's *Hollow Triumph* (1948), in which a criminal assumes the identity of a psychiatrist as a criminal escape. The film opens in a prison, as a prison assistant reads an information card about an inmate named John Muller, who went to medical school and specialized in "psych . . . psych . . . mental disorders." This halting attempt at pronunciation when referring to the vocabulary of the profession is quite commonly found in psychiatry *noirs*, as well as other early films that depicted psychoanalysis, highlighting the "foreign" nature of the practice (both literally and socially), and also as perhaps a euphemistic attempt to avoid saying the actual words that signify mental illness. In any case, Muller was evidently at home with psychiatry; he withdrew suddenly from medical school, but began practicing psychoanalysis without a license. Evidently exposed by the police at that time, he was released for lack of evidence and in turn began a life of crime that eventually landed him in prison. When we meet Muller (Paul Henreid), he is now released, but goes back immediately to the criminal life. Though his friends are working small-time gambling, like slots and poker, to make a living, this is not enough for Muller; he wants a larger score, to knock over a gambling joint. When the job goes bad and half the gang members are caught, Muller decides to lay low and take a drudgery office job.

His life takes a *noir*-ish turn when a man follows him on the street and stops him, thinking he looks like someone he knows, a Dr. Bartok. The man says he is a professional colleague of Bartok's, a dentist who works in the same building as he. The dentist is struck by the resemblance, except, he notes, for the fact that Bartok has a scar on his cheek, but he cannot remember if it is on the right or the left. Intrigued, Muller goes to Bartok's office (he is identified, like Lilith Ritter, as a "consulting psychologist") and talks to his secretary, Evelyn (Joan Bennett), who mistakes him for Bartok. Evelyn and Bartok are also lovers, and when she and Muller kiss, she knows immediately that he is not Bartok:

Evelyn: What can I do for you?
Muller: What more could any reasonable man ask?
Evelyn: No, no, I didn't mean that; it was a slip.
Muller: Slip, my eye, that's Freud.
Evelyn: What do you know about Freud?
Muller: You gave yourself away, the subconscious mind coming out in spite of yourself . . . you're just a wild bundle raring to go.
Evelyn: What are you anyway—an analyst or a patient?

Muller says he is neither, but rather "an innocent bystander." We have seen enough of Muller to know that he neither innocent, nor a bystander. The above banter between Evelyn and Muller signifies the way that the Muller/Bartok identity confusion is wrapped up in a psychoanalytic web. Muller tells her he was curious when he found out that he was supposed to look like Bartok, adding, "A thing like that upsets a fellow."

Muller's discovery that he has a double may be unnerving, but it begins to suggest a way out for him, as he not only has lost his job, but also is pursued by the crime boss who owned the gambling joint that was hit by Muller and his gang. The uncanny irony that not only does Muller have a nearly identical double, but also that this double just happens to be a psychiatrist, the identity that Muller had tried to pursue earlier in his life, is par for the course in the *noir* world. In a scene as Muller is hiding out and talking to his brother, there is a shot of Muller looking out behind horizontal blinds in darkness, neon flashing on his face. He appears stuck in a netherworld, as his brother, Freddy (Eduard Franz), says that everyone used to want to be like him, because "there were no rules" for John. This hubris is evident, as Muller is packing in his room, on the run from thugs, and voices in his head recall how much he resembles Bartok; he begins to think, "maybe I can get away with it." It is at this point, that he begins an elaborate plan to take over Bartok's identity, and it is unsettling how easy this ultimately becomes.

Part of Muller's plan is establishing a romantic relationship with Evelyn, who is drawn into his world, despite the fact that she is fairly cynical and savvy herself. She calls him an "egotistical smart-aleck with big ideas": "First comes you, second comes you, third comes you, and last comes you." She is also suspicious about his knowledge of psychoanalysis, quizzing him about conditions like scopophobia and Korsakov's syndrome. The choice of these particular psychological ailments, which are defined as fear of being seen and false memory syndrome, respectively, are significant, given Muller's situation. He is on the run and trying to hide himself from the world, using as the possible solution, the assumption of the identity of another man, a transformation that could never fully take place because of the inability to absorb the memories of that other identity. Physical appearance can be copied and even knowledge can be absorbed, but for Muller, even if he becomes Bartok, his memories will always be "false." Muller tries to set Evelyn's mind at ease by explaining that he studied psychoanalysis for years, and asks to see Bartok's files. Though she refuses, this does not deter him, and he breaks into Bartok's office to steal something with his signature, narrowly escaping being caught by Bartok himself, as seen in a deft shot with both of them in the frame, Muller standing behind a door.

Muller proceeds to become Bartok, as he practices writing his signature, imitating his voice, smoking as he does, and even doing further refresher reading on psychiatry. Though he and Evelyn end their relationship, he continues to plan the transformation, as he takes a night job at the garage where Bartok parks his car in order to position himself for the final stages of his plan. As we know from the start of the film, Bartok's scar is the key element in the physical resemblance, so Muller uses a photo of Bartok to duplicate the scar on his own face. This scene shows Muller, his face reflected in a mirror, standing next to Bartok's photo, using medical instruments to scar himself. As he performs the procedure, the camera shifts to show only his hands and the instruments; as he works, a cigarette burns down to ashes, forming a "scar" on the desk at which he works. As he scars himself, Muller becomes reduced to a new mirror image of himself that will be identical to Bartok's photo; only the devices needed to effect this transformation are important in this shot, as well as another mirror image of the cigarette "scar," signifying the further indelibility of Muller's action. This indelibility is brought into harsh relief, when the viewer learns that the photo developer reversed the negative when printing the photo of Bartok, and so Muller has scarred himself on the wrong side. Muller himself will only learn of this mistake later, but it is curious that the painstaking, medically educated Muller would have made such an error, since he had actually seen Bartok so many times as he studied his mannerisms and movements. It is arguable that Muller's mistake was a "Freudian" slip, much like the one Evelyn makes in their first conversation: inasmuch as he desperately wants to become Bartok on one level, he permanently marks himself on the opposite side of the face from Bartok's real scar, as if to assert his own identity, even as this would be the prime marker of his identity as Bartok.

Naturally, Muller only makes the fatal discovery after he has already killed Bartok, depicted in a well-shot scene incorporating close-ups of Muller's face, a flashback of montage images of his pursuit from the gambling house thugs, and radio music interwoven with stop and go intersection signs. These chaotic images correspond to the unraveling of Muller's plan, one that he must still carry out despite the danger of discovery. Another encounter between Muller and the dentist from the beginning of the film highlights this danger. The dentist tells him that he saw someone who looked just like him . . . not just resembled, but rather a real "double." The dentist goes on to say he resembles this other man in all respects, except the scar, motioning to side of face on which the scar is supposed to be. In this way, Muller becomes a "third" self, rather than Bartok's "double" or even himself anymore. But Muller forges ahead as Bartok, seeing Bartok's patients and listening to them, as he sits and smokes and looks lost in thought, almost calling into question the nature of the psychiatric profession—what, and how much, does one actually have to DO as an psychoanalyst, anyway? Penelope Pelizzon and Nancy West argue that *Hollow Triumph*

> blatantly mocks psychoanalysis—whose central figure, Freud, was the first to theorize the uncanny—as a practice devoid of both substance and credibility. As a doctor with many years of practice in a specialized field, Bartok would seem a difficult man to impersonate. Yet Muller, who appears in one scene studying a textbook of basic psychology, has little trouble. Bartok's patients even seem to prefer the crook to the real doctor. Indeed, the film implies that criminal skills and psychoanalytic aptitude are twinned forms of intelligence, both depending upon like modes of thought and resulting in identical personal tastes.[12]

Though we know that Muller has more than just a passing basic knowledge of psychiatry, it is true that the film's portrayal of Bartok/Muller seems to undermine both the nature and the effects of the profession. Though his patients may notice that he has "changed his methods," he is not suspected as being anyone other than Bartok. Becoming Bartok, however, ultimately turns out not to be the smooth ride for which Muller hopes, as he also learns that Bartok was about to go bankrupt because of his mounting gambling debts. Muller's assumption of Bartok's identity takes on even greater significance at this point, as yet another similarity between the two men is revealed: though their roles in the gambling vice are reversed, Bartok is a victim of the same type of criminal that Muller is and is also trying to hide from them in his new life.

Muller is further confronted by his past when his brother comes looking for him at Bartok's office. When the door opens, Freddy Muller says, "That's my brother," adding that the resemblance between his brother and Bartok is "striking." Muller defensively admits everything to Freddy, saying, "I'm Bartok. Who is going to know? Who will ever find out?" As it turns out, in perfect *noir* irony, no one is even looking for John Muller anymore, since the gambling boss was arrested and deported because of income tax charges. In a desperation-filled conversation with Evelyn, who has by now learned that Bartok is really Muller, she tells him that she is going away, taking a ship to Hawaii. An overwhelming sense of cynicism and bitterness bubbles to the surface in this scene. Evelyn is portrayed as fairly tough, as she admits earlier in the film that "it's a bitter little world full of sad surprises and you don't go around letting people hurt you." That the world has to prove a lack of fulfillment twice with the "same" man is a bitter irony to swallow, and the backdrop of psychiatry in this entire affair underscores the futility of hoping for real insight into human emotions or the human condition. Muller does seem to intend to make a genuine new start, with Evelyn, as he is seen making phone calls in darkness, giving his patients to other doctors. In an arresting scene as Muller is leaving his office building, his scar mistake is finally noticed by the cleaning lady, who says it was so clear in her mind that the scar was on the other side of his face. Muller tenderly brings her to her feet, as she says she knows she is wrong—how could she be right, when "Bartok" is standing right in front of her? In further irony, the one person Muller is least likely to notice has noticed him, and his almost loving reaction to her pronouncement indicates a certain relief that he is hoping to be free from the masquerade at last by his departure. This departure, however, is not meant to be, and constitutes the film's final and horrible irony. A group of gangsters pursue and overpower Muller in the ship terminal; however, these are not the hoods of the deported gambling boss, but a rather the gangsters that are there to collect the $90,000 that Bartok owes in gambling debts. Not only is there a double of Muller, there are also, as we see, doubles of his pursuers. Of course Muller tries to convince them that he is not Bartok, pointing out that his scar is on the wrong side of his face, but the resemblance is good enough for the thugs, and as he tries to flee to the ship, they shoot him down. First criminal and then victim, the fate of Muller remains the same.

As Pelizzon and West point out, *Hollow Triumph* exemplifies the elusive mood of *film noir* as it frames the tragedy of urban life within the realm of the uncanny: "The ease with which a felon like Muller assumes the identity of a 'respectable' citizen like Bartok depends on Muller's operating in an urban culture—a culture mythologized by *film noir*—where the boundaries between 'respectability' and criminality are easily blurred. In the world of *Hollow Triumph*, a criminal can pass himself off as a psychiatrist, a prominent psychiatrist can be murdered because of gambling debts, and a secretary supposedly in love with a respectable man can fall in love just as easily with his criminal look-alike."[13] Muller's impersonation of a psychiatrist brings into sharp focus the depths and shifts that this character type has in *film noir*—alternately seen as savior and criminal, the *noir* psychiatrist is at the heart of *noir*'s various ironies concerning the mysteries — and potential immorality — of the human mind. Beneficent, bogus, or downright evil, noir psychiatrists can be practitioners or panderers and their ability to treat or harm is a reflection of the anxiety at the heart of modern psychological inquiry.

Notes

1. Lutz Koepnick, "Doubling the Double: Robert Siodmak in Hollywood," *New German Critique* 89, (Spring-Summer 2003): 89.
2. Nicholas Christopher, *Somewhere in the Night: Film Noir and the American City.* (New York: Free Press, 1997), 209.
3. Glen O. Gabbard and Krin Gabbard. *Psychiatry and the Cinema*, 2nd ed. (Washington, D.C.: American Psychiatric Press, 1999), 56.
4. Mary Ann Doane, "The Clinical Eye: Medical Discourses in the 'Woman's Film' of the 1940's," *Poetics Today* 6, no.1/2 (1985): 212.
5. Christopher, 221.
6. Janet Walker, "Hollywood, Freud and the Representation of Women," in *Home is Where the Heart Is: Studies in Melodrama and the Woman's Film*, ed. Christine Gledhill (London: BFI, 1987), 207.
7. Peter Bogdanovich, *Who the Devil Made It* (New York: Knopf, 1977), 596.
8. Tony Williams, "The Naturalist Horizons of *Nightmare Alley* (1947)," *Excavatio* 22, no. 1-2 (2007): 133.
9. J.P. Telotte, *Voices in the Dark: The Narrative Patterns of Film Noir.* (Urbana: University of Illinois Press, 1989), 188.
10. Telotte, 189.
11. Williams, 135.
12. Penelope Pelizzon and Nancy West, "'A Perfect Double Down to the Last Detail': Photography and the Identity of *Film Noir*." *Post Script* 22, no. 3 (Summer 2003): 37.
13. Pelizzon and West, 38.

Chapter Two

Noir Asylums and Treatments

Through exploring the various roles of the psychiatrist in the world of *noir*, we have already been introduced to the modes of treatments that they use. Psychotherapy, dream analysis, hypnosis, and drug therapy are widely seen in *noir*, as well as the depiction of mental hospitals, sanitariums, and asylums. As one might imagine, these therapies are usually shown to have less-than-desirable effect, and the treatment atmosphere or mental hospital becomes yet another *noir* locale for alienation and peril. One of the most common reasons for the manifestation of psychiatric therapies in *noir* is the proliferation in popular culture of the 1940s and 1950s of stories about shell-shocked World War II soldiers and the solutions to their maladies that were being developed by U.S. military doctors. Though the appearance of the maladjusted (particularly amnesiac) veteran in *noir*, having important relevance to the general subject of *noir* psychiatry, will receive more detailed analysis in a subsequent chapter of this study, it is important to note here that the catalyst for various "new" treatments in mental health immediately preceding and during the *noir* period was the popular dissemination of treatments for veterans. According to Gerald Grob, "the war not only created a new therapeutic model, but also transformed the specialty of psychiatry. In 1940 the APA had only 2,295 members. . . . Under Brigadier General [Karl] Menninger about 2,400 physicians (most without specialty training) were assigned to psychiatry."[1] Menninger and others were particularly influential in not only advancing psychiatry as a science and mental illness as a medical condition, but also in advancing the idea that it was vitally important for soldiers to be treated for their war-induced psychological traumas in order for them to be able to reintegrate successfully in civilian society.

Chronicles of the kinds of mental illness therapies plied on servicemen were widely seen in popular magazines of the day. For example, a 1943 issue of *Time* published "Spit it Out, Soldier" in its Medicine section, comparing the modern "talk treatment" being used by the Army and its success to the high, lasting trauma rate of World War I veterans, whose only therapy for shell shock was removal from the front. The frame of the article interestingly applauds the modern methods for making it possible for soldiers to continue to fight after experiencing psychological distress rather than to be discharged home. "As soon as a front-line soldier loses his grip," the article tells us, "he is urged to tell what is the matter, preferably to an Army psychiatrist, just behind the battle lines."[2] An Army psychiatrist adds later, "It is amazing how much difference it makes to get to these men early. It's like releasing steam before it has a chance to build up to explosive point in a kettle." Other examples include an article in a 1944 issue of *The Saturday Evening Post* that describes techniques of psychodrama ("By bringing their problems out into the open, patients lose the dark, nameless fears which have been torturing their minds and warping their outlooks") and an article in a 1944 issue of *Collier's* that assures the following: "Most of our men are taking their isolation and C rations and airplane strafing and muddy foxholes with no cracking. Those who do crack are not necessarily softies. It is the toughest war that man has ever known. Many will break up and most of them will recover and many of them will fight again."[3] The article goes on to describe various methods of psychiatric treatment for those servicemen who do "crack," including the relatively new practice of "narcosynthesis," which involves administration of sodium pentothal, sodium amytal, or another tranquilizer as a technique that precedes psychoanalytic analysis in order to free the mind for subconscious release. The administration of such drugs to soldiers was found to reduce anxiety and break down defense mechanisms, while at the same time stimulating recall of original experiences, hence the popular name of "truth serum" given to it.[4] The *Collier's* article describes fairly accurately the technique that is documented in various psychiatric studies of the time: "If the men can be brought to describe what has happened to them and what has brought about the mental condition, the cure is not hard, but often they refuse to talk. They are then given a mild drug which brings about a slight hypnotic condition under which they discuss their fears, admit their failures and get release from inhibitions that have brought about that condition." Indeed, it is suggested that many psychiatrists at the time, according to Nathan G. Hale, Jr., "came to feel, on the basis of their wartime experience, that psychoanalysis possessed superior explanatory power" and also that "narcosynthesis provided dramatic confirmation of the existence of the unconscious."[5]

One of the most compelling true-life depictions of the way hypnosis, narcosynthesis, and other psychiatric treatments were used during and after World War II is John Huston's *Let There Be Light* (1948), a documentary that shows the real experiences of soldiers suffering from "neurospsychiatric disorders." The film was suppressed by the U.S. government until the late 1970s, even though it ultimately shows the triumph of American soldiers over the effects of battle-induced mental trauma. Nevertheless, and likely the reason for the suppression, the emotionally charged and often chilling depiction of actual psychiatric sessions between army psychiatrists and soldiers suffering from various maladies, such as depression, psychosomatic paralysis, and stuttering, show the very real consequences of war on the human mind. Oddly, the titles at the film's opening caution us, "The special treatment methods shown in this film, such as hypnosis and narcosynthesis, have been particularly successful in acute cases, such as battle neurosis. Equal success is not to be expected when dealing with peacetime neuroses which are usually of a chronic nature." There is no explanation regarding what makes other neuroses "chronic" or why the above treatments would only be effective for "non-chronic" ailments, but regardless, there appeared to be an effort to distance civilian mental illness from the "special" battle neuroses afflicting men from the war. What *noir* underscores is the scant difference between the two, and the fact that when the soldiers from the war return home, they bring mental disturbance with them, just as the horrors and uncertainty of modern war begin to permeate all aspects of the home front, even after peacetime.

In *Let There Be Light*, bandages and splints are compared to the less outward signs of those who are also wounded, the "psychoneurotic soldier," who suffers from "feelings of hopelessness and utter isolation . . . torments of fear and uncertainty and loneliness," and whose stories all focus on a common thread: "death and the fear of death." We hear stories of soldiers who feel "mixed up" and "not the same" as before they left home for the war, and who "got tired of living." We are told that "Modern psychiatry makes no division between the mind and the body" as we witness a treatment session for a soldier who suffers from psychological paralysis; jerking and twitching, he expresses anxiety about his mother's recent illness and his sudden crying spells. The doctor injects him with sodium amytal and explains, "The use of this drug serves a twofold purpose: like hypnosis, it is a shortcut to the unconscious mind. As a surgeon probes for a bullet, the psychiatrist explores the submerged regions of the mind attempting to locate and bring to the surface the emotional conflict which is the cause of the patient's distress. The second purpose of this drug is to remove through suggestion those symptoms which impede the patient's recovery." Sure enough, after the woozy soldier rambles about his parents in response to the doctor's questions, his legs feel "all right," and he can raise them. The doctor prods, "Now you are going to be able to walk, aren't you?" as the soldier indeed rises and walks. Another striking example of narcosynthesis is shown in a soldier who has developed a stutter becoming very emotional, crying repeatedly "I can talk!" The psychiatrist emphasizes that he will now be able to talk "just the way [he] always did," in what can be seen in the film as a continual emphasis to restore the solider to a pre-war condition. It turns out that this particular solder was laughed at by his fellow soldiers because of his pronunciation of "s"; such a sound, "sssssss," is characterized by the doctor as the "sound of death in combat . . . the sound of German shells coming in." The internalization of the soldier's experience of death and its psychological effects are particularly illuminating when one considers the effect of such cultural influences on the advent of *film noir.* Though the symptoms vary, the impact of imminent death on the lives of human beings invariably changes their outlook on life; likewise, lack of certainty and faith about the future and the nature of their own identities are imprints on human beings that are commonly seen in the world of *noir.* As the men are seen re-integrating with life in church and on the baseball field, *Let There Be Light* asks, "What is the mysterious ingredient that gives joy and meaning to living?" Regardless of how sound the psychiatric treatments seem to be or how resoundingly "When Johnny Comes Marching Home" triumphantly plays, the psychiatric "building rather than destroying" takes time, and its ultimate results are still unknown.

Various examples of narcosynthesis or induced hypnosis occur in *noir*; the idea of a "power of suggestion" is a compelling concept that roots itself in *noir* plots and scenarios. Human will is seen to be volatile and questionable, and the idea of outside influence on it is all too believable. A 1946 issue of *Science Digest* explains the process of narcosynthesis, which involves the intravenous administration of the drug to create a state of "narcosis," or "twilight sleep," a state similar to a partial general anesthesia; the drug is discontinued before the patient falls asleep. In this state, patients are encouraged to relive painful experiences and talk about them. Interestingly, the article offers that "this so-called truth serum was used not infrequently in military service during World War II to test soldiers on sick call suspected of malingering, or feigning illness" and further adds that "a major problem in its use revolves around the matter of ethics: Should a physician ever use a therapeutic drug for any other purpose but treating a patient? Is it ethical for a doctor to use his medical instruments to test criminal suspects rather than cure sick people?"[6] In the previous chapter, we have explored the depiction in *noir* of just such unethical physicians, and further examples can be found in *noirs* that feature these kinds of "treatments." In Robert Aldrich's *Kiss Me Deadly* (1956), for instance, Mike Hammer (Ralph Meeker) is subjected to narcosynthesis by the aptly named Dr. Soberin (Albert Dekker), who is trying to find out information about what the murdered Christina (Cloris Leachman) has told him. Hammer is tied to a bed, face-down, when Dr. Soberin enters, the shots focusing first on Soberin's feet, then legs then back, but never revealing his face; at this point, neither Hammer nor the viewer knows who he is. As Soberin prepares the injection, he says, "The young lady you picked up on the highway. She wrote you a letter. In it were two words: remember me. She asks you to remember. What is it you must remember? Do not be alarmed, Mr. Hammer. It is only a harmless drug. Sodium pentothal, a truth serum. Under its influence, you will sleep. And while you sleep, your subconscious will provide the answer. And you will cry out what it is that you must remember." Ironically, of course, and one of the features that make *Kiss Me Deadly* a *noir* rather than a simple murder mystery, Hammer is being tortured to remember something he does not know. Consequently, all Soberin and his thugs receive from Hammer is confused mumbling and his eventual escape when the drug wears off. Soberin, the thief of "the great whatzit" and its glowing atomic supremacy, is a chilling character in his anonymous menace and the use of his medical and scientific knowledge to pursue power.

A similar episode is seen in an earlier film, Edward Dymytrk's *Murder My Sweet* (1944), featuring the other well-known *noir* private investigator, Philip Marlowe (Dick Powell), who finds himself a victim of Helen Grayle (Claire Trevor) and her "psychic consultant," Jules Amthor (Otto Kruger). The opening shot of the film signifies Marlowe's psychological condition in the film quite clearly: he sits blindfolded in a dark room, illuminated by only one spot of light on his face, surrounded by police detectives. Still blindfolded, he begins to tell his story; this is an odd tactic, even for *noir*, a tactic more likely to be seen employed by criminals. Marlowe will relate how he became mixed up with Amthor and Helen, a convoluted tale of blackmail, infidelity, stolen jade, and mental therapy. Amthor describes himself to Marlowe as a "quack . . . which is to say I am ahead of my time in the field of psychic treatment." From Marlowe Amthor is trying to buy the jade necklace "stolen" from Helen, one of his "patients," though Marlowe does not have it. Like Mike Hammer, he is then knocked out and drugged, in order to make him volunteer information that he cannot know. Later, Marlowe will tell the police that Amthor does a "jewelry routine on gals who come to him with broken-down libidos." He has at his disposal "a little rest home where you learn to talk" operated by Dr. Sonderborg, a "whiz with a hypo," whose name, like Soberin's from *Kiss Me Deadly*, conjur up associations of sleep, *soma*. Marlowe experiences Sonderborg's treatment firsthand, as he loses three days consumed by a drug-induced disorienting dream. The stunning visual effect of cobwebs superimposed on the film adds to this disorientation, even when Marlowe awakens. In the dream, images of faces appear, threatening him and asking where the necklace is. As he tries to escape, the railing on a staircase bends, then disappears down in a whirlpool. Numerous doors appear, as a doctor comes toward him with injection; when the doctor gets to him, down the whirlpool he goes too.

Though narcosynthesis is never explicitly mentioned, both Marlowe's own perceptions and behavior upon awakening point at least to a similar drug being administered. Even when he awakens, the "gray web woven by a thousand spiders" lingers; he is sweaty and screaming, believing that his hands are "a bunch of bananas that look like fingers." As he becomes more conscious, he muses, "I wondered what I was shot full of: something to keep me quiet or something to make me talk. Maybe both." He does not realize the full extent of Amthor's power until he finds out from Helen that he routinely blackmailed his patients: "He did me a lot of good. He treated my centers of speech; I have a psychological impediment. His system's partly mumbo-jumbo, partly the real thing. He flatters you, he gets into your past, you talk and talk and . . . that's the awful way he works—uncovering a basis for blackmail." Amthor seems a precursor to *Whirlpool*'s David Korvo, who uses his hypnotic "treatments" on unsuspecting women to extort money. Like Korvo, Amthor meets a violent end, as his neck is broken by Helen's former lover, Moose Malloy (Mike Mazurki), who had hired Marlowe to find "Velma," the name by which Helen was previously known. Helen had triple-crossed everyone, staging the theft so that she would not have to give up her jade to Amthor. However, even though Amthor is not triumphant, the nature of his character's power over women, by both the potential use of drugs at his disposal, but more frighteningly, simply by his way of making them "talk and talk," is a chilling example of *noir*'s depiction of psychological "treatment." Kelly Oliver and Benigno Trigo suggest that Amthor, not Helen, is the film's real "femme fatale," a "psychological trickster."[7]

A more extended depiction of narcosynthesis is seen in Curtis Bernhardt's *Possessed* (1947). The entire film is actually framed around a narcosynthetic flashback of a disturbed woman, Louise Howell (Joan Crawford). From the opening shot of the film, Louise is depicted as being alienated and stricken with psychological torture. Crawford plays Louise strikingly with no makeup, as she wanders around a deserted street in the early morning; as Mary Ann Doane points out, *Possessed* follows a pattern of 1940s "medical" films in which "neuroses and even psychoses are evidenced not by contorted limbs and paralysis but by a marked lack of narcissism on the part of the sick woman. The illness of the woman is signified by the fact that she no longer cares about her appearance."[8] Louise is fragmented, her figure shot from the knees down, as she walks haltingly toward a bus, a church, a café, querulously calling every man that she sees "David" and saying, "I'm looking for David." Finally, she collapses in the café and is taken to the hospital. As she is put on a gurney from the ambulance, the perspective shifts to Louise herself, as shots of the ceiling of the hospital and the faces of doctors and nurses are seen by the viewer as the gurney wheels along. This sense of powerlessness and claustrophobia is heightened, as the Louise comes to rest under a large steel examining light, almost resembling a flying saucer; as two doctors peer at her, she stares non-responsively into space. Having identified her condition as a "coma . . . a non-traumatic stupor," the admitting physicians direct the orderlies to "take her to psycho"—what will soon be seen as being the "Psychopathic Department." Once there, she is seen by the elder Dr. Willard (Stanly Ridges) and his younger assistant, Dr. Craig (Don McGuire). Willard asks Craig, upon seeing Louise, "How many does this make?" and Craig responds, "Twenty today—one manic, three seniles, six alcoholics, and ten schizos." Willard muses, "Going up all the time. This civilization of ours has a worse disease than heart trouble or tuberculosis, and we can't escape it." The idea of mental illness as a growing "epidemic," as we have already noted in *Fingers at the Window*, is repeatedly seen in *noir* and reflects the post-war shift in *Weltanschauung*, as the gravity of modern problems seem to be proving too weighty for the human psyche to bear.

Willard and Craig attempt to treat Louise, who they characterize, in addition to her "catatonic stupor," as a "beautiful woman—intelligent, frustrated . . . just like all the others we've seen." Her lack of response vocally, as well as in her reflexes and extremities, and the fact that she has little to identify her, seem to encourage the doctors to use narcosynthesis in order to help her condition. When Willard asks her how she feels, she agonizingly struggles to say, "I . . . feel . . . " but can go no further. Willard responds, "You can't find the words can you? You want to, but you just can't. Something preventing you, is that it? We'll have to do something about that." He tries to explain to her what they are doing: "In order to help you, we've got to find out something about you. And to find out about you, we've got to make it possible for you to talk. We'll try narcosynthesis. . . . Now it's not going to hurt; it's just going to help you tell us what we want to know. . . . I want you to tell me what you're thinking." Willard adds, to Craig, "Every time I see the reaction of this treatment, I get exactly the same thrill that I did the first time." Though

Willard seems benevolent enough, there is no mistaking the somewhat creepy "thrill" that he describes, the implication of the God-like power that results in the application of narcosynthesis and being able to elicit speech and "truth" from a human being who cannot or will not communicate. This effect is compounded by the image of Louise, almost like Frankenstein's creature, coming to life as the head of her bed is raised, and she begins to respond. Though she insists that "won't tell him everything," she does follow Willard's instructions to talk about David, the frame dissolving into a flashback as she begins to hear the music of Schumann. We now meet David (Van Heflin), who is Louise's distant lover and player of the Schumann music at a piano after their swimming date. Though the scene seems tenderly romantic at the outset, it soon turns sour, as it becomes clear that Louise desperately wants more from David in the relationship than he is willing to give. She tries to convey the intensity of her feelings for him, how the word "love" is so inadequate, and how it makes one feel pain. She says that before she met him she did not feel one way or another about anything, and wants "a monopoly" on him. David counters her emotional outpouring with, "Don't, Louise . . . don't start bringing the subject around marriage again . . . It's a duet and I like to play solo. I'm not in love with you like that, Louise—you know that." Louise persists, "I used to be cold, shut-in . . . . I just can't go back being on the outside of people's lives, looking in." But David is not responsive to such a plea, as he tells her that it feels as though she is choking and smothering him. Louise's emotional isolation seems clear from the outset as well as her belief that her romantic love for a single individual has the power to rescue her from this isolation.

Louise's feelings toward David intensify in proportion to his efforts to push her away, and are contrasted by what she describes as her own distant feelings toward life before she met him. Even her employer, Dean Graham (Raymond Massey), comments on Louise's "magnificent detachment" when it comes to the way she manages her nursing duties of his neurotic invalid wife, Pauline. When she learns that Graham is contracting David's engineering services for a project in Canada, despite his pleading for her to let him go, she insists she will "find a way" to be with him. At this point, churning dark lake waters from the dock of Graham's house dissolve back to the hospital in the present, when Willard presses Louise for insight into her feelings when David left her. She says he did it to humiliate her, that he was only saying that she loved him too much, adding "they were all in on it . . . Dean, his wife Pauline . . . they all did it deliberately just to make me feel miserable." Willard, conferring then with Craig, notes, "Do you notice the beginnings of the persecution complex? No attempt to evaluate the situation or see the man's viewpoint, no judgment, lack of insight—classic symptoms. This is where the psychosis began." "Even further back, Doctor," says Craig. "She said herself that before she met him, she had never felt anything very keenly . . . typically schizoid detachments, split personality." Willard agrees, "Yes the seeds were there . . . and her obsession for this man made them grow." Though the full level of Louise's mental illness has not been developed yet, and though she does seem somewhat paranoid even in her initial reaction to David's departure, it is worth noting that David's rejection of Louise and the almost cruelly cavalier manner with which he approaches their relationship contribute greatly to her mental deterioration. However, within the narrative of the film, David is never implied to hold blame. The doctors even emphasize the fact that part of Louise's psychosis is due to the fact that she lacks the ability to "see the man's viewpoint" and therefore has "no judgment" and "lack of insight." The male "framing" of Louise's story is even seen visually from her first moments in the hospital, as she is scrutinized and surrounded by the eyes and instruments of the male doctors who seek to "classify" her and her illness. As Laura Mulvey argues, "The determining male gaze projects its phantasy on to the female form which is styled accordingly."[9] The gender issues implied in her mental illness are similar to those depicted in the character of Glenda Esmond from *The Sleeping Tiger*, whose desire for power and control is not only depicted as masculinizing, but also at the root of her neurotic behavior toward her husband, Clive and her lover, Frank. In Possessed, Louise's mental break may well have been heavily, if not entirely caused by the frustration and powerlessness to feel involved and actualized, in a male-dominated world. The only grasp at a solution is her clinging to a strongly independent man who rejects her attempts at the emotional conjoining of their lives.

Louise finds an eerie counterpart in Graham's wife, Pauline, who is mysteriously found drowned. Though the police seem suspicious of Graham, he maintains that Pauline killed herself, as she was prone to "spells of extreme depression." As they look down at the dark water, one of the detectives mentions that Pauline "got trapped by the weeds"; Louise responds, "The weeds grow very long here near the shore." There is an implicit comparison between herself and Pauline here, as Louise too is feeling trapped by forces beyond her control. Earlier, Pauline was shown to have repeated arguments with her husband over her "imagined" perception that he was in love with Louise. The fact that Pauline eventually became "trapped" by the "weeds" of her own mental torment and Louise's acknowledgment of the perilous nature of these weeds connect her fragile mental state to that of Pauline and foreshadow her own mental collapse. And a further connection exists in that Pauline's anxiety arose from her perception of rejection from a man, as does Louise's—a perception, by the way, that may have not been entirely a fantasy, since we see later that Graham indeed does have romantic feelings for Louise and will eventually marry her. Therefore, this connection also creates some doubt regarding the extent of Louise's own psychosis, or at least mitigates its severity by suggesting the role that David might have played in her suffering. After Pauline's death, Louise's situation is further complicated by the Grahams' daughter, Carol (Geraldine Brooks), who is distraught over her mother's suicide, for which she blames Louise and her father. Louise's situation seems increasingly one of total isolation, as she lacks any real roots anywhere. Even Graham's insistence that she stay with them to take care of the younger child, Wynn, seems a forced and unsatisfying gesture rather than an outgrowth of a meaningful bond.

Though Louise appears to have adjusted to her breakup with David, his return from Canada ignites the same passionate and self-destructive emotions all over again. Louise tries to remain calm, but as she prepares cocktails for him and Graham, her hands shake and she seems close to falling apart; dissonant music begins and fades as she suddenly grabs the sides of her face before regaining her composure. According to David, they were "through" before he went to Canada, and she does not react well to this pronouncement, becoming sarcastic, accusing him of being self-centered, and ascribing to him various motives for his behavior that do not seem to exist. In reality, he simply seems not to care, even when she slaps him as he leaves. At this point, she is ripe for Graham's proposal of marriage, which she almost seems to evoke by announcing her intent to quit her position. Her reaction to this proposal underscores her desperation, as she first laughs hysterically, then admits that such an offer is flattering and something she needed, because "something happens to a woman when she isn't wanted . . . something dreadful." Again, Louise's mental instability seems a more severe reaction to a too-common social condition: that of a woman's worth being dependent on her being desired by a man. She is then characterized as "sick" when she cannot accept the terms of her repressed existence. And from a broader perspective, her feelings of alienation, isolation, and emptiness are indicative of the entire *noir* condition.

Despite her entrance into a new life, David's appearance at Louise and Graham's wedding reception still creates discord, especially when it seems as though neither Graham nor Louise invited him. This detail is thrown out in the film without full explanation, but one imagines that either Louise did invite him, but does not want to admit it (doubtful, given the look of shock on her face) or that David had heard about the wedding and showed up uninvited. Given that we later find out that Louise may very well have married Dean to make David jealous, this seemingly small detail may actually illuminate aspects of Louise's "neurosis."One wonders why indeed David did attend if uninvited, and whether or not his morbid attachment to Louise is the cause, feeding into what is being characterized as her "delusions" about David having deeper feelings for her than he admits. His attendance also becomes an additional dangerous catalyst for Louise's instability in that his flirtatious interaction with Carol at the reception begins to trigger hostile impulses in Louise, as she realizes that if she were hoping to arouse David's jealousy about her marrying another man, the wedding may have actually backfired. Carol, oblivious to Louise's torment, cannot help but encourage David's affections, and invites him to sit with her and Louise when she later spots him at a concert. As Schumann is played, the camera lazily moves from Louise's face to David's; though she clearly shows more anxiety, David's face also expresses emotion, which causes him to go after her when she excuses herself to leave, feigning a headache. He does not offer comfort, however; when Louise angrily says, "I don't know why I don't hate you," he responds with, "You don't try hard enough—you should force yourself." Again, the role that David is playing is Louise's neurosis should be noted—his alternate encouragement and rejection of her emotional attachment seems to be a not-insignificant factor in her mental deterioration, yet is never attributed to by the film as a contributing source of her difficulty. This exchange also highlights he dual nature of the power of the will expressed in psychiatric *noirs*—on the one hand, the mind is powerful enough to alter perceptions of reality and lead the body down paths of self-destruction, but on the other hand, is often not powerful enough in terms of "will" to make itself whole or "healthy" if disturbed.

This upsetting incident leads to one of the most significant sequences in the film, which takes place later that evening after the concert. Louise has gone home, leaving Carol and David at the concert. In her bedroom, she is restless, and the camera pans around the room, from ticking clock to her pillow to her dressing table, as sounds of wind and rain are heard. Finally, we see Louise sitting forlornly in front of a rainy window, with Schumann music playing, seemingly in her head. The sound of the ticking clock gets louder and louder, and she silences it, only to hear the dripping of the rain and the beating of her heart taking its place. She almost seems agitated enough to jump out of the window, when she hears David and Carol arrive. She peers over the upstairs banister to hear David say, "We fooled her, didn't we?" They kiss, and then he leaves. Angered, Louise pushes a defiant Carol into her room to talk. Carol tells Louise that she and David had a long talk about her and her former relationship with David. When Louise claims these are lies, Carol says David does not hate her, but does not love her either and adds that he told her "other things, about [her] mother"—such as that Louise killed Pauline to marry Dean so that

David would be jealous and come back to her. When an anguished Louise admits that this is true, Carol threatens to tell her father, and when Louise goes after her to stop her, she hits her, causing Carol to fall down the stairs. While the viewer is trying to process not only the idea of Louise orchestrating Pauline's death and her subsequent marriage to Graham only in an effort to gain the love of David, but also her apparent murder of Carol, the image of the staircase and Carol's fall fades; it turns out this was a hallucination. Louise, sweating, now sees Carol come home for real, as her heart is heard beating furiously. When Carol comes upstairs, kindly soliciting concern for Louise's headache, she can barely answer Carol before returning to her room, agonizingly confused. As Doane argues, the seamless transitions among these scenes produce a particularly jarring effect on the viewer: "The revelation after the fact that the scene is hallucinatory is jolting, for it involves the image in a deviation from the truth. The viewer of the film is drawn into Louise's illness, into her hallucination. The spectator is therefore no longer diagnosing, but becomes a part of what is diagnosed, forced into sharing her illness."[10] This confusion between the real and the unreal in the filmic environment emphasizes the ease with which one can find oneself questioning one's own mental faculties and the frightening abyss that lies between the two.

At this point, the viewer believes, along with Louise, that she indeed was responsible for Pauline's murder. Therefore, when she and Graham arrive at the lake house (a trip designed to help Louise free herself from memories of Pauline), we are all too willing to believe that the hand seen in Pauline's window upstairs is ghostly, but in the end turns out to be that of the caretaker's wife. Likewise, when Louise wanders around the house in the shadows, and goes to kitchen where she hears a bell, as Pauline used to ring from her room, it seems perfectly reasonable to believe that in its metallic and chilling tones, sounds as though it is saying "Louise," even after Louise disconnects it and it still seems to continue to ring. We know this is only another instance of Louise's sensory hallucinations; aside from the staircase incident with Carol, Louise had thought she heard Pauline Graham calling to her, soon after she died, from her empty room adjoining, when the voice turned out to be Carol's. All of these instances draw us into the surreal atmosphere of Louise's mind, which is projected onto the film's reality. There is a likening to the supernatural in a way, as if to suggest that Louise's delusions are equally mysterious and too fantastic to be believed. Convinced that she helped Pauline commit suicide, Louise insists that the spirit of Pauline has told her to kill herself. However, Graham asserts that Louise was not even there when Pauline died; he says that he was with her the whole time. When she said she was cold, according to Graham, he went for her shawl and when he came back, she was gone. By this time, the viewer's head might be spinning, in an effort to discern whether or not Louise had any real part in Pauline's death. And this is entirely the intent of the film, which creates its *noir* environment by the continual questioning of objective reality. The hallucination involving Carol and the stairs sends an interpretation in one direction but Graham's reaction to Louise's anguish and his revelation about what really happened to Pauline calls into question what has been heard thus far. In any case, absolute certainty cannot be discerned. Louise's mental instability, her inability to distinguish reality from fantasy, is endemic to the film; with each turn and introduction of new information, it becomes increasingly difficult to accept any details as helpful in determining the "truth."

Though Louise appears to take control of herself in response to Graham's reassurance, what she cannot control is the love between Carol and David. Her efforts to sabotage their impending marriage are eventually thwarted by Graham, who now has become convinced that she needs a "mental specialist," though he had hoped that "things would work themselves out." In fear of this prospect, Louise sneaks out of the house to David's in a last desperate plea. In response to Louise's contention that she has "done some terrible things" because of him, he says the only thing he has "done is fall out of love with her, which is a man's privilege." David's usual flippant arrogance incites Louise to pull a gun on him. At the point she shoots him repeatedly, the shot dissolves back to the hospital in the present, where Dr. Willard comments that that a few years ago, he could have prevented Louise's breakdown: it was "there for any psychiatrist to see. . . . A child breaks a leg, he's taken to a doctor; he shows signs of mental illness, he's hidden away in a closet." The same parallel between physical and psychological illness surfaces here, with the dangers of not viewing mental illness in such a way borne out by the *noir* morality play just witnessed. When Graham is finally located and summoned, Willard pronounces that "it's a clear case of psychosis—completely unbalanced," but will not concede that Louise's case is "hopeless" and does not want to use the term "insane." His earnestness to try and "restore her" is admirable, but his explanation raises additional questions:

> We human beings act according to certain patterns of behavior. Sometimes—why exactly we don't know yet—the pattern is broken; the wires are crossed; the mind cannot evaluate, judge, or even function properly. Shock follows shock until eventually the mind gives way. The brain loses control and the body sinks into coma. Then, in a biblical sense, we might say that such a person is possessed of devils, and it is the psychiatrist that must cast them out. Substantially, this is what happened to Louise.

Here again, the link between psychiatry and spiritualism is emphasized, creating a moral structure that posits the psychiatric patient as a victim of forces beyond her control. The "why" is the most elusive factor, yet it is the one that most needs illumination. Willard theorizes that once Louise, because of the great emotional strain caused by the breakup with David, convinced herself that she was responsible for Pauline Graham's death, the rest of her breakdown was "inevitable." Though Louise has suffered, "only through greater pain and suffering beyond belief can she get well again," says Willard. Graham is seen staying by her side to help her through this pain, as the film ends with a shot of Willard walking down the hospital corridor. There is little romanticizing about the efficacy of narcosynthesis or psychiatric treatment in general in *Possessed*; not only is the point made that Louise's condition took time to develop and would have benefitted from early intervention, but also that treatment methods also take time to repair the mental damage done. Louise is not a femme fatale in the usual *noir* sense, but the struggles she endures that are uniquely female (and which make her uniquely dangerous) are unmistakable. The part that her frustration and powerlessness played in these struggles are portrayed as consequences of her own mental weakness and nothing else—a peculiarly retrograde conception of female "hysteria."

Depictions of narcosynthesis or hypnosis are not restricted to therapeutic situations, as we have seen with *Kiss Me Deadly*, but are often used in *noir* to add yet another threat to one's identity in a chaotic world. Such a scenario exists in Maxwell Shane's *Nightmare* (1956), which, like its predecessor, *Fear in the Night* (1947), was based on a story by Cornell Woolrich, whose plots often focused on loss of memory, emotional strain, loss of identity, and psychosis. Interestingly, Shane also directed *Fear in the Night* with the same production company; because of its lukewarm reception, he wanted to give the film another try with a bigger budget, better cast (Kevin McCarthy instead of DeForest Kelley; Edward G. Robinson instead of Paul Kelly), and richer atmosphere (transfer of locale to New Orleans, complete with jazz backdrop). This shift in tone is evident from the opening titles, in which appears a pinpoint of light that turns into the flame of candle; the camera pans down to dripping wax that dissolves into titles, behind which plays a moody jazz score by Billy Mays and his orchestra that will permeate the rest of the film, evoking eeriness and surreality, and characteristic of later *noirs* in its more overt despair. However, both versions of the film are nearly identical in many ways, such as the script, also adapted by Shane, which includes the effective voice-over of the character of Stan Grayson (McCarthy) from the beginning and the "dream" that frames the plot of the film.

The edges of the frame are blurry and floaty, as he describes a "beautiful babe's face . . . slow, crazy melody . . . a queer mirrored room and somehow I was inside it . . . there was danger there . . . as if my brain was handcuffed and I had to do what I came there to do." Grayson kills a man with an awl that the woman gives him and puts him into a closet, after which he escapes from the mirrored room and falls out of a window, shattering like a mirror on the ground. When Grayson awakens, the camera pans around the room, as he mutters, "What a dream"; though he seems to return to normal, he is shocked to see thumbprints on his neck in the mirror. "Couldn't be," he says, "It all happened in a nightmare." However, he cannot ignore the blood on his arm, the thumbprints on his neck, and also the button and key he finds in his pocket. This collision between dream and reality immediately creates a disorientation of identity for both Grayson and the viewer. As we have already seen, the use of dreams is particularly effective to highlight the intersection of conscious and unconscious and the questions of identity and reality common to the *noir* series. Grayson questions, "Could something like that happen, and I wouldn't know it? Was I going insane?" As he looks outside the window, he comments, "Out there everything was status quo; the hassle was in here, with me." When faced with what seems like the "normal" world outside the psychological "room" of his experience, the division within Grayson himself seems even more acute. However, as we will see, the world outside parallels Grayson's own mind with just as many unknown dangers.

Grayson struggles to make sense of his disorientation by retreating into himself: he calls in sick from work, and tries to rest in his room. However, when he cannot get the "weird nightmare music" from the dream out of his head, he feels the need to wander the streets, acknowledging that he felt as though he had to stay out of the shadows: "I knew tonight I'd be afraid of the dark." He rejects the thought of seeking help from his girlfriend, Gina (Connie Russell) and instead seeks the company of his brother-in-law, René Bressard (Robinson), a police inspector. As a figure of law, and particularly order, René seems to Grayson the best avenue for assistance in restoring his sanity. We have seen *noir* psychiatrists acting as detectives; in *Nightmare*'s René Bressard, we see a detective acting as a psychiatrist, as he works to help Grayson sort out the root of his mental anguish. Grayson even confesses to René as if he were a psychiatrist, telling him, "You're going to think I've flipped my lid, but I had a nightmare that I killed a man in a mirrored room." At the outset, though, René does not make the best mental practitioner, as he scoffs at Grayson's belief that he really killed someone, blaming it on Grayson's "artistic temperament" and his drinking, and even rejecting Grayson's use of the button and key as "evidence," saying, he must have had those things before: "You either dream a thing or it actually happens." When René prescribes taking a vacation, Stan angrily says, "You haven't helped me a bit." Ironically, Stan has gone to René because of his logic and practicality, but as it turns out, René's black and white way of viewing the world hardly helps Stan, who is caught in ever-shifting shades of gray. Though Stan still wants René to help him, to use the button and key as "clues," René rejects this idea. He tells him that he will take him down to "a head doctor" if he does not "quit it," implying the common assumption of mental weakness to be the cause of Stan's difficulty.

Stan continues to be tortured, suffering from insomnia, scouring the newspapers for mention of murders, and trying to pick out the "nightmare music" from the dream on his clarinet and on a xylophone, asking his musician friends if anyone knows the tune. He tries to find solace in a bar, only to find more confusion, as he thinks he sees the "babe from the mirrored room" who turns out to be a woman simply fixing her hair in the mirror. As they drink and talk, Stan does not want to tell her what is bothering him, afraid she would think he lost his marbles, to which she responds, "Take a good look around . . . people trying to find companionship . . . sometimes I think we're all minus a few marbles." Though the film focuses on Stan's particular problem, there is never a real sense that he is a lone crazy person in a sane world, only a sufferer of a particular form of disturbance in a much-disturbed universe. Stan cannot even spend the evening with the woman; in her apartment as they kiss, he sees the reflection of them in a mirror and terrified, abruptly leaves. Now skeptical about the society of others relieving his mental torture, Stan rebuffs René when he comes to his apartment to invite him on a picnic, and in the true denial fashion of a psychiatric patient, tells René, "Stop treating me as if I were cracked." He accompanies René, Sue, and Gina reluctantly and as it turns out, what is meant to be an innocent outing, designed to get Stan's mind off his troubles, turns into a terrifying recreation of Stan's dream.

In the process of trying to find shelter in a thunderstorm, they wind up, at Stan's direction, at a house that seems all too familiar to him. Sue's phobia about thunder, coupled with the chaos of the storm and the rainy blur on the windshield contribute to the buildup of tension that culminates as they enter the empty house. As they explore their surroundings, Gina comments that the "owner of this house must be a doctor or something" as she reads such titles of books on the shelves as "Freud's *Studies in Hysteria*," "*Manual of Psychotherapy*," and "*Narcoanalysis*." Gina turns on the phonograph, the record on which matches the "nightmare melody" from Stan's dream. Given that it was perhaps Stan's own mind that "slowed" the music that he remembers widens further the gap between dream and reality and to what extent the memory of his dream represents reality. The deserted house is haunted with the same empty memories of Stan's mind, their exploration of it revealing the same elusive truths. Already feeling an uncanny sense of familiarity with the house, Stan is compelled to go upstairs, where he finds a mirrored room identical to the one in his dream. René meets him upstairs, and when he sees the room, asks Stan for the mysterious key and uses it to open the closet doors. Behind these doors lie various elements that point to Stan's recollection: a safe with a burned door, dried blood on the wall. René's patronizing of Stan now turns to suspicion; he angrily accuses him of lying and of not having the "guts" to say he killed someone—instead, he had to "cook up a dream" and is trying to play on his sympathy or "think in terms of doctors" to get him off. But the arrival of a police officer further complicates matters, as he tells them the sordid story of how the wife of the wealthy owner, Belknap, was murdered there the previous week. This account, combined with the police description of the murderer ("his eyes were fixed and glassy . . . he could have been mentally unbalanced") only augments Stan's terror at the possibility that he could have committed these crimes without any volition or recollection.

No longer believing Stan's story that he was unaware of what he was doing, René only reconsiders when Stan attempts suicide and offers to stay with Stan to try and figure out what really happened. Now most like a psychiatrist, he tries to get Stan to retrace mentally his steps that night, asking him whether anything unusual happened to him and exactly who he encountered. René begins to be suspicious of his own assumptions, as Stan recounts how he met his neighbor, an older man named Britton, in the hotel bar that evening. Further recollections reveal Stan having a daiquiri at Britton's suggestion, even though he does not like rum, just to please him and Stan accepting a cough drop from Britton because he "felt sorry for him." Stan further remembers seeing Britton later when he knocked on his door asking whether his lights had gone out. René becomes even more suspicious when Stan mentions that Britton had a candle and kept repeating that he should go because, he told Stan, "You're tired." René has begun to piece the mystery together as he considers the police report about the murderer's "fixed and glassy eyes" and also muses to himself regarding Stan's interactions with Britton, "because he suggested it . . . testing will power, maybe." It is a telling detail that in the post-war *noir* world, what might be seen as compassion could instead be a lack of willpower that could get you killed.

Though René realizes, after confirming his suspicions by another trip to the Belknap house, that "Britton" is actually Belknap, he cannot change the fact that there is "no out" for Stan, since his fingerprints are there. However, what needs proving at this point is that Stan was not aware or responsible for his actions, a scenario that is set up by Stan returning to the Belknap house for a confrontation with the doctor that will hopefully result in re-hypnosis. Stan's fragmented self is well-represented by a compelling double-image shot of him emerging from the mirrored closet. He tries to convince Belknap that even though he "had the typical look . . . of the hypnotized subject," he remembers everything about that night, also pointing out (in confirmation of the moral code of hypnosis), "You couldn't make me murder; I killed that man in self-defense." Thinking Stan wants to kill him, Belknap hypnotizes him again, using his watch, urging "You don't want to kill me," as the light from the watch flickers on Stan's face. René waits for him to "really put him under" as "proof for a jury that he can do it," but as a result must rescue Stan from Belknap as he drives him to a river and tries to get him to drown himself. Stan remembers how, unable to defend himself, "that horrible curtain closed over [him] again." Upon Belknap's capture and his retrieval from the water, Stan relievedly states, "All of a sudden, I'm all right," suggesting that one's salvation may be just as unexpected as one's downfall. Like *Whirlpool*'s Ann Sutton, Stan Grayson is victimized by hypnosis, which is pervasively used in *noir* as a signifier for the ultimate loss of control and loss of identity. As in many *noirs*, the resolution is less a resolution than a temporary break from immediate tension. The lingering question still lies suspended at the end of the film's narrative: if Stan Grayson could be so easily hypnotized to commit crimes, how vulnerable are we all to such coercion and what does this suggest about human mental weakness?

Aside from the particular psychological treatments of hypnosis and narcosynthesis, the broader depiction of mental hospitals in *noir* is often a curious mixture of "Bedlam"-like conditions of the nineteenth century with more "modern" treatments of psychoanalysis. Moreover, as we have seen in *Strange Illusion*, they are places of mystery and criminality meant to be infiltrated. This is the case in 1948's *Behind Locked Doors*, directed by Budd Boetticher, in which another aptly named sanitarium, La Siesta, is a hotbed of both physical and psychological abuse, torture, and corruption. Once again, it is a private investigator who must navigate this dangerous environment as Ross Stewart (Richard Carlson) is hired by San Francisco reporter Kathy Lawrence (Lucille Bremer) because she suspects that a corrupt judge on the lam is hiding out in the sanitarium. Though Stewart rejects her offer at first, not wanting to be "locked up as a crazy person on a hunch," he eventually does take the case, and they agree that he will pose as "mentally unbalanced husband" with her as his wife who wants to commit him. The tone at this point in the film almost resembles the tongue-in-cheek treatment of psychiatry seen in *Fingers at the Window*. Kathy gives Stewart a book on psychological illnesses so that he can decide "what kind of mental case" he wants to be—"paranoid, schizophrenic, manic depressive" are some of the choices, a laundry list of possibilities from which he not only has to choose, but then use to practice how to act "queerly," the implication being that this would be a relatively easy thing to pull off. It turns out that it actually is, with the state psychiatrist believing Stewart's act, as he lays on a couch with his hat over his head, moaning, "Nobody can help me . . . nobody can help anybody." Ironically, this portrayal of insanity happens to ring true as the general state of affairs in the postwar *noir* world.

In fact, Stewart enters a chaotic, Kafka-esque nightmarish version of the outside world, in which his personal possessions, like suspenders and shoes, are confiscated, and he is trapped with others who seem to be suffering from illnesses of varying degrees, but who are all nonetheless portrayed as victims of an unpitying system. Violence is rampant, both from other patients and from the orderlies, one of whom, Nelson (Douglas Fowley), is overtly sadistic, treating misbehavers to a session with "The Champ" (played by Tor Johnson, widely known to B-movie aficionados), a mute, hulking ex-prizefighter who goes into boxing mode whenever a bell noise is simulated by Nelson's ubiquitously jangling keys. Nelson calls the patients "screaming monkeys" and routinely taunts and slaps them. Stewart's malcontented roommate comments, "You came here to be cured? You're more likely to be killed." The head of the sanitarium, Dr. Porter (Thomas Browne Henry) is aware of Nelson's abuses and tries to curtail them, but is more concerned with his powerful visitor, Judge Finlay Drake (Herbert Heyes), who is holed up in the "Locked Ward." Kathy's suspicions are proven correct to the viewer before Stewart can confirm that the judge is indeed hiding out there. Dr. Porter resents, though he is being paid a large sum of money for his hospitality, being at Drake's beck and call, to which the judge responds, "You'd be a small time quack if I hadn't come along." As we have seen, the use of "quack" terminology is often applied to dubious doctors, "psychic consultants," or "hypnotist fortunetellers," with often money and therefore, power, being the distinguishing feature of a "reputable" psychiatric physician. Porter only seems to have the money, as under his guidance, the sanitarium appears to offer no actual medical or psychological treatments, only confinement and terror.

Stewart manages to literally smoke out Judge Drake, when he gives matches to a firebug inmate, who sets a fire outside the judge's room. Doing this, however, exposes Stewart, himself, especially when Nelson finds a photo of the judge among Stewart's clothes. Though Dr. Porter wants no blood on his hands, "it's that, or jail or ruin," and so he approves of locking Stewart in with "the Champ." Stewart is ultimately rescued by the actions of the other and kindly orderly, Hopps (Ralfe Harold), who is a foil to Nelson's sadism throughout the film and who, it is implied, has been unable to speak out against the asylum's abuses because his own son is a patient, and his work there earns their keep. Nonetheless, he calls the police when Stewart is given over to "the Champ" and when they show up and all is revealed, Hopps' words are the final ones in the film: "I never did think he was crazy." Though Stewart enters the sanitarium to play the hero and expose the hiding place of the judge, it is Stewart himself who needs to be rescued, the trappings of psychological treatment represented by La Siesta being also exposed as fraudulent and dangerous. Normalcy is seen to be in peril, with law and order exposed to be corrupt and hiding in this environment of mental instability. What began as Stewart's cynical and darkly humorous coloring of mental illness finds a home in a violent and unjust microcosm of modern society in which the weak are victimized, the strong are malicious, and only chance compassion can provide salvation.

This kind of microcosm, and by far the most extended depiction of a *noir* mental asylum, comes in *The Snake Pit* (Anatole Litvak, 1948). *The Snake Pit* has often been critically evaluated not as a *noir* but either as a ground-breaking mental illness film in general terms, or through the lens of feminist critique.[11] Aside from the *noir*ish elements common to all asylum films, such as loss of individuality, alienation, paranoia, and hopelessness, the expressionistic photography, innovative use of voice-over, and narrative framing make the treatment of this film as a *noir* necessary. In the film, based on the book of the same name by Mary Jane Ward, Virginia Stuart Cunningham (Olivia de Havilland) finds herself struggling with various losses as she realizes that she is housed in a mental hospital—loss of her home (though she admits that she is married, she rejects the idea that she has a husband), loss of her ability to write, and loss of time and memory. The opening shot of the film shows Virginia sitting on what seems to be a park bench; though she looks disoriented and unkempt, it is only later that the viewer and even later, Virginia herself realizes that she is an inmate in an asylum. As she is sitting on the bench, an unseen male voice asks her if she knows where she is and how she is doing; as she tries to ascertain from where the voice originates, she says in voice-over, "He's clever, but he can't fool me with his magic," when she sees a woman, not a man, sitting next to her on bench. It is oddly disorienting to the viewer to hear two separate voice-overs open the film, with no context, especially when one voice is wondering about the other.

She recognizes neither her friend, Grace (Celeste Holm), nor her doctor, Mark Kik (Leo Genn), who she believes is "the warden of this prison." Before believing she was in a prison, she thought herself entering "a zoo . . . I'm sorry for the animals locked up." We see some glimpses of another self of Virginia, as she comments about "giving a speech" about prison conditions and insisting that she must be there because she needs to do research on prisons for a novel she is writing. She is neither cognizant of her identity as someone who is mentally ill nor of her identity as wife to Mark Cunningham (Mark Stevens), who has committed her.

Cunningham relates to Dr. Kik in flashback the events that led up to this point, including their courtship and hasty marriage. Cunningham admits that he was attracted to her partly because of her mystery; he never knew anything about her family, or where she went and what she did when they were apart. When she accuses him, characterized as somewhat paranoidally, of wanting to put off their marriage, they are married, but soon after, she begins acting strangely, culminating in her thinking it is November, not May, and hysterically screaming to Mark, "You can't make me love you, I can't love you, I can't love anybody!" In an effort to "make contact" with Virginia, Kik orders shock therapy for her, the first in a long series of psychiatric treatments that will be depicted in the film. Though the actual effect of the administration of the electricity is offscreen, the details of preparation, from the application of the conducting gel to her temples and the bite guard inserted in her mouth to the turning of the voltage knob, are painstakingly detailed. These shock treatments only begin to be successful after the fourth time, as "no insight or judgment" is initially reported, but after the fourth, she is "more alert, but still confused." When Dr. Kik begins to try to talk to her about her psychological problems, she seems to remember him, but is disturbed that she's "lost all these months." When asked what she remembers about her previous life before the hospital, all she can remember, she says, "I used to buy groceries . . . and I was writing a novel . . . and I couldn't sleep." At his suggestion that "it's like trying to push time out of your mind . . . and saying it's November instead of May," she begins to pace excitedly around the room, repeating that she's not able to love him or anybody. Dr. Kik responds that "it could happen to anybody." In this and in the subsequent interactions between him and Virginia, he is portrayed as a model of wisdom and patience, the ideal benevolent psychiatrist who is contrasted with his less progressive, less idealistic, and more utilitarian colleagues. Veda Semarne notes the peculiarity of Kik's name being abbreviated and never given in full that "because it is impossible to pronounce, as if he were a deity whose name cannot be spoken and who exists in some grander form elsewhere."[12] In the almost Inferno-like atmosphere of the asylum, Dr. Kik indeed seems god-like; Virginia even characterizes him as such when he stops another imminent shock treatment: "You're the one who saved me."

Much has been written regarding the film's accuracy of its depiction of mental hospital conditions and the treatments therein. What is probably indisputable is the dilemma of overcrowding that plagues any state institution, including those that housed the mentally ill. Here, as in other psychiatric *noirs*, there is an overwhelming sense of too many mentally unstable people in the world, an overcrowding of those suffering from neuroses and psychoses, with such overcrowding spilling over into the broader spectrum of society. Overworked nurses, abound, and the pressure by the head doctor to bring Virginia to the hospital evaluation meeting known as "staff" prematurely in order to authorize her release, thereby freeing up some beds from the hospital that is nearly at double capacity, signify this tension. Kik's savior persona is heightened as he struggles against this mentality and advocates for treating each patient as an individual. Knowing that he does not have much time to make headway in Virginia's case, he admits that "there's one more shortcut" he can try, and the film cuts to her counting backward as he gives her an injection. Even if he had not later identified the procedure as narcosynthesis in his dictation notes, her ensuing reaction shows the typical effects: she begins to recall the past and her relationship with her fiancé, Gordon, who was the first one she cared about since her father died. Even in this initial flashback, there is clear conflation between her father and Gordon, as she says," He always tied the bow in my hair." "Gordon?" asks Kik. "No," she says, "my father," with the next flashback showing Gordon fixing the bow on her sleeve. She then relates that her engagement to Gordon occurred by him not asking her consent but rather informing her that he planned to announce their engagement. It is this recoiling from the prospect of marrying Gordon that causes her to become ill and ask to return home, after which they get into a car accident that kills Gordon. Dr. Kik reassures her that she did not cause Gordon's death, a belief that he interprets underlies her psychological distress. Kik believes that they have had a breakthrough and that this will prevent her from being prematurely released. Much psychological illness in *noir* arises from guilt, as if all human relationships in the modern world are fraught with victimization.

Various signposts of Virginia's psychological journey are found in her perceptions when she is either alone or in relation to her private thoughts about her surroundings. As she gets dressed to meet Robert for a visit, for instance, she puts her hands in the pocket of a suit that she has not worn for a while and finds some random objects. "Look what's been in here all this time," she muses. "It's like putting your hands in someone else's pockets . . . a dead woman's." This particular suit, once rather snug, now fits her loosely, almost suggesting that aside from a literal weight loss, she has experienced a tangible loss of self. Virginia is not what might be characterized as a typical "nervous female"—as we have seen, she has had independence, both creatively and romantically, and though she seems to be punished for that independent spirit at this point, it renders her musings perhaps less paranoid than they may otherwise seem. As an example, when she sees Robert Cunningham again, she greets him cordially, but her internal voice-over says, "It looks like him . . . but watch yourself . . . they do a good job when they want to . . . you have to be careful—they're cunning." Referring to her loss of time, she says, "Sometimes before I came here, I used to wish I could make my mind blank. Now I know what a blank mind is." She even confesses to Robert, "I wouldn't mind having a cold or pneumonia or anything I could understand," as she actually has to ask him—incongruent to true psychoanalysis, in which the patient is a conscious participant—what is wrong with her; she believes it is a brain tumor, but he tells her that she had a nervous breakdown. In a subsequent visit in the asylum ice cream shop, looking too uncannily similar to any ice cream shop on main street America, she thinks in voice-over, referring to the "sick" vs. the "well," "I wonder which is which. If I can't tell, maybe they can't tell about me. . . . Question: Dear Dr. Kik—when am I real?" It is particularly telling that she asks these questions as she spends time with a man that she does not truly recognize as her husband. She is being asked to accept an identity that is foreign to her, and on which the "reality" of life seems to depend. The logic of being surrounded by those who are out of touch with what is deemed objective reality in order to cure this subjectivity seems insane itself, as Virginia tries to reason her way out of this dilemma: "I don't feel sick . . . but they say that if you think you're well, then you're really sick. Maybe if I say I'm sick, they'll think I'm well. The trouble is I can't be sure of anything." The real world appears to be as insanely constructed as the disturbed Virginia's mind, and the film's reflection of it makes the audience part of the deluded environment.

At the premature "staff" meeting, where Virginia is supposed to represent her level of sanity, enough to enable her to return home and free up much-needed bed space in the sanitarium, she is nervous and fearful, conveying confusion and only limited memory to recall her social security number, but hardly anything else about herself or her experience. She is unnerved by the head doctor waving his cigar in her face, and when she cannot remember her address, the scene dissolves into a flashback of her being overpowered by crashing waves and being pulled out into the ostensibly more secure, but actually no less threatening environment of the asylum's water bath. It is here that the viewer senses particularly acutely Virginia's plight, as she is in an environment, that of a "soothing" warm water bath, designed to calm her nerves, but which, because of its actual confinement, achieves the opposite result. She engages in some banter with the nurses in the hydrotherapy ward and later exhibits what is evident as a latent rebellious streak when she insists on walking (and later defiantly, sitting) on a rug in the ward that the nurses insist no one touch because it is "new and clean" and they "mean to keep it that way." Virginia wonders aloud whether they ought to "hang it on the wall" if that is the case, and proceeds to not only walk on the rug, but also to sit herself squarely in the center of it, as an expression of the ultimate functionality of a rug on a hard floor (that of comfort and warmth) as opposed to simply the illusion of these things. This is also the same environment that not only demands that patients serve themselves at table with communal food bowls, (thus ensuring unequal food distribution), but also demands assigned seats and silence at these same tables. The character of Virginia, who can very easily be seen as a victim of the asylum system, actually shows herself to be much more, and a much more *noirish* figure than might be supposed—a character who is struggling to master her destiny, but is being foiled by forces that seek to undermine the fundamental truths of her own psyche. Her presence represents an independent force that exposes the hypocrisy and inconsistent social mores that define existence in the sanitarium microcosm of society.

A further expression of Virginia's attempts at independence occurs when she "buys" a rag doll from another inmate in exchange for cigarettes. She values and cherishes this doll, emotions that will be mined upon later for latent Freudian lapses in development, but seems perfectly rational when Nurse Davis confronts her with the accusation by the other patient that she actually stole the doll. The more Virginia tries to explain her ownership of the doll, bought with the most tangible of collateral in the asylum (as in prisons), cigarettes, the more she is made to seem as though she is a liar and a thief. Within the social order of the sanitarium, as is the fluid social order of post-war modern life, mere affirmations of logic and reason can often not suffice when compared to vehement protestations of disorder and incoherency. When Virginia meets with Dr. Kik and cradles the doll for dear life as if it were a real baby, she is angry with him for "taking the part" of the other patient, likening him to her father. She then reveals to him the childhood incident in which she had traded a doll to her friend, only to find her mother's insistence that she return the doll juxtaposed against her own assurance that her father would take her part. This assurance is tempered by her realization that her father was more likely to acquiesce to her mother when her mother revealed that she was pregnant. In true Freudian terms, Virginia was resentful about her father's insistence that she return the surrogate child, born of her and her father's mutual trust and affection, to her friend. In her anger over this perceived betrayal, she smashes a soldier doll, won for her by her father at a fair, after which her father takes ill and dies. After this recollection, Dr. Kik muses to Virginia, "Wishes seem to come true sometimes, don't they?"—as if to emphasize the seemingly random nature of wish-fulfillment that may come to pass in waking life. Kik probes Virginia regarding the nature of her father's death, getting her to realize that the cause of this death, uremia, was "a complex illness that takes several years to develop" rather than something Virginia could have simply willed upon him. Perhaps the most telling effect from their session reveals itself when Virginia, as she leaves, unravels the much-coveted doll to find out "it's only a piece of rag . . . just a simple piece of rag." This realization, perhaps intended to paint Virginia as a silly, nervous woman, given to fantasies of child-bearing but being "ill-equipped" to achieve them, actually points more to her identity as a rational and critical thinking human being, as she is able to separate her emotional attachment to the idea of a doll in favor of a recognition that her ideal is not concurrent with the reality of the situation.

However, it is Virginia's apparent undoing that she acts in these ways, uttering ideas, such as her belief that Nurse Davis acts as she does because she secretly loves Dr. Kik, that seem to hold obvious, instinctual truths, for which she is ultimately punished. After her confrontation with Nurse Davis, she is sent down to an even lower ward than the one in which she started; this occurs, as Semarne argues, "in terms of the hidden logic of the film, she is demoted to a bad ward because she has overstepped the line between object and subject, patient and analyst, signifier and storyteller."[13] In other words, Virginia has ceased to be an object to be observed, but rather an observer, someone who is capable of discerning the limits and limitations of her present existence. This recognition brings anxiety, but also anger, as she attempts to carve out a measure of free will in this restrictive atmosphere. Her descent into this lower ward offers the film's opportunity to present successive scenes of doctors going from ward to ward, assaulted by crazed women. These scenes culminate in a long shot in which the camera pulls out for a bird's eye view of Virginia in the middle of the ward with chaos all around her, like an inner circle of Dante's *Inferno.* Virginia characterizes her experience as "being in a deep hole with animals, like snakes all around." She recalls to Dr. Kik that, "Long ago . . . they used to put insane people in pits full of snakes . . . as if they put insane people in bizarre situations, it would make them sane . . . to shock them into sanity." Though the film's title signifies this idea, the film's overall premise does not bear it out. This "shocking" experience is not what jolts Virginia to "sanity" (a state that the film does not clearly define), but rather her analysis experiences with Dr. Kik, who seems to be the only force that can penetrate the depths of her distress. Even he, the film ultimately reveals, can succeed only insofar as the status quo permits, since the gauge of her sanity is her reintegration, much as we saw returning World War II veterans depicted in *Let There Be Light*, into a society in which she may actually be ill-suited to reside. This disconnection is emphasized by the plight of the former nurse from the first ward who has now become a patient in one of the lower wards. There is little explanation regarding her journey to this point, but the implication seems to be an emotional over-identification with her patients, causing her identity to be subsumed by her inability to help them and to remedy some of the broader causes of disturbance engendered by the asylum. If a nurse, supposedly trained to care for and treat such patients with a certain amount of professional distance, is demonstrated to become not only unfit to perform her job, but also unfit to remain in normal society, one must not only question Virginia's chances to reintegrate into this society, but also on what basis she is being judged as fit to reintegrate into it.

One expects that the ministrations of a sensitive doctor such as Dr. Kirk would provide a subtle and sophisticated explanation of Virginia's mental difficulties. However, his surprisingly simplistic suggestion that Virginia failed to "grow up" and to realize that "husbands and fathers can't be the same thing" is very unsatisfying. No real or sound justification is given for why Virginia would suddenly come to this "realization."

Kik characterizes her "cure" in the following way: "It's as though you're in a dark room and you wanted to turn on the light, but you didn't know where the switch was. Now you do. You may never know why turning that switch makes the light go on, but as long as you know where it is, you don't have to be afraid of being in the dark again." Though Kik is presented as a kind and understanding force in a world in which Virginia is continually victimized and persecuted, his reassurance is oddly disturbing and somewhat patronizing, especially given what we have already learned to be Virginia's intelligent and questioning character. As part of her "treatment," she is encouraged to accept that it is not important to understand why she acts as she does or others act as they do, but that "illumination" rather consists of how her actions might be explained in relation to the prominent men in her life. She is presented to the audience as a victory of modern psychoanalysis, but seems disturbingly unenlightened as she is released to the strains of "Going Home" and advises her violent and mute fellow patient, Hester, "Don't be afraid to talk and you'll get well too." Though Hester now demonstrates her ability to say "good-bye" to Virginia, the mood at the end of the film, as it is in so many *noirs*, is outwardly cheerful, but inwardly chilling. What Virginia has learned, in effect, is how to be a good wife, and to accept her husband as the main male figure in her life with no guilt or resentment. There is no further mention of Virginia's writing or activism, and the audience must conclude that these fragments of her identity have been "cured" along with her other distortions of reality. The most probing treatment of mental asylums and treatment in *film noir* reveals the disconcerting choice between conformity and insanity as the definition of psychological soundness.

Notes

1. Gerald N. Grob, *The Mad Among Us: A History of the Care of American's Mentally Ill.* (New York: Free Press, 1994), 196. As one of the most influential psychiatrists in the history of the profession, Menninger's close ties to the military and influence in the therapies following World War II is important to note.
2. *Time.* "Spit it Out, Soldier." Sept. 13, 1943. 60.
3. Arline Britton Boucher, "They Learn to Live Again." *Saturday Evening Post* May 27, 1944, 105; Kyle Crichton, "Repairing War-Cracked Minds." *Collier's* Sept. 23, 1944, 22.
4. Nathan G. Hale, Jr., *The Rise and Crisis of Psychoanalysis in the United States: Freud and the Americans, 1917-1985.* (New York: Oxford University Press, 1995), 191-92
5. Hale, 205. For a detailed explanation of the use of narcosynthesis in World War II, see Roy Grinker and John Spiegel's accounts of their psychiatric practices in *Men Under Stress*, originally published in 1945.
6. Albert Deutsch, "Dramatic Effects of 'Truth Serum'," *Science Digest* 20, no. 4 (Oct. 1946): 67.
7. Kelly Oliver and Benigno Trigo, *Noir Anxiety.* (Minneapolis: University of Minnesota Press, 2003), 41.
8. Mary Ann Doane, "The Clinical Eye: Medical Discourses in the 'Woman's Film' of the 1940's," *Poetics Today* 6, no.1/2 (1985): 208.
9. Laura Mulvey, "Visual Pleasure and Narrative Cinema." *Screen* 16, no. 3 (Autumn 1975): 6-18.
10. Doane, 220.
11. See, for instance, Leslie Fishbein, "*The Snake Pit* (1948): The Sexist Nature of Sanity," *American Quarterly* 31, no.5 (Winter 1979): 641-55.
12. Veda Semarne, "*The Snake Pit*: A Woman's Serpentine Journey Toward (W) holeness," *Literature/Film Quarterly*, 22, no.3 (1994): 145.
13. Semarne, 149.

Chapter Three
Noir Amnesia

"Somebody turned on a light. It's a far-away light, but at least I don't have to be alone in the dark anymore."

—George Taylor, *Somewhere in the Night* (1946)

One of the most powerful examples of how psychiatry weaves its thread throughout *noir* is the depiction of *noir* amnesia. Given the ubiquity of the theme of the search for identity in *noir*—as the protagonist struggles to make sense of not only the world around him, but also of himself—it is not surprising to see striking examples of this concept in films in which the main characters suffer from amnesia, thus experiencing a literal loss of self that becomes metonymic of their figurative angst. Often such depictions center on the experience of the returning veteran, but there are just as many civilian *noir* characters that experience such a plight. Given the importance of the role of the veteran in the cultural popularization of psychoanalysis, as discussed in the previous chapter, this group of films, including *Crack-Up* (Irving Reis, 1946), *Dial 1119* (1950), *High Wall* (1947), and *Somewhere in the Night* (1946), is a useful place to start. Regardless of whether the characters suffering from amnesia in *noir* are veteran or civilian, these films present a central problem regarding the complex construction of individuality. The "absent selves" that these protagonists seek are akin to uncanny doubles, "others" that the main characters must find and either assimilate or destroy in order to reach psychological wholeness. Such characters in fact tell us much about anxiety-ridden characters generally found in *noir* cinema, in that such a figure not only represents the literal possibility of identity loss, often in the aftermath of war trauma, but also emblematizes the dangers of psychic loss in an uncertain world.

Freud explains the concept of the uncanny, or "*unheimlich,*" as being an experience of obscure dread, unexplained circumstances, or coincidences and, perhaps most importantly, a feeling that there is something unfamiliar about the familiar. Freud quotes the following definition from Schelling to illuminate the concept even further: "'*Unheimlich* is the name for everything that ought to have remained . . . secret and hidden but has come to light.'"[1] This idea of the uncanny is illuminating when considering the experience of the amnesiac in *film noir*. What becomes familiar and yet not familiar to the protagonist is the actual self. At each turn, the character glimpses shards of the self, as if in a fractured mirror, but can never see the whole image; each piece seems both known and unknown at the same time. The amnesiac is thus doubled by an entity or entities that are fragments of the self waiting to be discovered and reintegrated into waking consciousness. Confrontations with these uncanny versions of the self represent the search for identity that is so crucial to the depictions of existential loneliness and angst in *film noir*.

It is no accident that the amnesia victims in *noir* are so often returning veterans. The figure of the returning veteran in *noir*, as Frank Krutnik points out, was so common that it received a "standardised address within the generic mode" of the *noir* thriller.[2] The plight of the ex-serviceman as he must reintegrate into civilian life after witnessing the horrors of World War II was depicted in many *films noir* in which protagonists often suffered a myriad of psychological traumas, showing, as argued by Michael Walker, a distinct shift from filmic depictions of the physical trauma derived from World War I.[3] These psychological traumas, inspired by everything from Nazism to atomic warfare, often border on—and cross over to—the criminal. What is especially disturbing about the amnesiac in these films, however, is the unknowable quality of his identity and actions. He may have done things that he cannot remember or falsely remember things that he has not done, but in either case, all he has to rely on is the testimony of those around him (which often cannot be trusted) and his own shattered memory. According to Andrew Dickos, the *noir* amnesiacs live "in a betrayal of the mind that leaves them easy pawns to those that would exploit them. Their quest for self-identity often fuels this unknown with a dread in a narrative of fearful culpability."[4] Though there may be a short, significant span of time missing, as in *Crack-Up*, or an entire lifetime, as in *Somewhere in the Night*, in all of these cases, the main character must not only confront the fact that his mind cannot be relied upon, but also the question of his inner morality and capabilities of crime.

In *Crack-Up*, George Steele (Pat O'Brien) is an art curator who loses several hours of time when he believes he has been in a train wreck that never actually happened. The movie opens with a dark scene of a train collision, followed by Steele breaking into his own art museum. As he explains how he remembers getting to the museum after he regains consciousness, his realization that the train wreck in his memory never took place is unnerving to the viewer as well; it has the effect of waking from a realistic dream to see the questionable reality of waking life, as was also felt by *Nightmare*'s Stan Grayson. Steele's literal awakening is more a disturbing than relieving experience because in the place of the train wreck is nothingness: hours of his life that he cannot account for in which he was seeing, thinking, and acting, but of which he has no conscious memory. During this time, an uncanny "other" took his place, by assuming his consciousness and his body. It is the disturbing nature of this experience and the threat of loss of self (or the autonomy of this "blank" self) that causes Steele to relentlessly search for his "other."

Steele, like many of his fellow *noir* amnesiacs, must search for this "other" largely in secret, by retracing his steps and repeating his actions leading up to the missing hours. He attempts this search and thus the reconstruction of his psyche by returning to the train station, buying a ticket, and embarking on the same train ride as on the night of the blackout. As he compulsively repeats each action, he is faced with overwhelming uncanniness: everything about the train station and the train ride itself are both familiar and unfamiliar at the same time. He sees ticket sellers, conductors, and candy men again, asking them, "Do you know me?" or "Was I on this train last night?" However, they do not know him, even though his blackout occurred only twenty-four hours before. He knows he was there, but to judge from the perceptions of others whom he encountered, it is as if he were never there, as though he did not exist—or worse, as though someone else was in his place. This experience, of course, represents the existential questions that plague nearly every *noir* antihero regarding the nature of the self: how does one exist—on what basis? The only way George Steele can verify, can truly know, that he took a train ride the night before is to trust that part of his mind that still speaks logically to him—but even that becomes suspect as other evidence dissolves. After being finally rebuffed by the sandwich seller on the train, Steele murmurs, "I thought you might remember . . ."—a phrase that highlights the futility of his search. If he expects to find the "other" self that remembers what really happened on that train ride, he can rely on no one but himself. Ironically, in the upside-down world of *noir*, eyewitness accounts often only appear when they serve to incriminate an innocent man; when they are necessary to validate someone's identity or to provide the pieces to a puzzle that save a man from insanity, prison, or death, such verification is non-existent. It is no wonder that Steele feels as though he is a ghost, the shadowy döppelganger to a real self somewhere experiencing a part of his life without his consent. The intermittent shots of his face reflected in the train window highlight this doubleness: Steele can no longer tell with any certainty what lies beyond the train window; he can only stare at a face that is his, yet uncannily unfamiliar at the same time.

A frustrated Steele exclaims, "All of a sudden, I don't know myself. In twenty-four hours, everything has become unfamiliar." His girlfriend, Terry (Claire Trevor) replies, "Your ego's been bruised because all of a sudden, you don't know all the answers." This exchange is illuminating in many ways. For one, it speaks of the alarming speed at which his life has turned from familiarity to unfamiliarity, and the fact that a mere missing few hours can call into question the entirety of one's life and oneself. Terry's response to George's distress is important in that his power, male bravado, and independence—all of which we clearly see in both flashbacks and the events subsequent to his blackout—must necessarily suffer at the hands of the "other" Steele who inhabited the missing hours after the imagined train wreck. And in many ways, Terry's assessment holds true during the course of the entire film, as George, mostly ineffectually, tries to solve the mystery of his missing self. What few clues he discovers he cannot or does not use to any real advantage, and he is stymied and confused at every turn, often acting in a certain way simply for the sake of doing something. Relying heavily on intuition, Steele begins to connect a Nazi art forgery scheme that he had investigated during the war to a nearly identical scheme currently going on in New York that is using his art museum as a pawn. But, as Robert Watson argues, "The villains easily manipulate his mind and his body is made a puppet for the authorities."[5]

Ultimately Steele is merely a plaything in his own deliverance because it is a Scotland Yard art expert detective who solves the mystery of Steele's missing plight as he single-handedly saves both him and Terry from the clutches of Dr. Lowell (Ray Collins), who has orchestrated the forgery scheme. Lowell uses narcosynthesis on Steele to determine whether the police know that the paintings were forgeries. Lowell's comments prior to injecting Steele reveal the shadow of the war—and the hidden traumas it may have caused men like Steele: "Odd, isn't it, that truth should be a byproduct of war? Only in the recent war did we perfect a direct communication with a man's true self. It's called 'narcosynthesis.' . . . One small injection of this and the brain is illuminated with accuracy . . . the subconscious mind takes over." Examples of narcosynthesis in *noir* abound, but when applied for nefarious purposes to characters who are veterans, it takes on an even more sinister implication, as we know that the development of the technique arose to help and cure veterans, rather than victimize them. The larger implication is perhaps that war exposes the minds of men to brutal, primitive motivations and actions that, like Schelling's *unheimlich*, are better left undisturbed. We never find out what sort of private traumas George Steele experienced during the war, but their implication here is obvious. Ironically, the one thing in the film that can elicit "truth" and thus lead Steele out of his subconscious darkness to reunite with the phantom "other" is used against him, to provide knowledge that will lead Lowell to attempt to murder him and Terry. And nearly to the very end of the film, Steele still appears to be raving and unsure of reality, the film's deus-ex-machina resolution doing little to prove that Steele's mental rupture is really healed. Those surrounding Steele seem to understand what has happened to him, but not Steele himself. If we only exist insofar as those around us permit us to exist, then Steele is truly "whole" again. But as far as Steele himself is concerned, there is no clear sense that he has met, recognized, and been reconciled with his uncanny "other" self.

Narcosynthesis rears its ugly head again in *High Wall*, where we see Steven Kenet (Robert Taylor) accused of the strangulation murder of his wife and, because of amnesia, unable to tell investigators what really happened. Unlike its use in *Crack-Up*, sodium pentothal is used more traditionally as a therapy to help Kenet reconstruct his memory and thus reassemble his psyche. However, most of the film leading up to these reconstructive moments is filled with Kenet fighting against the uncanny "other" who inhabited the moments of his wife's death. Kenet at first seems to fear re-experiencing what really happened during that missing hour between confronting his wife about her infidelity and waking up next to her dead body. Then, as it becomes likely that he did not kill her, he becomes obsessed with finding out the truth, with exposing the actions of the phantom self that murdered his wife—the person, when faced with all logical evidence, who *must* have killed her. Like George Steele, he attempts to reconstruct the scene leading up to his blackout and enlists the help of his female psychiatrist, Dr. Ann Lorrison, (Audrey Totter), who is an example of the benevolent and nurturing variety of *noir* psychiatrist, much like *Spellbound*'s Constance Peterson. When Kenet and Ann return to the apartment of Helen Kenet's boss and lover, Willard Whitcombe (Herbert Marshall), Kenet disarranges the furniture and belongings in order to walk himself through the previous experience. Doing this does not really cause him to remember much more than he did before, but it serves an additional function: since Kenet already suspects Whitcombe of murdering his wife, he thinks that when Whitcombe returns to see the apartment looking like the original murder scene, he will become unnerved. In this way, Kenet almost acts as Whitcombe's double—both men were at the murder scene, and both had a reason to kill Helen, but only one of them actually did it. Kenet spends the rest of the movie playing mind games with Whitcombe, each of them trying to expose the other as the true murderer.

Part of Kenet's resistance to facing the missing hour in which his wife was murdered is the rage he felt toward her when he found out about her infidelity. He is already a scarred man: a war veteran who had sustained a serious head injury during combat, and who unhappily sought flying work in Burma after the war to satisfy his war bride's insatiable desire for money. When he is in custody in the psychiatric hospital, he seems to accept his fate because it is an almost fitting end to the mess his life has become. The opening scene of the film clearly portrays his state of mind: driving a speeding car with his dead wife slumped beside him, Kenet has an equally dead expression on his face as he elbows her dead body away from him and drives the car off a bridge in an effort to kill himself. His self-discovery thereafter becomes so important because in order to find out that his life is worth redeeming at all, he must realize that, regardless of his hatred and anger toward his wife, he did not commit murder. The "other" murderous self restrained itself in his psyche—drastically perhaps, as such restraint caused a blackout—but it was restrained nevertheless. Dr. Lorrison uncovers such truths in her narcosynthesis session with Kenet, and finally (and ironically) does the same with Whitcombe when she and Kenet confront him in the apartment. The police, as symbols of logic and authority, are there to witness the so-called truth that emerges from Whitcombe's narcosynthetic trance and thus the extinguishing of Kenet's criminal double. The film's flowery resolution of Ann Lorrison (the morally "strong" woman) replacing Helen Kenet (the morally "weak" woman) and bringing Steven Kenet and his son back together does little to erase from the viewer's mind the propensity of Kenet to commit a murderous act, even as it seems he will be officially cleared of the deed itself. Kenet hopes that the elimination of the phantom "other" that inhabited his amnesiac state will erase the frustration and violent urges that were a by-product of his war and post-war experiences. This is what Nicholas Christopher points out as the "shadowy borderline between repressed violence and outright vulnerability" that is evident in so many *noir* protagonists.[6]

This "shadowy borderline" is also evident in E.A. Dupont's somewhat lesser-known *The Scarf* (1951). The opening of the film shows John Howard Barrington (John Ireland) escaping from Alcanta Hospital for the Criminal Insane, beginning a journey both literally and figuratively in the desert, one that he hopes will prove to him definitively whether or not he murdered his girlfriend, an incident that he cannot remember, but for which he has been convicted and imprisoned for life. Barrington cannot decide not only whether or not he is guilty, but also whether or not he is insane. He is a man without a past in many ways: not only is he unable to remember what happened on the night of his girlfriend's murder, he is also the adopted son of wealthy tycoon Cyrus Barrington, and so his biological background is shrouded in mystery as well, including, implied by the film, any evidence of hereditary insanity. He refuses to go back to Alcanta (also called "The Dungeon"), calling it "a pesthole of creatures with bodies and no minds." Barrington acknowledges that "insanity is the lack of knowledge between right and wrong . . . not in the abstract, mind you, but in the particular act . . . whatever you've done against society." However, he cannot remember what his "particular act" was, and it is his lack of a sense of guilt that his instincts tell him may be the signifier of his innocence. Barrington's greatest assistance after his escape comes from the unlikely—and initially reluctant—"wilderness man," Ezra Thompson (James Barton). He acts almost as a surrogate psychiatrist, trying to nurse Barrington back to physical health with work on his turkey farm and to emotional health with his friendship and security. Barrington shares with Thompson his fears and insecurities, including a flashback memory from the asylum when he witnesses a trustee being attacked by one of the violent inmates. Barrington is tortured by the fact that he was paralyzed and cannot assist his fellow worker. "I couldn't get to her," he says, and then realizing the slip, adds, "Did I say her—I meant him." Though Thompson is not a medical doctor, he supports Barrington, including in his discussion with the warden and doctor from the asylum when they come looking for Barrington. In response to the warden's assertion that "loss of memory is a passport to immunity from the hot seat," Thompson argues, "If he's insane, he's sick. And if he's sick, he needs help." As we have seen, this type of mental-as-physical illness rationale is a common argument used by psychiatrists in *noir* in support of their patients, adding to the victimization quality of mental illness.

Another key individual in Barrington's recovery and eventual exoneration is the hard-bitten bar waitress, Connie (Mercedes McCambridge). When she pulls out a scarf and puts it around her neck, he is visibly shaken and demands to know where she got it; it turns out that the scarf looks just like the one with which his girlfriend was strangled. He shares with Thompson that seeing the scarf seemed to almost spark his memory, but it was like "a bubble that burst." Rather than reassure him, the incident leaves him even more frightened because, as he tells Thompson, at least he had some doubt before about his guilt, but that even that seems to be fading: "Doubts may wreck you but they let you believe what you want to believe—facts don't." When Barrington first came to Thompson, he was troubled by similar doubts as to his own propensities, fueled by his loss of memory: "If I did it the first time, I might do it again if it's in me." Barrington's phantom "other" self is beginning to look more and more like himself and he is terrified at the prospect of something alien "in" him that he cannot see, let alone control.

It is ironic that the faux psychiatrist-detective, Thompson, offers just as much, if not more assistance to Barrington than the other two "real" psychiatrists in the film. Dr. Gordon (Lloyd Gough), the asylum doctor, grows to believe in Barrington as the film progresses and ultimately provides crucial help to Barrington later in the film. The other psychiatrist is the mentally unstable Dr. David Dunbar (Emlyn Williams), who is the British "family friend" of the Barringtons, having met John in the war and returned home with him afterward. The two doctors meet when the elder Barrington comes to the asylum, Dunbar in tow, concerned about his own protection now that John has escaped. Barrington challenges Dr. Gordon by querying him, "You're a physician?" to which Gordon responds, somewhat defensively, "I don't know how I'm expected to answer that; I'm a psychologist." The strength of Gordon's psychiatric chops will later prove particularly important to John Barrington's salvation, but at this point, from John's perspective, Gordon is the enemy and David Dunbar is still his friend, and Barrington seeks Dunbar's counsel because he still trusts him. Having recalled small portions of his memory since he has escaped, he remembers that he and Dunbar were together with his girlfriend, Rosmary, when the murder happened, and believes that Dunbar is the "one that can give [him] the answer." The exchange between Barrington and Dunbar is highly charged, and Dunbar is eager to use the opportunity to seal Barrington's fate as the killer, since it is actually Dunbar himself who is guilty of the murder. Dunbar uses his psychiatric expertise to capitalize on Barrington's trust by using semi-hypnotic suggestion to attempt to "prove" to Barrington that he really is guilty. As mentioned earlier, what chiefly bothers Barrington is that he has no sense of guilt, while simultaneously recognizing that all available evidence seems to point to his guilt. This puts him in the terrifying position of not only being guilty of a heinous crime but also being so morally bankrupt that such an act would not cause him any remorse or shame. Dunbar senses his weakness and fear, as he closes the blinds in his office, intoning "night is the mother of thoughts" and asking Barrington if perhaps it is possible that he has simply just forgotten that he has done it. As Dunbar suggests significant pieces of information, such as the scarf, it is clear that he is also attempting to extract exactly how much Barrington actually remembers. Dunbar goes so far as to tell Barrington that he was a witness to his murder of Rosemary, and it was only his own shock at Barrington's actions that kept him from stopping him. Barrington is so weak at this point that his former trust in Dunbar's friendship convinces him enough to resignedly admit "I did it," as Dunbar opens the blinds and reveals the police there waiting to collect him.

Barrington is no longer capable of saving himself and his only remaining savior is Thompson, who still believes in Barrington enough to enlist the help of Connie and Dr. Gordon to orchestrate a plan that will exonerate him. Just as Barrington seems powerless to have defended himself against the seemingly random original situation that placed him as the murderer of his girlfriend, he needs the assistance of not one or two, but three different individuals to come together in order to save his life. Again, playing the role of the "surrogate" psychiatrist who believes in the patient against all "logic," Thompson admits that he does not have any reason to help Barrington except for faith: "Faith is the evidence of things not seen, says the Bible—now that's what I mean when I say that boy's not guilty." Despite the fact that the newspapers report that Barrington confessed, Thompson persists, "Let him shout it from the rooftops; he's not guilty." It would appear, as is so often the case in *noir*, that the more modern the world becomes, the less we can rely on our logic or reason, needing to resort instead to instinct or faith to keep us going from day to day and to solve the most morally difficult of problems.

To save Barrington and expose Dunbar, Thompson, Connie, and Gordon plan an assault on Dunbar from two angles—first, Gordon's attack on his psychiatric ability and mental competence and second, Connie's attack on his sexual insecurities and memory of his relationship with Rosemary. Gordon and Dunbar then begin a session of psychiatric sparring, as Gordon ridicules every interpretation that Dunbar offers, including Dunbar's own "mental coma" regarding his witnessing of the murder. Gordon asserts that "there must be a vital difference in the interpretation of medical ideas between our two countries" since he was taught that such shock reactions as Dunbar describes do not exist. Gordon offers instead that Dunbar is the actual killer and Barrington the actual witness, using as further evidence his discovery of Dunbar's war record—a record that reveals his confinement to a psychopathic ward in England in 1942 and again in 1943. Dunbar defensively replies, "As a soldier, is that necessarily something to be ashamed of?" to which Gordon counters, "As a soldier, no; as a doctor, it might have proven an obstacle." The role of the war and the psychological difficulties of the veteran are emphasized here, only not sympathetically when they are being used to imperil another veteran. And finally their visit ends with arguably one of the most priceless exchanges in a psychiatric *noir*:

Gordon:	You settled in California not because of the sunshine, but to cover up your past.
Dunbar:	You're not a doctor, Doctor; you're a mind reader. Where's your turban?
Gordon:	You're not a doctor, Doctor; you're a patient.

Gordon is clearly the winner of this psychiatrist v. psychiatrist bout. Dunbar's manipulation of Barrington using psychiatric techniques is challenged with contempt by Gordon, who Dunbar in turn tries to discredit by the usual appropriation of the "fortune-teller" mythology of quack psychiatry. But Gordon's characterization of Dunbar as more of a patient than a practitioner is a cutting and accurate blow, especially as we see Dunbar soon after attempt to strangle Connie with her own scarf.

He bitterly recalls that "Rosemary and John giggled behind [his] back, and giggling's worse than laughing." When he finally wraps the scarf around her neck, he muses, "She was beautiful; so are you . . . she laughed at me; so did you." As the police intervene and arrest Dunbar, Barrington declared, "I was only haunted by four walls; you were trapped in the dungeon of your own conscience." As in many amnesia *noirs*, though the real killer is brought to light it is unclear to what extent the protagonist has become truly free of the demons that plagued him. It is not even clear to what extent Barrington has regained his memory, but as we have seen, in some *noirs*, it is preferable not to have full memory restoration. When Barrington leaves Thompson and Connie and says he is "going home," there is no sense of where that would actually be or how he might re-integrate into society.

Similarly, in Victor Saville's *The Long Wait* (1954), based on a Mickey Spillane story, John McBride (Anthony Quinn) finds himself in much the same predicament at John Barrington. An auto accident leaves McBride with horribly burned hands and complete amnesia. McBride's doctor in the hospital sympathizes with his condition, telling him that "amnesia is one of the most unnerving things that can happen to a person. . .not really sick and yet you're not yourself. . . . You look in the mirror and say, 'who am I,' 'where'd I come from?' . . . and you have what we call a general amnesia. Your past is a total blank." This blankness is compounded by an entire erasure of tangible evidence of identity since all of McBride's identification cards were destroyed in the accident. However, the doctor acknowledges that his case is not hopeless: "One of these days that part of your brain that remembers will start working again . . . how we don't know—it just happens that way." In addition to the hit-or-miss effectiveness of narcosynthesis for amnesia treatment, the role of psychiatric expertise in helping amnesia victims, as portrayed in *noir*, does not inspire confidence. Not only is the doctor incapable of telling McBride whether or not he will ever regain his memory, even if he does, it could take "days, months, even years." In addition to all external identification of McBride being destroyed, he has also lost his most uniquely identifying human features: his fingerprints, which have been burned off. When the doctor fixes the bandages on his hands and says he will eventually be able to use them "as good as ever," McBride says, "How good is that? How do I know?"

In an effort to literally find himself, McBride emerges into a world that seems to offer few answers. He works as a laborer for two years before starting a fight with fellow workers when they ridicule amnesia, calling it "some racket" and joking about why they did not come home last night, or wondering where their paintbrushes are. After the loss of this job, he finds himself adrift until he meets a man in a bar who says he has come back from "his part of the country." An angry McBride says, "Nobody knows where I come from, not even me." This man tells him that he saw his face in a photographer's store window in a town called Lyncastle and gives him the photo. This is the first that McBride even knows his "real" name. What McBride does not know, as he leaves for Lyncastle, is that this photo was actually cut from a wanted-for-murder poster: he is being accused of bank robbery and murder of the district attorney. The one piece of airtight evidence is the fingerprints on the gun—fingerprints that they can no longer prove are McBride's due to his accident. McBride is released, but knows his time is limited to discover whether or not he is truly a thief and murderer. When he learns that he was a bank teller when the robbery took place, he revisits the bank, standing like a prisoner behind the bars of his old teller window, in an attempt to spark his memory, but to no avail. He begins to realize that finding the answer depends upon locating a woman, Vera, who was pictured with him in the newspaper clippings about the crime. The further he delves into her whereabouts in order to find some truth about himself, the more confused he becomes and the more mysterious his surroundings appear. This sense of disorientation is compounded by his discovery that Vera now "looks different" because she has "changed her face." He now finds himself in the position of searching for a woman that he cannot physically identify, a woman who has become the symbolic counterpart to his own amnesiac state.

McBride's total amnesia reflects a *noir* world in which identity is a fluid and ultimately unknowable thing, and Vera's elusive identity is part of it. All he knows, pointing to his temple, is that "There's a locked door up here, and Vera's got the key. Maybe when it's opened, [he] won't like what's inside, but good or bad," he has to find out. There are four possible women who could be the missing Vera, and they are all in some way connected with casino crime boss, Servo (Gene Evans): Carol, Servo's secretary; Wendy, Servo's casino floor manager; Troy, Servo's girlfriend; and Venus, manager of a dress shop owned by Servo. McBride quickly learns that Servo "owns everything in this town," and all are in some part intimidated enough by Servo to give McBride only limited help, as he all the while knows that one of them is the real Vera and for reasons he cannot understand, will not admit to her real identity. When McBride seeks out Servo for answers, Servo tells him, "You can have amnesia and still be a smart cookie," adding that McBride is better off the way he is now: "Like they tell you when you're a kid: what you don't know won't hurt you." Realizing that McBride suspects that he had some involvement with the DA's murder, Servo gives him three hours to get out of town . . . but if he does not heed his warning, he's "not callin' it amnesia; [he's] callin' it suicide." McBride's only ally that he can trust through all of this is reporter Alan Logan (John Damler), who seeks him out initially to get a story, but then becomes his confidante. He responds to McBride's assertion that he never killed anyone by asking him, "How do you know?" Like Thompson in *The Scarf*, Logan is a non-physician who acts like a benevolent psychiatrist, trying to help McBride find his way and acting as a reflecting mirror to help him piece his identity together.

"The way I heard it," explains Logan, "when you came back from the war, you had a load of medals. But you were scared of everything. Once they had a burglar alarm . . . at the bank and they told me you almost passed out . . . you turned yellow. . . . I'd say you're guilty, McBride; you've got it in you to kill a man." Logan sheds important light on McBride's post-war psyche, but also emphasizes that in spite of what appears to be McBride's shell shock, he has the capability, perhaps because of his killing experience in the war, to be guilty of the crimes for which he is accused. McBride says he does not "remember much about the war or what [he] did in it," but Logan reminds him, "The memory may be gone, Johnny, but the instinct lingers on." This comment raises the continued question in amnesia *noir* regarding the inherent capability of crime, especially as it relates to wartime scarring. In *The Long Wait*, largely because it is a Mickey Spillane vehicle, the question of masculinity is inherently tied up with all of these questions. As McBride pursues the elusive Vera, he tests each of the four women contenders sexually, partly to discover some kind of clue in their responsiveness to him, but also it seems as a desperate effort to assert some kind of identity through aggressive sexuality, in the absence of any other marker. A significant symbol of this anxiety is the garter, which McBride first encounters in Venus' dress shop. The garter reads (translated from the embroidered

French), "Evil to him who evil thinks," an ironic nod to the fourteenth-century Order of the Garter motto. McBride will later appropriate this very feminine object in order to save his life, as he takes off Wendy's garter and puts it on his own leg in order to hide the very masculine symbol of his identity, his gun. Later, as he is trying to save Venus from Servo, and is captured himself, he repeats the French motto, a signal in order to get her to retrieve the gun from his immobilized leg. In his paralysis, he relies on what is female to preserve his life—the symbolic absence of self allied with the feminine embodied in Venus.

When McBride confronts Gardiner, the bank president who McBride he says he knew he was not a murderer, and that "losing your memory makes your mind work sharper. . . . The average person remembers things, but half the time, he remembers wrong. A guy with amnesia has nothing to fog up his mind . . . he's got nothing to remember. So he makes deductions, like a detective." Though not Mike Hammer, McBride has become, like many other *noir* amnesiacs, a private eye to solve his own case of unknown identity. And though he cannot remember, McBride is bitterly resentful of Gardiner trying to capitalize on the fact that his "nerves were shot in the war, especially of the implied attack on his masculinity. This comment further reveals the ironic freedom that amnesia affords, as it "cleans" the mind to be able to reason more clearly without the emotional baggage of memory to interfere. It turns out that Gardiner had pulled a bank alarm to make all the tellers draw their bank-issued guns, all the while planning McBride to be the unstable patsy. Now McBride takes pleasure in ridiculing Gardiner trying to escape from him, saying that Gardiner fleeing with his cane tapping is like a "dame with high heels" running away, projecting onto the Gardiner the robbing of masculinity that he had felt. After the police arrive to collect Gardiner, Wendy fills in the final piece of the puzzle by admitting to being Vera, telling McBride that once he was wanted for murder, she thought the only way she could find out the real killer was to change her appearance and work for Servo. The bizarreness of this scheme, only made more bizarre by McBride's loving you-went-under-the-knife-just-for-me reaction to her confession, glosses over the fact that McBride has merely discovered external facts, like a detective, that prove his innocence, but there is no evidence that any of this is due to internal restoration of his memory. McBride asserts to Wendy/Vera that he will love getting to know her face all over again and that he is "remembering everything . . . forgetting nothing." However, what he remembers may very well be a figment of his imagination, especially since the woman he is "remembering" could never be outwardly recognized again. Once McBride has convinced himself what he is *not*—at least in relation to the specific crimes for which he was pursued—his search for his past identity is abandoned in the arms of his "anonymous" wife. His identity therefore becomes a conglomeration of questionable memory and imposed facts—a disturbingly unstable resolution.

While the journeys of Kenet, Barrington, and McBride reveal that their amnesia buried their innocence, for other returning veterans in *noir*, amnesia reveals a far darker reality—that of unremembered criminality. Robert Florey's *The Crooked Way* (1949) provides such an example, in which a veteran searches for answers that increasingly indict him as a criminal and a stool pigeon. The film's documentary-style opening voice-over posits Eddie Rice (John Payne) as one of the unfortunate souls inside a hospital where "war is still going on." The idea of the long reach of the war's effects surfaces in a myriad of ways in *noir*, but the plight of the amnesiac veteran is one of the most often-seen vehicles through which this idea is expressed, as the amnesia-stricken veteran represents the most extreme case of the pitfalls military personnel faced when attempting societal re-assimilation. Rice's amnesia is "organic," a result of shrapnel lodged too deeply in his brain to remove, and surrounded by scar tissue. There seems no illusion that Rice can recover his memory; his doctor informs him that unlike the "psychological" form of amnesia that can be cured with psychotherapy, his is "permanent." However, the doctor also tells him that he is healthy, capable of living a normal life, and encourages him to "go home" to California to see if he can encounter anyone who knew him, so that at least this might lead to his recovering his identity—to find out at least who he really *was*, even if his memory can never be restored. This situation of never being able to restore one's memory, one's sense of self, only adds to the uncanniness of the amnesiac experience and provides the disturbing uncertainty seen so often in *noir*. The best the hopeless amnesiac can expect is that he can encounter others who knew him and *tell* him who he used to be—he then becomes a product of others' perceptions (and perhaps, grievances) but can never have any first-hand knowledge of his own self. Oddly, such a situation also positions the amnesiac as the ultimate existential hero, able to begin with a blank slate and create any identity he wishes.

Rice is understandably frightened at such a prospect, and rightfully so, as he returns to his hometown and discovers all manner of shady characters who recognize him, as well as the police, who are quick to pick him up for interrogation. The cynical police lieutenant Williams (Rhys Williams) reacts unsympathetically to his veteran status: "You think you come back with a dumb look and a silver star—that changes a no-good heel?" It turns out that he apparently is really Eddie Riccardi, who had multiple criminal charges against him, including weapons possession with intent to kill and suspicion of murder. Despite having any evidence to the contrary, Rice's voice-over ponders, "That's not me; it can't be . . . it only looks like me." His strategy is to "play along" and not reveal his amnesia, in order to get the most accurate information. This kind of survival strategy speaks to the often artificial constructions of identity found in *noir*; Rice is having the uncanny experience of "playing" himself, since this self is a foreign "other" entity. He has no psychiatrist attending him to assume the detective role, but he assumes it himself, and the extent to which everyone believes the charade, by his use of broad, vague language and an attitude of familiarity, seems a testimony to the lack of worth on the genuine individual human character emergent in the post-war world. He allows himself to be beaten up by his former criminal cronies, including longtime "friend" and crime boss, Vince Alexander (Sonny Tufts), who is angry that Eddie turned state's evidence against him. Vince is somewhat unstable himself, as he is seen treating his water with drops of "sodium arsenite" prescribed for a "nervous condition." Vince gives him twenty-four hours to get out of town—everyone, from the police to the criminals, wants Eddie to get out of town, as a matter of fact; his "homecoming" is the antithesis of the sunny mythology of the WWII returning veteran. These feelings are also shared by his former girlfriend, Nina (Ellen Drew), who we learn was likely married by Eddie Riccardi in order to prevent her damaging testimony against him at his trial. Nina is the only one to whom Eddie reveals his amnesia, but ironically, she thinks he is lying, bitterly believing that she was cruelly used as a pawn to secure Eddie's exoneration. Despite his plea that she should call his hospital doctor for corroboration and his appeal that "Eddie Rice wants to make Nina forget that Eddie Riccardi was ever in her life," she rejects him, adding to the irony that Eddie's only "true" revelation of his current state of mind is seen as untrue and not believed.

Vince actually changes his mind about wanting Eddie to leave because now he has a better idea: to attempt to pin his recent murder of Lieutenant Williams and Kelly, a criminal associate, on Eddie. In an impressive display of forensic technology, Williams had confronted Vince with his discovery of an arsenite-tinged fingernail found on Kelly's body. Eddie finds himself in a situation similar to that of *High Wall*'s Steven Kenet: knocked unconscious by Vince's henchmen, he awakens to find himself inside a moving car with the dead Williams by his side. When he flees the car, he is given a ride by a mortician. Death surrounds Eddie like a cocoon, and his lack of conscious identity makes him like an ambient interloper between the living and the dead. With both the police and Vince now pursuing him and an added layer of uncertainty in the fact that he cannot be sure that he did not kill Williams, Eddie is plunging further and further into a whirlpool of existential dread. Eddie's manner throughout his ordeal is strangely artificial and robotic—initially it seems to guard against people discovering his amnesia, but later, for pure self-protection as he cannot find help from any source. Once Nina finally believes in him, and wants to help, he tells her to go away. Knowing that abandoning Eddie means being subject to Vince, Nina responds, "That's something Eddie Riccardi would tell me to do, not Eddie Rice." The "new" Eddie is now at odds with the "old" Eddie for the claim of Nina's love and by extension, the assumption of a reborn, newly moral identity for himself. In his conversation with Nina, her face is illuminated by a spot, while his is backlit in darkness, except for his cigarette. His eyes are then lit, as Nina comments that he is "far away." With a cut back to his face entirely lit, he muses, "Five years . . . a lifetime . . . beyond that, a blank. . . . I don't want to be pushed back to Eddie Riccardi. . . . Now all that's left is wondering what it'd be like if there had only been an Eddie Rice, if I had just met you for the first time."

Nina insists that Eddie Rice *can* have this new life, repeating to him that he is "good." But from where does this "good" emanate? Evidently, Eddie Riccardi was quite the "heel" before the war, suggesting that Eddie's blank slate may equate to a return to Edenic innocence. Once Eddie is cleared of Williams' murder because of a blood match to Vince (more *noir* forensics at work), he is clearly on this more righteous path, as long as he follows Nina's admonishment to "be Eddie Rice." Eddie says, "I will be for the rest of my life; I have the doc's word for it." The implication here is that the war-caused damage to his brain has actually been a blessing in that it allows Eddie to erase his troubled past and begin anew. Still, the disturbing shadow of Eddie's capabilities remains: what is "in him" that made him the way he was before and what are the chances that mysterious property has been erased too?

Perhaps the most complex treatment of the amnesiac (and criminal) antihero can be found in *Somewhere in the Night* (1946), in which George Taylor (John Hodiak) portrays a character in whom we can see the profound effects of confronting the phantom "other." Like Steele and Kenet, Taylor is a newly-discharged veteran; his amnesia is directly caused by a grenade explosion during the war, subsequently plunging him into an unwelcome journey of self-discovery. We literally see the world through his tortured eyes, as we hear Taylor's thoughts after he regains consciousness in a military hospital; he is absolutely unsure of who he is or how he got there. The viewer's perspective is that of Taylor's and his uncanny experience as he frantically looks around the room at alien faces with no internal reference point to make sense of his existence. Nothing seems familiar, but everything does, as he fights against the doctors and fellow soldiers telling him that he is George Taylor: he resists acquiescing to an interpretation of his identity that feels false to him. His solution is to stay as quiet as possible, revealing nothing, as if he were a POW in his own life. Initially, this silence is aided by his jaw being wired shut, and this condition symbolizes the helpless mute state of the amnesiac, who is powerless to articulate who he really is. He assumes a confrontational stance toward "George Taylor," the man that everyone keeps telling him he is, hating this phantom self because of the blankness of what he perceives as his own present self. Taylor's anger toward this "other" solidifies after he finds a letter in his wallet from an unknown sender, one who vehemently despises him. The letter reads: "'I shall pray as long as I live for someone or something to hurt and destroy you, make you want to die, as you have made me.'" This discovery solidifies Taylor's resistance to assuming the identity that was "given" to him after his blackout and leads to his secret search for his "true" self. He questions, "Who writes letters like this? Who do they write them to?" And the answer is not one that he wants to face.

Taylor's search leads him to the discovery of baffling clues and the company of suspicious and threatening characters—who may only be suspicious and threatening because of Taylor's paranoia or the unknown possibilities of their hidden knowledge of Taylor before the war. Finding a letter from someone named Larry Cravat that will allow him to withdraw money from a bank leads Taylor on a dizzying search for Cravat because he believes him to be the only key to his true identity. Indeed, Cravat's letter, which will "identify" Taylor at the bank, is the only apparent proof that George Taylor even existed at all, beyond the military and the war. And it is no wonder that this is the only proof, considering that George Taylor is actually Larry Cravat, a fact that he will not discover until the end of the film. Before this point, however, Larry Cravat is Taylor's doppelganger who he relentlessly hunts in an effort to solve the mystery of his identity. Like other *noir* amnesiacs, Taylor resists help and stubbornly tries to conceal his amnesia as he searches for his true identity. Nearly halfway into the film, he finally confesses his predicament to Christy Smith (Nancy Guild). She is a lounge singer, not a psychiatrist, but fulfills the same type of role in that she supports Taylor and helps him find his way out of his dark labyrinth, even when this means a threat to herself. She comments on the shady reputation of Larry Cravat, by musing to Taylor, "That's quite a pal you've got"—to which Taylor replies, "I can't be choosy; it's the only one I've got." Taylor knows more than he realizes: in this *noir* world of confusion and chaos, one's only friend is oneself. And when Taylor asks her what she knows about amnesia, she responds that it is "when you forget who you are or where you belong."

Christy has essentially summed up the existential plight of the *noir* protagonist, amnesiac or not. It is almost as if the phantom "other" has taken over his rational pre-war life, and left him with only the bits and pieces of an identity.

It turns out that the reason everyone looks askance at George Taylor is that Larry Cravat had left behind him a trail of shady alliances and a missing two million dollars of Nazi money; the police are after him, as well as some of his former associates who believe that he double-crossed them. Taylor also believes himself to be implicated in a murder since he was Cravat's friend; there turns out to have been an unknown person involved that night, and the one man who actually witnessed the murder has been murdered himself, but only after languishing for three years in an insane asylum. He gives Taylor enough information before his final breath, however, to find the hidden money. This money is located in a case under a fishing dock that also houses the final piece of Taylor's identity puzzle: a coat that bears a label with Larry Cravat's name, along with another label that reads "made by W. George, Tailor." George Taylor's identity was actually manufactured by Larry Cravat himself, as he frantically hid the two million dollars and escaped into the wartime military, leaving his old identity (and the old grievances of many) behind. But, as we have seen before, this reunion with his original self is not without anxiety: he has been profoundly changed by his wartime and post-war experiences. The film really does not address the fact that Cravat was not in any way a hero, was actually not even a very nice person—one who at best could be considered a somewhat weak-minded, cowardly opportunist. And perhaps these intimations are what so disturb him during the time that he must pursue the phantom "other" that represents his former identity. After all, as Foster Hirsch argues, in *noir*, "[a]ccused of violent crimes, the victim is forced to examine his own outlaw potential."[7] Especially in Taylor/Cravat's case, such potential is found to be disarmingly accurate.

As Taylor delves deeper into the life of the mysterious Larry Cravat, he realizes that it is going to be impossible to "start with a brand new score pad," as he originally hoped when he first re-entered civilian life. The more he discovers about Larry Cravat, the more he discovers about himself, even before he realizes that he and Cravat are one and the same person. He realizes that he is "really alone in the whole world—a billion people, every one of them a stranger—or what's worse, not a stranger, somebody, maybe, who knows you, hates you, wants you to die." His reintegration into society is an uncanny experience because he is at a social disadvantage: he knows nothing about anyone or himself, yet he is not truly anonymous since any of the "billion people" in the world might have interacted with his phantom "other" self and knows things about him that he cannot know. What is worse is the fear that who he was is not someone he wants to be anymore, and he questions the extent to which any man can remake his personality, his life, as he makes an entire existential leap into an abyss of non-identity and considers the prospect of creating being from nothingness.

In his frustration over his helpless amnesia, George Taylor exclaims, "The war is over for me—I don't have to be afraid anymore!" But the irony is, of course, that there is just as much to fear after the war as during it. The reconciliation of the self back into normal human relationships is psychologically daunting and is an effort that is emblematized in these amnesiac experiences. What these characters must face, as they are pursued by mysterious, persecuting forces, is that "their entrapment may spring from guilty *thoughts* more than guilty deeds."[8] None of these men is particularly virtuous; all have murderous, angry thoughts, and death has followed their actions, whether accidental, driven by soldierly duties, or the misfortune of being in the wrong place at the wrong time. After being presented with a blank self, and thereby forced to seek a phantom "other" that parallels his pre-war identity, each man seeks some semblance of psychological unity, one that in the end, like the restoration of the pre-war world, is disturbingly imperfect. This amnesia-induced blank self is analogous to the fresh start that veterans theoretically have in the post-war world, but which for many is anything but fresh, only blank. As Dana Polan points out, such searching often realizes the subject's "own capacity for violence. The amnesia narrative, where an investigator finds out that he may also be the object of his investigation, suggests a certain blurring of the classic boundaries between knower and known, between character and a supposedly separate reality."[9] The first thoughts of George Taylor after he regains consciousness, and the first lines of *Somewhere in the Night*, actually tell much about the returning veterans' misconceptions about reintegrating their lives: "Somebody turned on a light. It's a far-away light, but at least I don't have to be alone in the dark anymore." Confronting and understanding the uncanniness of their phantom "other" selves, as well as absorbing them, are not seamless processes for the veteran antiheroes of *noir*, but a glimmer and a whisper become preferable to the darkness and silence of a completely empty self.

A fascinating bridge between the treatments of veteran and civilian amnesiacs in *noir*, and one that exhibits a striking example of this empty self, is found in *Dial 1119* (Gerald Mayer, 1950). Aside from the main story surrounding the plight of mentally disturbed, would-be veteran Gunther Wyckoff (Marshall Thompson), the film is a cynical exploration of psychiatry, the police, and the media, as most of the film's action centers on Wyckoff holding a group of people hostage in a bar, demanding to speak to his psychiatrist, while police, reporters, and crowds of curious onlookers gather outside. Wyckoff has been broadcast over television as not only an escapee from a hospital for the criminally insane, but also wanted for killing a bus driver after his escape. The backdrop to the story is the constant presence of media—from the television in the bar to the reporters outside to the vendors selling newspapers in the crowd. Much of what is actually "seen" in the film is through the lenses of the television cameras, complete with lens changes for the "best effect." It is actually a television bulletin about Wyckoff's escape seen in the bar that causes him to pull a gun and hold the bar hostage. In addition, one of the bar hostages is a reporter who was in the process of drinking himself into a self-pitying stupor, on the verge of quitting his job at the newspaper because he believes he is not appreciated. Wyckoff's entrance into this scene provides an ironic catalyst to reinvigorate the reporter's career: he is witnessing one of the biggest stories of his career but cannot communicate it to anyone. These devices, which allow a mass audience for Wyckoff's crimes, past and present, create an eerily voyeuristic and sensationalized tone for the film's message regarding the many varieties of post-war trauma that existed.

A pale and rigid young man, Wyckoff plans to hold the bar patrons hostage until he can speak to his former doctor, police psychiatrist John Faron (Sam Levene). Though it seems as though Wyckoff desperately wants help, what he really wants is revenge against Dr. Faron, because he believed that his psychiatric confessions to the doctor that caused his institutionalization were a breach of trust. He tells the police that if Faron does not come in twenty-five minutes, he will kill everyone in the bar. While they wait, Wyckoff rebuffs the bar patrons' attempts to reason with him, and begins to rant about the injustices of the newspapers that "lied" about him, since "they didn't want the true story." He is adamant that "there's still time to put it on the record," since now "they'll have to listen" to him. The nature of Wyckoff's "public" concern with his "story" highlights the cultural dissemination of information associated with the war and how important these stories were to the public. He seems to be trying to make his case to his hostages, appearing quite convincing as the disgruntled and maladjusted veteran: "Gonna give us a break, they said. Well, what kind of a break did they give me? I'm a good man with a gun. Who gave it to me—who told me to use it?" Wyckoff goes on to assert, "I was no officer. Get that straight right now! Four times they wanted to make me an officer. Think I wanted the medal?" As the viewer will learn at the end of the film, Wyckoff never was a soldier, let alone one that faced the war or earned any medals; however, he has become subsumed in this false identity to the point that he not only recounts what appears to be an participatory account of the Normandy invasion, but also assumes a post-war traumatized persona. It is this persona that Wyckoff uses as a defense for the murders he has committed and which resulted in his prior psychiatric treatment by Dr. Faron.

Faron is a benevolent psychiatrist figure, much like many of the ones explored earlier in this study. He wants to try to help Wyckoff and believes that his assistance is instrumental in saving the lives of the hostages in the bar. However, he clashes with the police captain managing the hostage situation, who happens to be the one who built the case against Wyckoff that ultimately led to his commitment in the asylum. Their debates reveal typical distrust (or distate) regarding mental illness as a mitigating circumstance for crime. While Dr. Faron calls Wyckoff a "demented man with a dream," the captain is angry that "you people stepped in" and came along to ruin his death penalty conviction. Dr. Faron counters with, "We no longer execute the sick—we're not in the Middle Ages." Though Faron makes a compelling case for "confinement and treatment" for the criminally insane, given his ultimate failure to defuse the hostage situation (he is killed by Wyckoff who in turn is killed by the police), the thrust of the argument for psychiatry as a solution to this sort of problem is not especially strong. He cannot make any headway with Wyckoff when he is finally able to see him. Wyckoff insists that he has to kill the doctor and rejects Faron's assertion that they are friends, by asserting, "No, Doctor—we've talked, but we're not friends." Though Faron believes that reminding Wyckoff about the truth of his illness—that he has fabricated an alternate identity as a veteran because he felt inadequate after being rejected for the draft—will shock him back to reality, this approach has the opposite effect. Wyckoff wants to assert this false identity to Faron, saying that he is not afraid, just as he was not afraid in the war when "they gave [him] a gun; they told [him] to kill." When Faron will not accept this, Wyckoff shoots him to silence his disagreement and his rejection of Wyckoff's preferred identity.

Wyckoff's obsession with the war and being a soldier enabled him to absorb enough knowledge, coupled with his delusions, to believe he really had been a veteran. After his draft rejection, he killed others because this was an accepted part of the identity of a soldier and subsequently created the false memories of being in the war that therefore justified his actions. Faron points out what can be seen by the viewer as a tragic societal irony: "Soldiers were the only people permitted to kill without committing a crime." This seeming contradiction, along with the attack on Wyckoff's masculinity by the draft rejection, cause his "reverse" amnesia, as he remembers events that did not occur, rather than not remembering events that did occur. Faron had earlier made the point that Wyckoff struggled with "fighting his inability to function normally, trying to overcome insecurity and proving to a hostile world that he's a hero." However, oddly enough, Wyckoff undermines his own original delusion—that of his being a heroic veteran of an honorable war—by ultimately needing to assume still another identity—that of a victimized soldier whose efforts have not made one bit of difference in this "hostile world." To his hostages Wyckoff argues, "Blood, sweat, tears . . . that's what the man said. What good did it do? We were gonna have a better world—that's what they said during the first one. That's what they told us this time. But what happened to that world? Look at the people's faces in the streets. What do you see? Sadness . . . sadness everywhere." Ironically, Wyckoff's false memories only highlight the futility of wars and the trauma of those who fight in them, rather than promote a heroic ethic of the soldier who can save the world. This is a world in which "most of us" are "unbalanced . . . in one way or another," according to Dr. Faron, in which memory and identity are frequently blurred, a world holding very few stable truths.

Though the depiction of veteran amnesiacs provides particular insight into the construction of cultural identity in *noir*, amnesiac *noir* characters are not limited to wartime experiences (or delusions). In the aptly titled *Man in the Dark* (1953), the amnesiac protagonist is convicted mobster Steve Rawley (Edmond O'Brien) who, in exchange for a parole for his crimes, has agreed to undergo an experimental brain surgery that aims to eliminate his criminal tendencies. The only catch is that this surgery will leave him with amnesia. Rawley's attitude toward the impending surgery (and life in general) is appropriately sardonic, as he tells the police officers who assure him that he will be released soon if the surgery works out, "How would you like *your* lid opened?" Rawley insists on watching the operation, and though the doctors indulge him by positioning a mirror by which to view the surgery, he succumbs to the anesthesia before his "lid" is opened. Here, as in other psychiatric *noirs*, the use of the mirror signifies an effort to breach the divide between the conscious and unconscious, as Rawley struggles to hold on to what may very well be the last moments of his identity. When the surgery appears to be a success, Rawley emerges with a complete loss of memory, but as a more mild-mannered man even with a new name (James Blake). He wants to remain in the serene confines of the mental hospital and assist the benevolent Dr. Marston (Dayton Lummis); his identity having been erased, Rawley cannot imagine a life outside this world into which he has been reborn. However, as is the case with *Somewhere in the Night*'s George Taylor, there is a life outside the hospital that still remembers him, even if he does not remember it. For starters, there is the group of gangsters with whom Rawley worked and most recently before his arrest and surgery, pulled off a $130,000 payroll robbery, the money from which is still missing. In addition, Jawald, the insurance investigator of the company that insured the payroll, is also eager to talk to Rawley after the surgery. As Jawald tells Marston, now that Rawley has been made an honest man, he "wants some honest answers," though he quips that to make Rawley an honest man, "you'd have to cut off his head." As *The Dark Past* and other *noirs* have shown, the idea of criminality as a psychiatric illness capable of being cured is a thorny *noir* issue. Though in some ways it indicates a progressiveness of thought that was beginning to find its way into the popular culture of the late 1940s and '50s, the application of psychiatry to solve criminal issues nearly always finds an ambivalent outcome in *film noir*. Even if psychiatric treatment can get at the root of criminal behavior, the criminal in question cannot often break free of these burdens. In the case of Rawley, the drastic step of total amnesia and identity change is used as a treatment, but even such a marvel of modern science cannot prevent him from being pursued and nearly destroyed by his past.

Once the other members of his gang kidnap Rawley from the hospital, he is subjected to their repeated tactics to elicit the whereabouts of the stolen money. These tactics include physical beating and exposure to artifacts that could jog his memory, such as the newspaper clipping reporting the heist and a trip to his previous house. Additionally, both Jawald and the police are pursuing him, as the police believe he broke out of the hospital. Everyone wants a piece of Rawley for their own purposes—perhaps even the kindly Dr. Marston, who seeks out Jawald to discover Rawley's whereabouts, may be more concerned with the possible failed prestige of the revolutionary brain operation than with Rawley's well-being. Like other *noir* amnesiacs, Rawley finds things that may or may not be clues to his previous identity, such as a scrap of paper with the number 1133 written on it. He must write the number again in order to confirm that the number was written in his own handwriting, and this discovery, rather than relieve him or shed light on his predicament, only adds to the psychic pressure of seeing tangible evidence of another self that is completely foreign to him. As Hugh Manon argues,

> the [*noir*] amnesiac drifts into and out of various hermetically sealed scenes, risking recognition by unknown past acquaintances, while hoping some object, statement, or locale will spark recollection. In doing so, the amnesiac is forced to gaze suspiciously at the minutiae of everyday life—exactly the sort of playful speculation *noir* wants to incite in its viewer's real-world wanderings. The fact that the amnesiac moves about the world in a complete vacuum, then, should be understood not only as a novel twist on the classical detective's quest to sort out a murky enigma, but also as *noir*'s most emphatic statement about the knowledge-deflecting potential of real world surfaces themselves."[10]

Rawley's carnival dream brings the conflicted aspects of his multiple selves into sharp relief. Rawley, then, is blindly groping for answers in a world that is only uncannily familiar because of the external clues to his previous identity that are floating randomly to be (or not be) discovered. But I would argue that he is not, as Manon asserts, in a "complete vacuum," then, because of these very clues and the tether they must hold on him while he is existing in the same world. Rawley has very much attained a "third self" through which he has cobbled together remnants of his previous existence and his present experiences. In the dream, he finds himself lost in an amusement park. He gets into The Whip, a motorized spinning car ride, as the police pursue him, shooting at him. Other strange elements emerge, including a large spider web, and his girlfriend Peg (Audrey Totter) who mans a wheel of fortune and gives him a box of candy. The backdrop to all of this is a mechanical figure whose laughter seems to pursue him as much as the police in the dream. It seems no accident that the venue of the carnival keeps surfacing in psychiatric *noirs*; we have already explored the connections between psychiatry and the surreal element of fortune-telling, as well as the role of the psychiatrist as a mysterious "seer" with supernatural powers.[11] The symbolism in Rawley's dream adds another layer of understanding to his torturous predicament, as it includes real elements and clues to his original identity (the candy box in which Rawley had actually hidden the money and subsequently checked at a carnival) interwoven with objects signifying his anxiety (the dizzying motion of The Whip, the random spin of the wheel of fortune, and the maze of the spiderweb). Later, when conjectures he arrives at based on the dream do not pan out in reality, Rawley mutters to himself, "Dreams . . . next thing, it'll be tea leaves. I must be getting soft in the head." The workings of his own mind seem as unreliable and mysterious as fortune-telling, and his efforts to sort them out promise little more security. Rawley breaks down to Peg following this dream, crying, "My brain is in a scramble! What am I? Who am I?" He cares less about his physical ailments than his psychological ones, claiming, "These are nothing—they hurt on top, not inside. And you know why? Cause there's nothing inside to hurt. I'm dead. Your friends ought to be arrested for beating up a corpse." Like many *noir* amnesiacs, Rawley is indeed like the walking dead—physically alive, but mentally void. Peg poses this blankness, however, as an opportunity rather than a liability, an idea that is central to the ethos of the film: Rawley has the chance to become a better person, a different person than the cruel and angry criminal that he once was. She comments that he is always running in his dream because "Steve Rawley was always frightened." When Peg pauses, unsure if she is revealing too much truth about his former self, he urges her to continue, saying that if he is this character that everyone says he is, "maybe I'd better find out about myself." Peg would like him to be a "new Steve" who is willing to turn his back on recovering the stolen money in favor of starting over and beginning a new life. Unfortunately, however, Rawley cannot divorce himself from who he used to be; he cautions Peg, "This is me, whoever I am. Don't put a halo around my head—it doesn't fit." He cannot help himself from discovering about his past, to fill in the "blank wall" that was his former self, but the ultimate nature the third self that is taking shape remains to be seen.

When Rawley and Peg visit the pier carnival where he hid the money, just as in the dream, the Whip ride appears, as well as the wheel of fortune and the laughing mechanical figure, which turns out to be at the entrance of the "Bug House" attraction. Rawley is indeed in the "Bug House" during the film: he is housed in and kidnapped from one "Bug House" in the first half of the film and is in the figurative confines of another "Bug House" in his own mind during the rest of the film, as he tries to retrace the path of his former self. Peg highlights the duality of Rawley's former and current selves when she tells him that the "candy" in the box that he finally discovers is "poison" and if he keeps it, she can no longer be with him, since she's "in love with another man." As she leaves, Rawley is pursued by both his gangster cronies and the police. Just as in his dream, he flees through the carnival to the backdrop of mechanical hysterical laughter that mocks his hopes to escape—it is clear that such hopes are illusory, since, like George Taylor, he cannot escape from himself. His flight through the fair mimics his desperate attempts to simultaneously make such an escape while making his painful self-discovery. This flight culminates in his climbing aboard a roller coaster, a symbolically appropriate ride for Rawley: it moves fast, taking the rider through disorienting ups and downs, and ends when the rider arrives at the same place from which he started. As Rawley attempts to flee down the roller coaster ride scaffolding, the gangsters drop like flies—literally, as one falls off the scaffold and another gets caught by the police. In the end, Rawley eludes both the law and the unlawful, but in order to be truly free, he must relinquish the stolen money, the fruit of his original, corrupt self. Once he does this, he not only receives the reward of Peg's love, but also the freedom to adopt a new and ostensibly cleaner life.

The intertwining of criminality and amnesia is also seen in *Street of Chance* (1942), based on Cornell Woolrich's *The Black Curtain*. One of the earlier *noirs*, it was also very likely the earliest *noir* dealing with amnesia. Sheri Chinen Biesen points out that the film's "dangerous random accidents" parallel the unnerving effect of the Japanese attack on Pearl Harbor having "lethal consequences and a labyrinth of chaos spiraling out of control. The film's convoluted, elaborate, and unlikely psychological crime plot was just the stuff *noir* was made of."[12] Another of Woolrich's numerous (amnesia and "wrong man") novels that he adapted for the screen, *Street of Chance* captures the same kind of unnerving, uncanny experience of the *noir* amnesiac that we have already seen. The jarring opening of the film shows pieces of construction debris unexpectedly falling off a building and striking a man unconscious. The man who identifies himself as Frank Thompson (Burgess Meredith) regains consciousness and seems relatively unscathed, until he realizes that not only is he in an unfamiliar part of town and has no recollection of how he got there, but also that both his hat and cigarette case bear the initials of "DN," rather than "FT." The abrupt beginning of the film posits the viewer in the same experiential boat as Thompson; to us, we have never known him as anyone else beyond who he claims to be following the accident, and though it becomes increasingly clear that Thompson had been living under another identity, he has very little knowledge to help him piece the puzzle together. The first mystery he encounters is going "home," where he discovers that his wife had moved away over a year ago. For him, no time has passed since he said goodbye to her that morning in the winter, but when he finds her again, she is living under her maiden name in another location in the summer. Thompson muses, "It doesn't make sense; it's like a bad dream." The dream-like state of the amnesiac is well-represented in other films as well, an experience akin to awakening from one state of reality (a dream) to another (waking life) and being momentarily uncertain of one's own location or identity. Thompson's amazingly understanding wife, Virginia (Louise Platt), assures him, "We've both read of cases like this . . . amnesia." She tells him that she is willing to stick with him and find out what happened, but that he must try to hold on to the things he knows, like "home." However, the idea of "home," just like the idea of one's own name, has become a fluid, rather than a constant, concept. As "DN," he must have had a different home, and possibly a different wife—which one can be determined to be "real"?

Thompson tries to immerse himself in the trappings of his old life, including getting his old job back; ironically, Virginia had told his employer that he had a nervous breakdown, rather than saying that he had disappeared. He is, however, haunted by nightmares and disturbing thoughts, especially that of the face of a sinister-looking man who is following him and wants to get at him so badly that he breaks the window of a cab in which Thompson is trying to flee. When this man, leading a group of other suspicious characters, beats on his door in the middle of the night, Thompson sends his wife away to her mother while he tries to figure out what is happening. She wants to stay and help him but he says, "When a man falls in quicksand, he doesn't reach up and pull those he loves down with him. . . . I've got to find out what this is before I dare come into your life again." Thompson's predicament is that he is drowning in a sea of uncertainty, pursued by unknown entities because of an unknown past. His desperation brings him back to the neighborhood in which the construction accident occurred in search of some clue or more importantly, some person who can recognize him as "DN." In voice-over, he maintains, "Somewhere down here's the answer. Someplace there's somebody who's got to recognize me, remember me, say hello. Nobody I ever saw in my life, nobody that ever saw me, from the looks on their faces." The only recognition he receives is the contempt of a pawnshop owner, to whom he has previously pawned the same cigarette case three times, in addition to giving the owner a false address, that of "a vacant lot." It is, of course, entirely appropriate that he has represented a former address as a vacant lot, since that emptiness characterizes both his self as "DN" and also his present self that is missing one year of life.

Desperate for something to break through and give him information, he wearies himself by walking up and down the street all day. The endless retracing of steps in order to regain memory (with or without a psychiatrist or other "detective guide") is a pattern that we have seen in films like *Nightmare* and *Crack-Up* and which is described by Edward Dimendberg as the "walking cure" of *noir*: "For like Freud's psychoanalytic method, this cure also hinges upon memory and repetition as the means by which past and present combine into a comprehensive personal identity. Yet here the technique employed does not involve a patient's verbal narration of dreams or earlier events but rather the physical act of passage through the city."[13] Thompson reaches the point at which he acknowledges, "I'm dead . . . I've got to find something that'll help me remember." He has come to the realization that any of his selves, even his present, more accepted one, is in jeopardy while a rogue self exists, unknown to him, but known to others.

Finally, by chance, Thompson meets Ruth Dillon (Claire Trevor), the only person who truly recognizes him as Danny Nearing, the mysterious "DN." Her initial reaction to him that he should get into the upstairs apartment and "out of sight" brings into focus the nature of Thompson's alter ego: he is evidently wanted for the murder of Harry Diedrich, Ruth's employer, and the mysterious man following him is Joe Marucci, not an underworld thug, but a police detective. Upon reading a newspaper clipping about his wanted status, Thompson looks quizzically in a mirror, touching his face pensively, as if it were an alien appendage; his own face has become uncannily unfamiliar to him. Ruth cannot even seem to vouch for his innocence, since she claims she was not in the room when the murder happened. As baffling as these circumstances are, Thompson is fairly sure that he is not the murderer—he says, "I couldn't be: 'the me' that is inside me wouldn't let me kill anyone." Similar to the Constance Peterson's claim in *Spellbound* that John Ballantine could not be a murderer because she would not be in love with one, the idea of a moral center, a core identity, is often at odds in *noir* with the seemingly random forces that could lead anyone to commit an unethical or criminal act. The idea of Thompson's inability to be a murderer also seems inconsistent with the way Danny Nearing is characterized by those who knew him, from the pawnbroker to Ruth herself, who calls him "no good," though she loves him anyway. Granted, being "no good" does not make one a murderer, but it does call into the question the idea that Thompson's character as Nearing is beyond reproach.

Though Nearing is the only one officially wanted for Diedrich's murder, he is one of several sordid characters who might be guilty, including Diedrich's wife and brother, who happen to be having an affair with each other. However, it turns out that the killer is Ruth herself, who stabs Diedrich when he beats her after discovering she is stealing money. Thompson discovers all of this in a curious way. He goes back to the Diedrich house with Ruth late at night, and with a flashlight, prowls for clues, like other amnesiacs *noir* "detectives." To solve a murder in order to exonerate oneself, one must find the true murderer—even as there is a risk that the true murderer *is* oneself. Thompson discovers Grandma Diedrich (Adeline deWalt Reynolds), the murdered man's mother, who is mute and paralyzed, but the only witness to the murder. Through a complex method of her eyeblinks representing no, yes, and letters of the alphabet, Thompson painstakingly discovers that Grandma saw Ruth kill Diedrich through the reflection in a mirror on her bedroom wall. Grandma's mute and paralyzed state parallel Thompson's inability to prove his innocence or identity, and once again, the appearance of a mirror in a psychiatric *noir* "reflects" the protagonist's dual states of mind and search for (or rejection of) insight. Ruth claims to Thompson that she stole because he had told her that the only way they could get married is if they could get some money together. There is, of course, no way for Thompson to corroborate the claim, but since she does not know that Thompson does not remember his life as Nearing, she would likely not be lying. This admission calls into further question the nature of Nearing's character, and even though Ruth is shown to be rather tough around the edges, especially when Thompson lets her know that he will turn her in, the unanswered questions surrounding Thompson/Nearing himself are the most troubling aspect of the film. Aside from the suspected murder, the fact that Nearing worked for the Diedrich family, and the few bits of information gleaned from Ruth and the pawnbroker, we know almost nothing about what Thompson was doing or what kind of man he portrayed himself to be during the year that he was missing. The implication is that Nearing was the "Mr. Hyde" of a "Dr. Jekyll" Thompson, hooking up with a frowsy blonde, scraping for money, and being generally "no good." As Thompson, he appears to be the opposite: happily married and working in a responsible and safe office job. What is most disturbing, however, is that we never learn in the film what happened to cause Thompson to turn into Nearing—where, even, the name "Danny Nearing" came from. There are often many odd occurrences in *film noir* that are never explained, but the magnitude of this ignored question is unusual, even for *noir*. The fact that Thompson discovers at the end of the film that he is not a murderer and can return to his former, original life does little for viewer closure; we are left with a dead Ruth (shot in a gun struggle with Thompson) and Detective Marucci pensively emerging into the street, smoking a cigarette. As morally questionable as Ruth's own character might be, it is almost as if she is sacrificed to Thompson's aborted foray into the underworld, somewhere that he could not allow himself to venture in his normal life. His short journey as Danny Nearing is a journey into his own unconscious, a dream-world from which he eventually awakens, but not without two dead bodies in his wake.

Perhaps the most unusual—and haunting—amnesia *noir* is Patrick Jackson's *Shadow on the Wall* (1950). Rather than an amnesiac veteran or a civilian man in search of a lost identity, *Shadow on the Wall* depicts a young girl, Susan Starrling (Gigi Perreau) who suffers from amnesia after witnessing the murder of her stepmother. From the start of the film, family dysfunction abounds, from Susan's little friend Bobby, who wants to see her father shave because "his father doesn't live with him," to Susan's dislike of her stepmother, Celia (Kristine Miller) to Celia's toxic relationship with her sister, Dell (Ann Sothern). Just about the only loving relationship depicted is the one between Susan and her father, David (Zachary Scott), who brings home to Susan the gift of an "injun" doll that Susan treasures and names "Cupid." The odd appellation has multiple associations, including the strong emotional connection between Susan and her father (in opposition to her lack of feeling for Celia) and also as a representation of the spurned love for which the doll eventually becomes a symbol. Susan happens to be right about the fact that Celia "doesn't like" her and her father—she is cheating on David with Dell's fiancé, Crane (Tom Helmore). The discovery of this affair puts a string of tragic events in motion that leads to Susan's amnesia. First, David confronts Celia about the affair with violence on his mind, as he threatens her with a gun; however, before he can act on whatever murderous impulses he might have had, Celia knocks him unconscious with—our favorite object in psychiatric *noir*—a mirror. As if this does not constitute enough drama, Dell's appearance at the door does not provide Celia with the relieved help she hopes for, as Dell is the second person in line to want to confront Celia, and David's gun provides an all-too convenient opportunity to act on her own hurt feelings: she shoots Celia dead. As Celia slinks away, she casts a huge shadow on the bedroom wall, a shadow that Susan sees before she discovers her dead stepmother and unconscious father. This most significant detail is also the most elusive in the film, since Susan cannot remember it after the trauma.

The structure of the film does not create experiential anxiety in the viewer; rather, there is very little actual mystery, since the viewer knows the "truth." However, most of the other characters in the film are in search of answers or in possession of misinformation. Susan cannot remember what happened before she finds her father and stepmother, and even David believes that he could have killed have Celia; in fact, David thinks he did probably kill her, that the gun went off when Celia hit him with the mirror, and he also cannot remember anything further about what happened. Dell is the only one who does know, and while Susan is in a psychiatric hospital and David is found guilty and sentenced to death, she remains silent. Dell is a tortured character herself, first being pathologically jealous of her sister as a child, then having to endure the indignity of infidelity. She is torn about revealing what happened, as she writes a confession, but tears it up, and is obsessed by guilt over David's death sentence, to the point that she imagines herself in an electric chair as she is in a beauty salon being put under a hair dryer. Once she seems to get accustomed to these feelings, however, she turns her attention to figuring out how to deal with Susan, who she knows could be the only witness to the crime. Susan, meanwhile, is sequestered in the psychiatric hospital, having remembered the shadow on the wall, but has transposed the shadow in memory to the doll that David had gotten her. She is being treated by one of the most benevolent psychiatrists in *noir*, Dr. Caroline Canford (Nancy Davis), who agrees with Susan's family doctor that her mental condition is not "organic," but rather the result of something traumatic, since she was in shock when they found her. Assumedly the mere discovery of one's unconscious father and dead stepmother is not "traumatic" enough to cause the loss of memory. Susan's condition, aside from her amnesia, is one of utter depression and apathy; she does not want to eat, shows no interest in anything, and only wants to do things that others want her to do, showing no initiative on own—her mantra becomes "If you want me to," and she behaves much like a robot, showing no emotion. Dr. Canford calls Susan's condition "a form of shell shock," asserting that such a traumatic condition can happen to children too, causing blindness, paralysis, or loss of speech. The reference to shell shock is significant as Susan's condition so closely parallels that of the many disaffected veterans suffering from trauma that we have seen in *noir*.

As we have seen with many *noir* psychiatrists, Dr. Canford must make the case for the "normalcy" of her profession as just another kind of physician. When David raises concerns about Susan being treated, Dr. Canford asserts that he should "not be afraid of a word. For a bad appendix, a surgeon; for a broken bone, an orthopedist. Susan's had a severe mental shock; that's why she needs me, a psychiatrist." The progressive attitude toward mental illness is again evident here, as Susan's amnesia is likened to just a different kind of childhood injury. Through various sessions of "play therapy," Dr. Canford's initial goal of trying to discover the nature of Susan's trauma turns into, as the occupation of psychiatrist often does in *noir*, a detective pursuit, as it becomes clear that Susan's account of the night that her stepmother died differs from the evidence brought forward in David's trial. Dr. Canford plays doll games with Susan, encouraging her to talk and begin remembering, through the use of the dolls as surrogates for the people in her memory. The use of mirrors is also important in these scenes, as these sessions are observed and recorded by Dr. Canford's assistant through a one-way mirror. Dr. Canford is attempting to create a secure "home-like" environment for Susan in order for her to begin to relax her defenses; curiously, the artificiality of this surveilled environment offers more safety than Susan's own "normal" home and bedroom. After some time passes, Dr. Canford reports to David that she has discovered that Susan saw what happened: "She won't admit it, but it's deep in her mind," adding that Susan has a "psychic block" and what she witnessed is "locked it away in her subconscious." Aside from her own mental health, the recovery of Susan's memory is the only thing that can save her father from execution, so there is particular urgency to Dr. Canford's work when she realizes that Susan saw another person in the house that night. Not realizing that Dell is this person, Dr. Canford encourages her to visit with Susan, thinking this contact will help spark Susan's memory. The primary effect, however, is to create increased anxiety in Dell, as she realizes that Susan may very well be able to report her crime. She desperately tries to sabotage Susan's treatment, first interrupting a "play interview" she is witnessing before Susan might have a breakthrough, and then more drastically, poisoning Susan's chocolate milk. When that fails, she goes so far as to try to drown Susan by untying her sedative bath hammock. Dell's character shifts subtly but darkly as she is driven to attempt her own niece's murder in order to save herself.

Dell's final attempt to secure Susan's silence is to convince David that she should be made Susan's legal guardian; as her guardian, she would have the power to have Susan released from the hospital and away from the doctor's inquisitive treatment.

The cure for Susan's amnesia, and salvation for her father, depends on Dr. Canford solving the mystery surrounding Susan's "Cupid" doll, who does "awful things," according to Susan. She also cryptically says that she is afraid of Cupid, but that Cupid is not an Indian. Dr. Canford asks if she knows Cupid, she says she thinks she does, but that it looks different, somehow. Following this revelation, Susan does not want to go any further, because she says "it's awful" and asks Dr. Canford not to "make her." In addition, that night Susan has a dream with blurry images of her doll and the shadow of Dell on the wall, one shadow moving into another, with Dell and Cupid appearing in the same frame. The dream imagery confirms the conflation in Susan's mind between her doll and the image of her aunt on the wall on the night of the murder. Dr. Canford, however, must find a way to uncover the last hidden details in Susan's memory before she is taken away by Dell, and must convince David's lawyer of the same, even as he tries to assure Dr. Canford that Dell assuming guardianship of Susan is "the only rational way." As perfectly logical and reasonable as Dr. Canford is throughout Susan's treatment, she is nevertheless placed in the position of the "emotional" female psychiatrist who eschews the facts in favor of an idealistic "notion." Ironically, of course, her theory is most consistent with true psychiatric investigation, but in order to prove it, she must take a step more drastic than she had planned at this stage in Susan's treatment, what she calls "play therapy with a vengeance": she will take Susan back to her old apartment and her old room to try to get her to relive and remember the experience.

However, in typical *noir* fashion, though this recreation is chillingly suspenseful, and successful in the sense that it does seem to prove to Dr. Canford that someone else was present that night, she still cannot discover who it was, and though she now suspects Dell, there is no proof. What does prove to be the catalyst for Susan's memory restoration and thus her father's deliverance is a random occurrence. As Dr. Canford and David's lawyer are leaving after dropping Susan off at Dell's house, Susan runs after them and says she wants to go with them. Susan looks back toward the house and sees Dell, wearing a hairpiece with a feather, waiting outside; the shadow she casts on the wall, all too familiar now as the alternate "Cupid," brings Susan to screams, the identification of Dell, and Dell's final confession. Though it is clear that Susan's ability to identify Dell at the end is assumed to be the culmination of her treatment with Dr. Canford, it is worth wondering on how thin a thread David's life hung for Susan to be able to make the leap to ultimately identifying Dell as the murderer. She is seen harmoniously reunited with her father, who is most grateful to Dr. Canford, but it cannot be ignored that the most important revelation of the film did not occur during her actual treatment, and the film does not make much of the necessary cumulative effect of psychoanalysis. *Noir* amnesia narratives in general call into serious question the efficacy of the psychiatric process and the practically random quality of the search for identity that these amnesiac characters experience. Whether returning veterans, criminals, returning veterans who used to be criminals, or children, the role of amnesia in *noir* crystallizes the disorienting search for identity in an increasingly chaotic post-war world. As portrayed in amnesia *noirs*, the self is an elusive and fluid concept that can change in an instant, and this portrayal necessarily raises disturbing questions about the relationship between morality and memory in the human psyche. Does a criminal cease to be a criminal if he cannot remember his crimes? What does a veteran become if his identity has changed from a law-abiding civilian to someone who killed for a living at the bidding of the government? Are we all equally susceptible to crime if the memory of our lawful lives is erased? Amnesia *noirs* are for this reason among the most terrifying sub-category of *film noir*, since they represent the very real possibility of ultimate revelation and ultimate loss in the conscious self.

Notes

1. Sigmund Freud, "The Uncanny." *The Standard Edition of the Complete Psychological Works of Sigmund Freud*. Trans. James Strachey. Vol. 17. London: Hogarth, 1957. 224.
2. Frank Krutnik, *In a Lonely Street: Film Noir, Genre, Masculinity*. New York: Routledge, 1991. 66.
3. Michael Walker, "*Film Noir*: Introduction." *The Movie Book of Film Noir*. Ed. Ian Cameron. London: Studio Vista, 1992. 35.
4. Andrew Dickos, *Street With No Name: A History of the Classic American Film Noir*. Lexington: U of Kentucky P, 2002. 184.
5. Robert Watson, "Crack-Up." *Film Monthly* 3, no. 6 (August 12, 2001). <http:www.filmmonthly.com/noir/articles/CrackUp/CrackUp.html>.
6. Nicholas Christopher, *Somewhere in the Night: Film Noir and the American City*. New York: Free Press, 1997. 208.
7. Foster Hirsch, *The Dark Side of the Screen: Film Noir*. New York: Da Capo Press, 1983. 178.
8. Hirsch, 178.

9. Dana Polan, *Power and Paranoia: History, Narrative, and the American Cinema: 1940-1950.* New York: Columbia University Press, 1986. 240.
10. Hugh Manon, "X-Ray Visions: Radiography, Chiaroscuro, and the Fantasy of Unsuspicion in *Film Noir*," *Film Criticism* 32, no. 2 (Winter 2007/2008): 2-29.
11. *Ministry of Fear* also employs a similar use of the carnival as an entrance point into a "wrong man" intrigue, as Stephen Neale (Ray Milland), recently released from a mental asylum after serving a "sentence" for euthanizing his wife, finds himself, after winning a pie from a carnival fortune-teller, neck-deep in international conspiracy.
12. Sheri Chinen Biesen, *Blackout: World War II and the Origins of Film Noir.* Baltimore: Johns Hopkins University Press, 2005. 89.
13. Edward Dimendberg, *Film Noir and the Spaces of Modernity.* Cambridge: Harvard University Press, 2004. 127-28.

Dr. Andrew Collins (Lee J. Cobb) tries to psychoanalyze escaped criminal Al Walker (William Holden) in *The Dark Past* (Rudolph Maté, 1949). Courtesy of the Wisconsin Center for Film and Theater Research.

Hypnotized attempted murderer, Bixley (Charles Wagenheim) on display, while Dr. Cromwall (Walter Kingsford) gives his diagnosis to Edwina Brown (Laraine Day) and Oliver Duffy (Lew Ayres) in *Fingers at the Window* (Charles Lederer, 1942). Courtesy of the Wisconsin Center for Film and Theater Research.

The setup of the shot depicting Louise Howell (Joan Crawford) under male medical scrutiny in *Possessed* (Curtis Bernhardt, 1947). Courtesy of the Wisconsin Center for Film and Theater Research.

The inner circle of the psychiatric Inferno for Virginia Cunningham (Olivia de Havilland) in *The Snake Pit* (Anatole Litvak, 1948). Courtesy of the Wisconsin Center for Film and Theater Research.

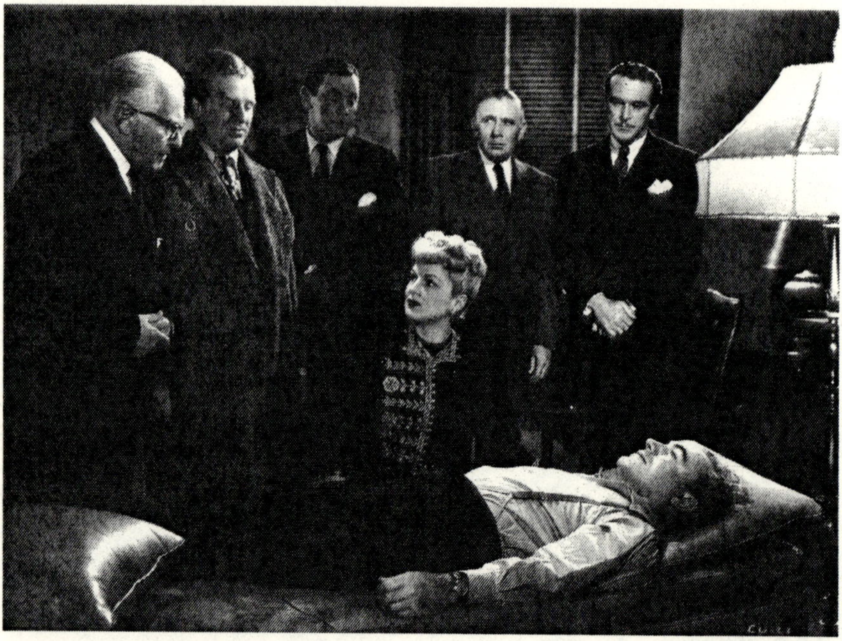

The helpless George Steele (Pat O'Brien) on the couch in *Crack-Up* (Irving Reis, 1946). Courtesy of the Wisconsin Center for Film and Theater Research.

Steven Kenet (Robert Taylor), haunted by his blank past, is examined by Dr. Ann Lorrison, (Audrey Totter) in *High Wall* (Curtis Bernhardt, 1947). Courtesy of the Wisconsin Center for Film and Theater Research.

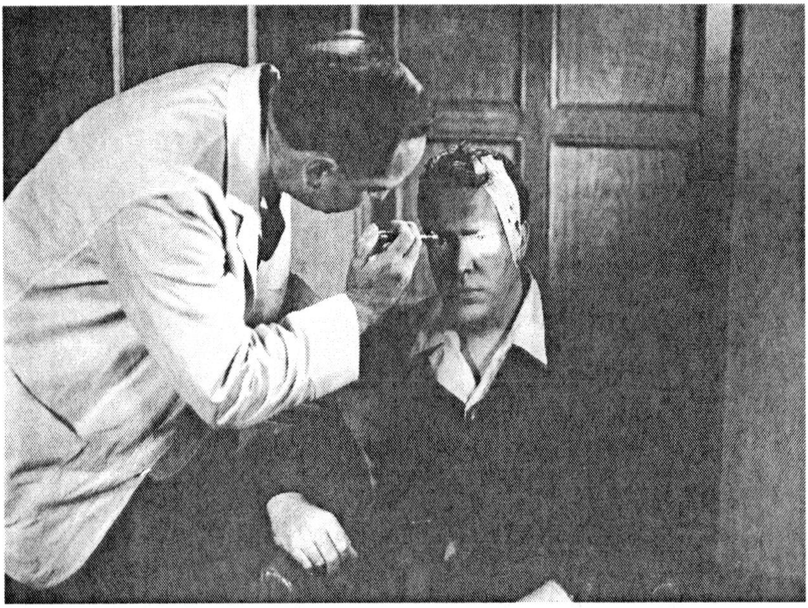

Ex-mobster Steve Rawley (Edmond O'Brien) is cleaned of criminal tendencies by surgically-induced amnesia in *Man in the Dark* (Lew Landers, 1953). Courtesy of the Wisconsin Center for Film and Theater Research.

Frank Thompson (Burgess Meredith) is stunned to discover that his hat is not his own in *Street of Chance* (Jack Hively,1942). Courtesy of the Wisconsin Center for Film and Theater Research.

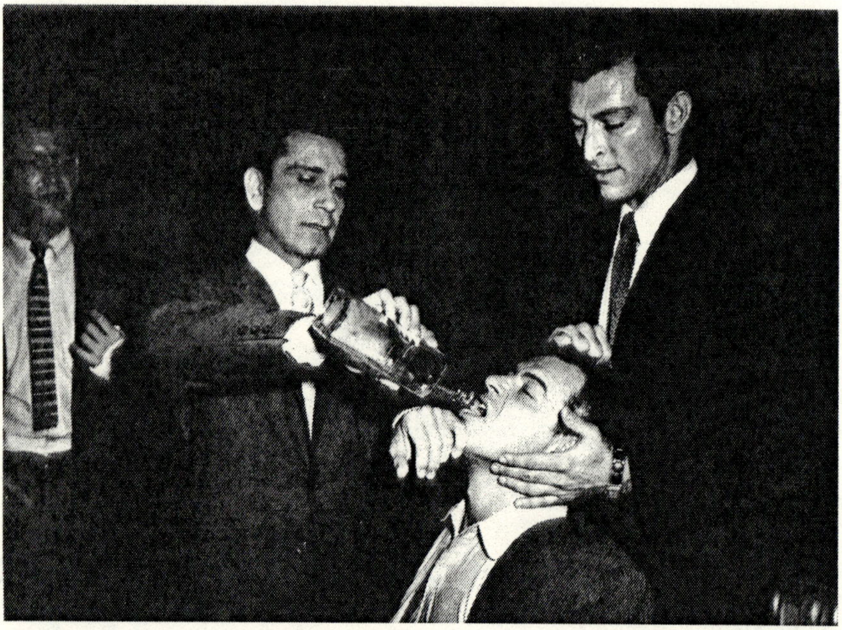

The psychotic Mr. Brown (Richard Conte) gives Lt. Diamond (Cornel Wilde) the hair tonic treatment in *The Big Combo* (Joseph Lewis, 1955). Courtesy of the Wisconsin Center for Film and Theater Research.

Ellen Berent (Gene Tierney) icily watches her brother-in-law Danny (Darryl Hickman) drown in *Leave Her to Heaven* (John M. Stahl, 1946). Courtesy of the Wisconsin Center for Film and Theater Research.

Ruth Collins (Olivia de Havilland), hanging by her last thread of sanity, in *The Dark Mirror* (Robert Siodmak, 1946). Courtesy of the Wisconsin Center for Film and Theater Research.

Janet Stewart (Anabel Shaw) in the clutches of nefarious psychiatrist Dr. Richard Cross (Vincent Price) in *Shock* (Alfred Werker, 1946). Courtesy of the Wisconsin Center for Film and Theater Research.

Mark Lamphere (Michael Redgrave) in the scarf-gripping misogynist neurosis that threatens wife Celia (Joan Bennett) in *Secret Beyond the Door* (Fritz Lang, 1948). Courtesy of the Wisconsin Center for Film and Theater Research.

Chapter Four

Noir Neuroses and Psychoses

It is virtually impossible to turn around in the world of *noir* without bumping into someone who is either peripherally or grossly maladjusted, and as I have argued in previous chapters, *noir* would not be *noir* without this backdrop of psychological instability; it is woven deeply into the fabric of the cycle. As we have seen, amnesia is a pervasive example of this instability, but often other kinds of neurosis or psychosis take center stage in a *film noir*, not necessarily having the curative frame of a psychiatrist, asylum, or other treatments. Raymond Durgnat, in his seminal 1970 essay, "Paint It Black: The Family Tree of *Film Noir*," calls *noir* psychopaths, "legion," arguing that they fall into three main categories: "the heroes with a tragic flaw, the unassuming monsters, and the obvious monsters."[1] As we have seen, the potentiality of crime and transgression is often what drives *noir*, especially in films that do not depict the fruition of crime, but darken the screen with its possibility and the psychological instability of its characters. This scenario is evident in a film like *The Blue Dahlia* (George Marshall,1946), in which neither the cuckolded returning veteran husband, Johnny (Alan Ladd), nor his shell-shocked, half-crazed buddy, Buzz (William Bendix), is found to be the killer of Johnny's wife, though both show more than the potential to do so. A similar situation involving screenwriter Dixon Steele (Humphrey Bogart) in Nicholas Ray's *In a Lonely Place* (1950), as he is accused of murder and eventually cleared, but not before exhibiting his raging temper by nearly choking his girlfriend, Laurel Gray (Gloria Grahame). The overarching ethos is that anyone can snap at any moment; it certainly helps if you are a returning veteran scarred by the war, but that is not requisite. The war's aftermath creates an environment of unpredictability, especially in human behavior. Men who left home with moral and legal sensibilities return as killers; this incongruity seeps into every aspect of *noir* and colors previously-held beliefs regarding mental illness and anti-social behavior. Nicholas Christopher points out that such subjects are inherent to *noir*, being portrayed, along with previously taboo issues, such as sexual deviance, with more "frankness" than ever before.[2]

This rejection of taboo is evident in such films as Fritz Lang's *While the City Sleeps* (1956), in which police and newspaper reporters hunt for the latter-named "Lipstick Killer," a serial murderer who exhibits a mother/female fetishism and who "steals ladies' things." As we have seen in other psychiatric *noirs*, the media play a significant role in this film, underscoring the influence that newspapers, magazines, and eventually television had on popular conceptions of psychology, as media voices become amateur psychoanalysts, speculating on the killer's motives and weaknesses. Reporters are in competition to discover the killer's identity and use television to enrage the killer and draw him out of hiding. They describe the killer as having a "sick ego" and being "exactly like a little girl" in order to infuriate him, a tactic that succeeds. But in contrast to this depiction of a media frenzy over a psychopathic killer, many *noir* psychopaths emerge, despite their sadism and disregard for social mores, as merely commonplace in the *noir* universe, figures whose behavior, while usually punished, is never explained, as if there is no need to do so, given the world they inhabit. For instance, Mr. Brown (Richard Conte), from Joseph Lewis' *The Big Combo* (1955), believes that "first is first, and second is nobody," and the way that he insures he stays "first" is his disregard for the humanity of others, from his long-suffering and suicidal girlfriend Susan (Jean Wallace) to the police detective, Lt. Diamond (Cornel Wilde), who is investigating him. His love for Susan takes the form of requiring her to wear white dresses, as he sexually controls her, a practice likely similar to the way he treated his former wife, Alicia (Helen Walker), who is now in an insane asylum. Mr. Brown's idea of mercy is to remove the hearing aid of one of his victims before he kills him, telling him, "I'm gonna give you a break. I'm gonna fix it, so you don't hear the bullets." His sadism is also economical, as he uses the same hearing aid as part of the "technique" to torture Diamond, installing it in Diamond's ear and then first yelling into it, after which Mingo (Earl Holliman), one of his henchmen, blasts a radio into it as well. These niceties are capped by them forcibly pouring hair tonic down his throat. Mr. Brown is so powerful that he does not even need a first name; and his last name, menacing though its effects are, is deliberately ordinary, as is the terrifying suggestion that in the modern world, his sadism might be as well.

Speaking of sadism, one would be hard-pressed to find a more textbook case than Tommy Udo (Richard Widmark) in Henry Hathaway's *Kiss of Death* (1947). The grinning, giggling, milk-drinking Udo, who says he shoots squealers in the belly so they "roll around for a long time, thinking it over," famously sends the wheelchair-bound mother of a crime associate tumbling down a flight of stairs, simply at annoyance that the associate is not at home. Like Brown's, Udo's motives are not explored, and he is a mystery in every way, including his unusual name, almost an inverse of the commonality of Brown's name. Jack Shadoian has argued that Udo represents the particular evolution of the criminal in the post-war world: "He can be seen as . . . a force that the world must contend with, a presence that activates people, a concentrated symbol of what the world is, at its depth. Or perhaps more like an emblem full of significations, the postwar equivalent of the plague in past cultures. . . . The 'criminal element' has not only gone off the deep end, it can't be easily defined."[3] Even in the case of Cody Jarrett (James Cagney) in Raoul Walsh's *White Heat* (1949), who is usually seen as the most iconic *noir* psycho-killer, more insight is provided regarding his mother-fixated psychosis and perhaps organic origins of his insanity, than is provided in *Kiss of Death*, rendering a figure like Udo all the more frightening.

There is no shortage in *noir* of non-gangster psychopathic murderers, either. One need look no further than John Farrow's *The Big Clock* (1948), in which Earl Janoth (Charles Laughton), head of a publishing conglomerate, murders his mistress Pauline (Rita Johnson). She makes the fatal mistake of ridiculing him and suggesting that it is only the power from his position that would attract any woman. Brilliant close-ups of Janoth's crazed eyes and sweaty face are a prelude to him stabbing Pauline with a sundial clock that she has just bought him. Cruel, petty, and time-obsessed Janoth—who docks a worker's pay for leaving a light bulb burning in a closet—tries to frame one of his magazine editors, George Stroud (Ray Milland), for the murder. Janoth meets a fitting end by falling down an empty elevator shaft as he tries to shoot George, but not before wreaking havoc in George's previously undisturbed life. Jealous and possessive murderer Sam Wilde (Lawrence Tierney) from Robert Wise's *Born to Kill* (1947) is an even more disturbing force as he not only kills a former unfaithful girlfriend and her lover, but also provides a catalyst for the parallel corrupt and depraved impulses in his new love interest, Helen (Claire Trevor). This film is in some ways a precursor to the toxic love relationship seen in *The Sleeping Tiger*, sans the mitigating factors of benevolent psychiatrist and redemption of the non-homicidal criminal. Though Wilde's friend, Marty (Elisha Cook,

Jr.), fearfully describes that the way Wilde goes "off his head" has been worse "ever since that nervous crack-up last summer," there is no further insight regarding his behavior; he is a destructive and enigmatic force whose behavior with every scene notches up the level of anti-social transgression seen in the film. More refined, but leaving just as many bodies in his wake, is Alan Garroway, from Vincente Minnelli's *Undercurrent* (1946). Garroway is an inventor who tries to convince his new wife, Ann (Katharine Hepburn), that his brother Michael (Robert Mitchum) is corrupt and has victimized him. As it turns out, it is Alan who is so corrupt that dogs and horses recoil at his approach. Michael is actually the only one who knows that Alan has murdered one of his engineers in order to obtain the invention through which he has prospered. However, it is Ann's fascination with Michael that drives Alan to try to kill her, as he seems to have fought against his feelings of inferiority toward his brother his entire life. Alan meets his death by being trampled by Michael's horse, a fitting Freudian end.

One of the most intriguing sub-categories of the *noir* psychopath involves pathologically jealous characters who orchestrate vengeful punishment on others after their own deaths. *Cause for Alarm!* (Tay Garnett, 1951), *Rage in Heaven* (W.S. Van Dyke, 1941), and *Leave Her to Heaven* (John Stahl, 1946) are among these films, and the passive-aggressiveness of the characters in them incites the potential for more destruction than the overt actions of other *noir* psychopaths. Unlike the gritty city streets of an urban milieu, these films are all set in domestic situations, highlighting the dysfunctional arrangement in *noir* of the most fundamental social institution. *Cause for Alarm!* opens, in fact, with a June Cleaver-like Ellen Jones (Loretta Young) cleaning her house in a sunny suburban neighborhood. Things are far from sunny, however, as the viewer soon realizes from Ellen's opening voice-over, in which she comments that though the day had started out like any other, she did not know it would turn out to be "the most terrifying day of [her] life." We soon learn that her invalid husband, George (Barry Sullivan), is not only ill physically with a heart condition, but also mentally, with dangerous paranoia. The seeming ubiquity of mental illness in the post-war *noir* world is visible here, as R. Barton Palmer also argues: "In *Cause for Alarm*, *noir*ness is thus not an alternative world of temptation, illicitness, or irresponsibility; it is simply the repressed underside of an otherwise ordinary domestic life."[4] Ellen's own conception of her predicament is actually somewhat misguided, as she muses, "I tried not to think about us, how he'd changed." In reality, Ellen's mental flashbacks reveal that George Jones showed the seeds of mental instability long before his full-blown paranoia surfaced.

When Ellen first meets George, a military pilot, she is secretary to his friend, naval doctor Ranney Grahame (Bruce Cowling), who is quietly in love with her. George aggressively pursues Ellen, first pretending to be a sick patient so that he can take advantage of her massaging his head and attempt to steal a kiss, and then more openly, when they find themselves alone during a beach picnic with Ranney. By the time George returns overseas, he has become Ellen's lover, and as he and Ellen embrace at the airport, he seems to smirk triumphantly at Ranney over Ellen's shoulder, as if gloating that he had bested him. George's brazen behavior seems to attract Ellen, but takes a darker turn later when he is rendered bed-ridden by his heart condition. His only exercise of power possible is his pursuit of paranoid delusions that he expresses in a letter to the district attorney: "My wife and close friend, who is also my physician, are planning to kill me. . . . He was in love with her before I met her." Ranney has remained his friend and physician, and attempts to encourage George, who reacts morbidly to every encouragement. Ranney urges, "When you get these ideas, try using a little mental therapy," to which George responds, "Next thing you'll be telling me is to see a psychiatrist. . . . You doctors: if you can't cure a patient, you tell him it's all in his mind." Though Ranney tells Ellen that George's "brooding . . . could develop into something serious," they both fail to realize that it already has. And though Ellen tells Ranney that George has taken "sudden dislikes to people," by her own voice-over soon after, she reveals that George would not approve if she stopped and chatted with the neighbors. She says that "George didn't believe in neighbors," suggesting that George's misanthropy was not a new condition.

George's psychosis is further revealed as he tortures Ellen throughout the morning by refusing her ministrations, demanding that she call another doctor instead of Ranney, and leading her to dream about what she will do when he is "out of this bed." He accuses her of dreaming of a life with Ranney. Then, George relates to Ellen a story about his childhood that seems to confirm the long roots of his mental illness. He describes how he hit another little boy with a rake when the boy took his prized possession, a ship in a bottle, and thought he would have killed him if the boy had not run off, adding that he "felt safe after that." That is, until his mother, as punishment, told him to give the ship to the little boy. George then purposely broke the ship to prevent him from having it and muses to Ellen, "the ship was mine, more than it had ever been before." George adds that the little boy looked like Ranney Grahame, and he predicts that Grahame will find himself in the same position: "He may have you all right, but he'll be disappointed with what he gets." It is clear that George is consumed by impulses of morbid possessiveness and self-destruction. He reveals to Ellen that the letter to the D.A. she had mailed for him that morning contained his detailed account of how she and Ranney were trying to kill him so that they could be together and that all her actions of that day—innocent though they may have been—will actually incriminate her later. But impatient for this justice to be carried out, George intends to kill her, perhaps in "self-defense"—except that he dies trying. Ellen experiences a panicked *noir* moment, as she tries to find the key to the locked bedroom door after his collapse: "It was one of those awful dreams . . . that man lying there was George, my husband. He was dead. He died trying to kill me." When Ellen escapes, she has only cleared one hurdle of her nightmarish day, however. She now finds herself in the position of having to retrieve George's letter to the D.A. and actually does not report his death when it happens because she believes that she must find the letter first. George's psychotic reach has extended not only in the tangible existence of the incriminating letter, but also in his ability to convince Ellen that all her actions during the day will damn her once the D.A. receives his accusations. George's self-fulfilling prophecy causes Ellen to run frantically all over town looking for the mailman, to view with fear every person that sees her, and to begin to accumulate a trail of lies throughout the day that threaten to incriminate her more than her simple reporting to the police what had happened.

Earlier in the film, George berates Ellen for (he believes) encouraging Ranney to suggest that he needed psychiatric help, telling her, "I know what happens to a man when you take away his self-respect." A returned veteran, who relied enormously on his self-confidence and sexual bravado, George cannot abide his invalid status. According to Palmer, George's illness "can be seen as a fitting punishment for his asocial exercise of sexual power, for his drive to take what he wants, even by deception; that is, because he is not a real man emotionally, he must endure being helpless as a child."[5] George's possessiveness creates the only outlet it can, in his attempt to destroy Ellen, and fittingly destroys him first. However, Ellen must still endure, in typical *noir* fashion, desperate anxiety before she is saved by a seemingly chance occurrence: lack of sufficient postage on the letter to the D.A. She and Ranney seem destined for togetherness at the end (ironically fulfilling George's "delusions"), but her hysterical laughter at the film's close is a bit chilling and underscores the insidious and far-reaching effect of George's murderous paranoia.

A similar dynamic is found in *Rage in Heaven*, in which deeply disturbed steelworks heir Philip Monrell (Robert Montgomery) is tormented by insecurity, especially when it comes to his friend, Ward Andrews (George Brent), a strong and confident engineer. Faced with the prospect of taking over the management of the steelworks from his ailing mother,

Philip becomes desperate and suicidal, checking himself into a Paris sanatorium. His attending doctor, Rameau (Oskar Homolka), explains his case to the British consul who has come to identify the wayward Monrell in the following way: "To you as a layman, he would appear to be a normal, charming, highly intelligent young man, but if you watch him closely, you'll see a curious lack of emotion . . . what we call paranoia . . . he may be sane for long periods, but if anything happens to upset him, he could become very dangerous indeed, capable of anything."[6] The two factors that are chiefly upsetting Philip are his impending role as steelworks manager and his love for Stella Bergen (Ingrid Bergman), Mrs. Monrell's secretary and companion. He and Ward meet Stella at the same time, and both are clearly attracted to her. Philip seems somewhat blasé at the prospect of courting her, however, telling his mother, "In order to love someone, you must be a little afraid of them. People are afraid of Ward; no one is afraid of me." He is jealous of Ward, believing him to be all the things that he is not: brave, self-assured, successful, and attractive to women. And during his crisis in Paris, he went so far as to begin calling himself "Ward Andrews," because, he tells Stella, "it made him feel better." However, since he cannot be Ward, or even be like him, he resents him, especially when it comes to Stella. In a perverse appropriation of Ward's identity, he can only ask her to marry him by asking her in the third person, as if he is oddly pretending that it is Ward asking her.

Philip's obsession with Ward takes an increasingly darker turn after he marries Stella, as he struggles with his insecurities both at work and at home. Philip attempts to destroy everything that threatens him, including the kitten that Ward had given Stella. Philip takes it to work, and soon after it is found by the chauffeur behind the steelworks building with a broken neck. When Stella wonders how the kitten got there, Philip argues with her, becoming belligerent and paranoid. When he later apologizes, he turns in the opposite direction, begging her not to leave him. Philip cannot help bringing up Ward at every opportunity, including this one, to the point that she asks Philip to never mention Ward again, saying, "Ward, Ward, Ward . . . if you can't rid yourself of this idea you'll . . ." "I'll go mad?" he responds. Philip does not feel any more secure at work, where he sits idly during the day, working on crossword puzzles and waiting for time to pass. His only actions there are destructive ones that seek to manufacture respect and power rather than earn them. One afternoon, he brings Stella up to the office so she can witness him berating some of the long-standing executives of the company. He believes they still treat him as if he were a child and therefore makes rash demands that contradict everything they say, a tactic that results in the resignation of the veteran chief engineer and the alienation of all of the men he supervises.

Philip's actions are exactly those of the petulant child he is fighting not to be and he—perhaps deliberately—further puts himself in the position of having to ask for Ward's help. He takes perverse delight in inviting Ward back to the house, so that he can "see what happens" when Stella is faced with Ward again, but he also needs a chief engineer to keep the steelworks running. He watches Stella's reactions obsessively, noting that after Ward arrives she is reading a book upside down. When she asks him whether or not he has eyes in the back of his head, he responds, "I always notice what you're doing . . . and what you're thinking too." Part of his bizarre "experiment" involves his pretending to leave town so that Ward can "take care of her" and then surprising them the next day as they dine at a hotel restaurant—the same hotel that Philip stayed in the previous night, unbeknownst to them. What Philip does not know is that in his brief absence Ward and Stella have been innocently commiserating about Philip's instability—Ward is concerned that Philip is acting unreasonably and handling the workers the wrong way, and Stella is convinced that Philip wants to kill her love by his possessiveness. Ward comments, that Philip "needs affection" more than anyone he ever knew, and this simple statement perhaps sums up best the depth of Philips's mental illness—his constant need for reassurance to bolster his struggling self-confidence manifests itself in all manner of destructive behaviors that thwart his very desires.

Meanwhile, both Ward and Stella are caught in the snarl of a domestic love triangle that becomes even more *noir*ish after Philip orchestrates his own death. Philip seems to come to this drastic decision after a crisis at the steelworks during which the workers revolt. Philip retreats and runs away, leaving Ward to handle the situation, telling him to "give them anything they want." Philip seems to have reached a full mental breakdown at this point, as he wanders in the rain, rambling about how nothing can hurt him now and there is no need to be frightened, a journey culminating in a physical fever and the resolution that he must rid himself of Ward. Philip muses to Ward, "Fever is a funny thing; it makes everything look ugly like a mirror in a funhouse." However, the truth is that Philip's mental "fever" existed long before this, turning all those he loved into ugly threats in his psychic "funhouse." After Philip's attempt to push Ward into a vat of molten steel fails and Ward finally confronts him with his love for Stella, Ward fires him and orders him out of the house. These events also drive Stella away from Philip more than ever before, as she becomes distant and depressed and eventually leaves him. Philip's final act of twisted revenge is to lure Ward back on the pretense that he needs advice about his impending divorce; however, his actual purpose is to orchestrate evidence that will incriminate Ward for his murder after Philip commits suicide following their meeting. Philip seems to account for every detail that might point later to Ward as his killer, from their angry conversation, timed so that a servant overhears, to his rigging a false bell pull with the knife he will use to stab himself so that Ward's fingerprints end up on the murder weapon. Philip has psychologically projected himself into a reality that he will no longer be a part of, and it is this projection that signifies the depth of his disturbance, as he egomaniacally imagines the reach of his power in death that could not have reached those depths in life.

Inevitably, Ward is found guilty of Philip's murder and sentenced to death. It is psychiatry that interestingly ends up coming to his rescue, as the somewhat dotty Dr. Rameau resurfaces on the day before Ward's execution to reveal to Stella that Philip not only was clinically insane, but also that he was likely a suicide, rather than a murder. Rameau, displaying a preference for the "faith-based" practice of psychiatry, rather than a scientific approach, scoffs at the evidence presented in the case in court: "I spit on evidence! . . . Too convenient, too perfect—look into the human heart, and you'll find the motive for this crime. . . . Philip was murdered by his only enemy—himself. . . . He hides from the world in the tree of his childhood. He creates a neurotic jealousy and nourishes it like a plant." Again, one might conclude that faith or intuition has little place in psychiatry, assumed to be a "science" that had the potential to unlock the mysteries of the human mind. However, in *film noir*'s representation of the formative years of psychiatry, the notion of an instinctual sense of human morality prevails, as if that is the only bedrock element that can be depended upon. The preference of Rameau to "the human heart" rather than "evidence" suggests that what is considered by society in *film noir* to be objective truth can often be lacking . . . and that perhaps the "science" of psychiatry may rely equally—if not more—on an intuitive sensitivity to human motivations that elude rational explanation. Rameau goes on to say that they do not even have to prove that he was his own killer because Philip "will prove it for" them by his need to leave behind some kind of "message" that he wanted Stella to find—that his longing for "recognition" demands that Stella realize after his death that he was "cleverer" than all of them. Without this, Rameau says, "his triumph will not be final." Earlier in the film, Philip had illogically told Rameau that he wanted to commit suicide, because he "wanted to know what people would say about [him] after [he] died," a declaration that foreshadowed the eventual level of his morbid self-absorption. As in *Cause for Alarm!*, the importance of a written document by the madman proves the key to damnation or salvation of his targets: Philip's "message" is found in his diary, in which he is seen writing his delusional thoughts throughout the film. The discovery of the diary exonerates Ward, but he and Stella are still displaced, as they seem to need to flee their tortures by sailing to America, throwing Philip's diary off the side of the ship in a symbolic, but not wholly satisfying rejection of the suffering that he imposed on them.

Perhaps the most terrifying domestic *noir* of this type is *Leave Her to Heaven*, in which the psychopath is not an insecure man but a homicidally possessive woman. But unlike *Possessed*'s Louise Howell, Ellen Berent (Gene Tierney) does not confine her destructive impulses to her own fantasies; she is bold enough to carry them out. The object of her perverse affection is novelist Richard "Dick" Harland (Cornel Wilde), who is taken by her striking beauty (coupled with the fact that she is reading one of his books), but from the start her behavior signals an unusual intensity. She is very forthright, and before they even begin talking, she actually stares at him for so long that he is visibly unnerved, an action that Mary Ann Doane connects with "a certain excessiveness, a difficulty associated with women who appropriate the gaze, who insist upon looking."[7] Ellen seems to lack the sense of traditional female social timidity, and there are numerous descriptions of Ellen throughout the film that indicate her somewhat superhuman strength, such as "Ellen always wins" and "Nothing [bad] ever happens to Ellen." Her mother (Mary Philips) and adopted sister, Ruth (Jeanne Crain) seem to be resignedly accepting of Ellen's ways, including the possessive relationship that she had with her own father, a relationship that appears to form the catalyst for her attraction to Dick, given their physical resemblance. Their meeting is also occasioned by the trip that Ellen, her mother, and Ruth take to New Mexico for the "funeral" of her father—the scattering of his ashes along a mountain ridge that he had deemed "the front lawn of heaven," and a spot only frequented by him and Ellen. As Ellen on horseback, framed in close-up against the sky, defiantly scatters the ashes, Dick, almost voyeuristically, observes from a distance, his presence signifying the assumption of his role as the reincarnated love object. Ellen reveals to Dick that she and her father had a "pact" that whoever died first would scatter the other's ashes along that ridge, adding that "people you love don't really die." For Ellen, the idea of her father, a strong, masculine influence with whom she could identify, would never die.

Ellen's relationship with her father seemed more than close, and not entirely mutually obsessive. She tells Dick that she and her father were "inseparable. . . . From the time I was able to walk, we were both happiest when we were together." However, Ellen's mother and Ruth both hint that Ellen's possessiveness of her father took a toll on him too, as well as on the rest of the family. Her mother tells Dick that Ellen "loves too much," a simple statement perhaps, but one that encapsulates Ellen's single-minded desire. After a few short days with Dick, Ellen makes the quick decision to call off her engagement to soon-to-be district attorney Russell Quinton (Vincent Price). She rashly pronounces Dick as her "fiancé" and later when Dick tries to confront Ellen about this, she charms him by asking him to marry her, and he cannot resist. Their embrace is punctuated by her dreamily pronouncing, "I'll never let you go. Never, never, never." Once they are married, Ellen refuses to hire a cook or a housekeeper, to Dick's surprise, because she says she does not want anyone else to do anything for him. She also says, "I don't want anyone in the house but us," and though these conceits seem like playful devotion to Dick, they have a far darker motive. A similar dark motive underlies her seemingly generous suggestion to forego their honeymoon to take a cottage in Warm Springs, Georgia, where Dick's younger brother, Danny (Darryl Hickman) is recovering from polio. Though Danny and Dick are thrilled, especially with Ellen's attention toward Danny, what Ellen really wants is to encourage Danny to recover as quickly as possible—to become independent enough to go away to school and leave her and Dick alone. Ellen's face clearly falls when Danny excitedly shows Dick that he can walk on crutches, expecting that such an achievement means that "all three" of them can go home to Dick's "Back of the Moon" cabin in Maine. She even tries to get Danny's doctor to convince Dick that Danny is better off at school; the level of her dark resentments surfaces for the first time when, as the doctor is resistant to her idea, she blurts, "But after all, he's a cripple." The athletic and robust Ellen cannot brook the idea of having anyone come between her and Dick, let alone an invalid who she might have to serve. Her intense dislike for Danny seems fueled by his disability, and not only the potential drain he (and it) has on Dick's affection, but also a reflection of her own mental instability, a weakness she would never recognize.

Like George Jones and Philip Monrell, Ellen displays an extreme misanthropy, a complete dislike of spending time with anyone other than the object of her love, who would necessarily reflect the best features of herself. This dislike especially surfaces if the society of others, even her own family, comes upon her suddenly. She makes it clear to Dick that she has no use for Thorne, the Back of the Moon caretaker, coyly lamenting that she would love it at the cabin, "if only it weren't so crowded." When Dick surprises her by inviting her mother and Ruth to visit, she becomes enraged, and her perceived claustrophobia with Thorne and Danny around becomes unbearable to her as the group enjoys themselves by laughing and singing around the fire. Dick seems to really realize Ellen's instability at this point and angrily confronts her about her "beastly" treatment of her family, saying that he cannot understand her cold treatment of her "own people." Ellen has no "people," however; there is only one "person": Dick, about whom she is so jealous that she accuses him of being in love with Ruth. Her declarations of, "I love you so . . . I love you so, I can't bear to share you with anybody" begin to ring hollowly to Dick, especially after her mother and Ruth decide to leave after only a few days. Now that her family has left, and Thorne has moved into the boathouse, all that remains is for Ellen to rid herself of Danny. In one of the most shocking scenes of murder in film, let alone in *noir*, she takes Danny out in a rowboat to practice his swimming, encouraging him to swim farther, despite his fatigue. When he gets a cramp and sinks, she coolly and calmly, behind her dark sunglasses, watches him drown as he screams for her help. Though some may criticize the choice of Technicolor as harmful for the film's expressiveness, there is hardly a *film noir* scene more chilling, in black and white or color, than the verdant colors of the forest and lake as a backdrop to Ellen's inhuman and starkly cold behavior. Because she cannot imagine loving anyone other than Dick, Ellen cannot conceive of Dick loving anyone other than her, and so underestimates the effect that Danny's death will have on Dick—hardly the increased bonding she had hoped for the two of them.

Dick responds to Danny's death by pulling away from Ellen, not clinging closer to her. He becomes despondent and is unable to work or tolerate being at the cabin any longer. At Ruth's suggestion that "a child of his own" might make a difference, Ellen, fearful at losing him, is inspired to try this new tactic. Her happiness is short-lived, however, as it becomes clear to Ellen that a child would be yet another obstacle between them, another conduit of Dick's love potentially directed away from her. She is angered when her mother, Dick, and Ruth turn her father's old laboratory into the baby's nursery; this room was ironically her nursery before it was her father's lab. These intertwining connections between infantile nurturance and masculine independence frame Ellen's anger at the contemplation of her own motherhood. She is irritated with the doctor's restrictions on her diet and activity, and becomes increasingly convinced that Dick and Ruth are in love with each other. At the zenith of her frustration, as she looks at herself disgustedly in the mirror, she confesses to Ruth that she never wanted the baby at all, saying, "I hate the little beast; I wish it would die." It is likely this outburst, combined of course, with Ellen's decision to abort her own child by falling down the stairs, that inspired Jacques Siclier in 1956 to call *Leave Her to Heaven* "the most misogynistic Hollywood production since *The Maltese Falcon*."[8] There is an undeniably grotesque quality to Ellen, particularly as she prepares to make her fall; she joyously dons high heeled satin slippers, a matching silky peignoir, and painstakingly applies her makeup, as if she were a bride readying herself on her wedding night; she is, in fact, hoping for a rebirth of herself and her love with Dick. She is never more powerful than when she stands at the head of the stairs, as the camera shifts to a glassy-eyed close-up while she contemplates the height of her fall. Hateful though she may seem, Ellen's delusions spring from female frustrations that are all too understandable—frustrations that, though wildly exaggerated here, convey enough truth to make her not entirely detestable. Many newlywed women would be aggravated by the automatic presence of an invalid child, especially one in such close proximity that he can knock on the wall of her bedroom. And Ellen voices the sentiments regarding pregnancy that no "normal" woman is supposed to feel: anger at losing a slender body and a feeling of parasitic subjection to a creature growing inside of her. If these sentiments are taken to be monstrous, then of course the film can be seen as particularly misogynistic. If they, instead, are taken to be elements of Ellen's particular power, more complex than those of many *noir* femme fatales, then perhaps not.

After the death of his unborn son, Dick is inured to Ellen's professions of love, almost as if the amount of time he has spent with Ruth has cleared his internal vision of Ellen. Livid that Dick dedicated his new book to the nurturing Ruth, "the girl with the hoe," Ellen cannot even employ her usual coy and passive-aggressive admonishments toward him, as he stands cold and impassive to her influence. Where once he might have dedicated the book to "Patchouli," the exotic and mysterious allure of Ellen has long passed, as he has come to realize her murders of both his brother and his child. Like Philip Monrell, Ellen refuses to allow herself to be bested by Ruth and Dick, and so orchestrates her own suicide in such a way as to incriminate Ruth, even writing a letter to her old beau and now-D.A. Quinton, asking for his help. True to her dying words to Dick ("I'll never let you go, Richard . . . never, never . . ."), she reaches beyond the grave in an attempt to destroy Ruth. Surprisingly, despite Quinton's energetic efforts to convict Ruth, Dick's testimony about Ellen's crimes is enough to acquit her but ironically, also enough to incriminate him as an accessory to her crimes. Though Dick serves two years in prison, "Ellen had lost . . . the only time she didn't come out first." She ironically sacrificed herself to the greater cause of her insatiable desires, nearly absorbing all she had professed to love in her wake. Ellen's dangerous possession nonetheless reached beyond the boundaries of her physical life, undeniably scarring the lives of everyone close to her.

Though she does not seek to destroy her enemies beyond the grave, Diane Tremayne (Jean Simmons), from Otto Preminger's *Angel Face* (1953) is similarly father-fixated and possessively devoted to her love object, Frank Jessup (Robert Mitchum). She meets Frank, an ambulance driver, when he arrives on an emergency call for her stepmother Catherine (Barbara O'Neil), who has suffered from gas inhalation, seemingly by her own will. Catherine Tremayne insists that someone has tried to kill her, and it is difficult to imagine the refined, innocent-appearing Diane as a potential suspect. But Diane is indeed of a mind to commit murder, especially when it comes to anyone who threatens the relationship she has with her father, Charles (Herbert Marshall), a popular novelist who has hit a dry spell and has not published anything for several years. Though Frank has a serious girlfriend, Mary (Mona Freeman), he responds immediately to Diane's rather forward pursuit of him. Slight, doe-eyed, and British-refined Diane, is not the typical *noir* femme fatale, but she possesses the same kinds of manipulative powers as a Kathie Moffat or Phyllis Dietrichson. And for much of the film she does not even seem particularly disturbed, though she cunningly tries to ingratiate herself into Frank's life. One of the ways she does this is through her sports car, a racing vehicle that is close enough to her to be an extension of her personality, and an object that Frank covets, since he used to be a race car driver before the war and hopes to open his own garage someday. This symbol of masculine power is similar to Ellen Berent's horse, a vehicle of movement and freedom usually associated with men. Frank is clearly in search of excitement; since the war, he is still a driver, but one who drives to respond to emergency civilian calls rather than to war casualties or even for his own amusement. As Richard Lippe argues, "Diane's sports car associates her with risk-taking and adventure, and, to Frank, both Diane and her car are equally attractive."[9] Coupled with Diane's ability to give Frank the illusion of control and the allure of adventure, Diane's entrance into Frank's life begins a spiral of disaster that cannot be unwound.

Diane's goal seems not to replace her father, whom she clearly adores, but to have someone she can possess as her very own. Or perhaps she is beginning to think that she will not have her father forever, and so rather urgently must find his replacement. She tells Frank that her stepmother is jealous of her father's work, so her father only talks to her about it. Diane says that she found out that her father has not written a line since he married Catherine, just blank pages in his desk—and that Catherine has "humiliated and destroyed him." Diane seems intent on saving Frank from a similar fate; she connives to break up his relationship with Mary by calling her for a lunch meeting to intimate that Frank is cheating on her. For her part, Mary says she wished Diane had not told her, and is particularly confused when Diane offers her money to finance Frank's garage venture. Mary is right when she tells Diane that she knows she brought her there in order to shake her faith in Frank and to "find out how stupid" she was. Mary is not the typical "good girl" in *noir*—she seems particularly street-wise and world-weary. Her response to Diane's question about what she will she do about her offer, is "not one thing," not even paying for her meal as she coolly departs. Meanwhile, Diane capitalizes on the opening, telling Frank that she has found a race that he could drive in, with her car, and suggesting he take a position with her family as chauffeur. Though Frank says he does not think he is "quite the type" for that, Diane lures him with security, the prospect of the race, and a passionate embrace that she initiates. Once Frank takes the job, the prospect of his garage financing dissolves away and his closer proximity to Diane makes her paranoia more apparent to him, as she continues to insist that Catherine is trying to kill her. Finally, Frank decides to quit the chauffeur job, a decision that seems to draw Diane to the brink of both a psychological and literal cliff, as she senses that he is slipping away from her. Because she seems unable to do anything to Frank directly to secure her hold on him, she takes drastic action against Catherine by dismantling the brakes on her car, causing her to go sailing over a cliff. What she does not count on is that her father would be in the car with Catherine, and her very action to "save" her father destroys him.

As part of the aftermath of the accident, Frank is suspected, since he was the last to drive the car, in addition to the suspicion of his imminent departure, but Diane is a suspect too. Her characterization at this point almost suggests that she may not be as insane as she seemed before, since, though she appears catatonic, she seems to want to take responsibility for her actions, saying she says she does not want anyone to defend her and confesses to doing it all by herself. In a sordid bit of legal strategy, her lawyer pushes her to marry Frank, so the hint of an affair would not taint the legal process. This marriage only adds to Diane's delusion that she and Frank have a future, a future that she especially needs now that her father is gone. Frank will not continue with the charade after their acquittal, however; he is adamant that he wants a divorce. Again, the portrayal of Diane casts doubt regarding the depth of her instability as she very genuinely seems to express to Frank the reasons for her fixations. She explains that she was only ten years old when her mother was caught "in that air raid," after which her father "became everything" to her. But after he married Catherine, Diane says she used to fantasize about what she and her father would do if her stepmother were dead. As bizarre as this may be, especially for an adult, Diane does say to Frank that she realizes now that Catherine never meant to harm her and that she would give her life to bring them back. So when Diane tells Frank that he cannot leave her because she would not know what to do without him, she seems less psychotic than desperately lonely. Frank is unmoved, declaring that he says he does not hate her, but he is "getting out just the same." It is particularly poignant when, after Frank's departure, Diane closes up the family house, dismissing the servants and wandering around aimlessly before retreating to Frank's old room above the garage, where she spends the night curled up in an armchair, wrapped in his jacket.

Diane's desire to come clean and make a statement to her lawyer that she did indeed kill her father and Catherine also suggests that she is not completely delusional, or at least recognizes that what she did was wrong. Ironically, her lawyer tells her that the only thing that would happen if she kept repeating her story—the truth—is that she would be put in an insane asylum. Having no way to deal with her guilt and faced with a lifetime of being alone with it, Diane's rash decision to kill herself and Frank by driving off the same cliff near her house is perhaps more understandable than the actions of some *noir* psychotics. It is difficult to know for sure at what point she makes this decision—whether she thinks that his acquiescence to her offer to take him to the bus station represents the end of their relationship or that she believes she may still change his mind as they share a bottle of champagne on the trip is uncertain. But there is clearly something in his admonishment of the way she puts the car in gear, as he exclaims, "Easy!" that seems to spark her reaction to floor the car in reverse off the cliff. Similar to Ellen Berent, she says, "I can't let you go, darling—I just can't." And she does not. She cannot go "easy," and her drastic action to hold on to her thwarted desire places her beyond the bounds of "normal" behavior, especially the standards of normalcy expected for a woman.

As we have seen, much *noir* psychological pathology involves the obsessive fixations of a love object. However, in a film like Robert Siodmak's *The Dark Mirror* (1946), the fixation of the psychotic personality is directed toward a sibling, not a lover. Olivia de Havilland plays identical twins Teresa (Terry) and Ruth Collins in the film, and it is one of the most overtly psychological *noirs* that was produced, signified right from the start of the film by the Rorschach blots under the titles. Ruth and Terry are inseparable, living together, generally dressing alike both publically and privately, and even sharing the same job, so they can "switch out" when one wants time off. They even wear eerie wire necklaces that bear their names, as if each might be in danger of forgetting who she was. They have been orphans since childhood, and though Ruth is the "older" by seven minutes, Terry seems like the elder and more protective, controlling sister. The film's premise relies on the "old wives' tale" about twins that one must have some sort of abnormality—in this case, a psychological one—as is made clear even from the publicity materials of the film that proclaimed, "To know this twin is to *love* her . . . to know this twin is to *die*!" After one of the twins is suspected of murdering a doctor, they are both under suspicion and ironically protected by the law, since it cannot be proven which one was spotted by an eyewitness. The investigating officer, Lt. Stevenson (Thomas Mitchell) enlists the unofficial help of up-and-coming psychiatrist Dr. Scott Elliott (Lew Ayres), who is an expert on twins. Though Stevenson must believe that Elliott could help, he approaches Elliott with the "fortune-teller" mentality, wanting to see Elliott's "gimmicks" and asking, "Don't you witch doctors treat people with tinkertoys?" Elliot may not use tinkertoys, and he may dismiss the "superstition" that twins are usually "penalized in some way, physically or psychically," but his assessment of the situation with the twins seems just as misguided. He insists that "character, personality is the key"—equating the two elements, though one is a moral and the other is a scientific designation. He goes further to say that "not even nature can duplicate" this quality, "even in twins," so this is what would tell who is the murderer. He adds that "one could and one couldn't commit murder, and that's all there is to it." This dichotomous appraisal is inconsistent with the advances of psychiatry and reduces the complexities of Terry and Ruth to black and white categories. Indeed, Foster Hirsch seems on target when he argues that "the insistent separation of the characters into icons of good and evil makes the film a superficial melodrama rather than a probing psychological study. Good and evil do not engage in an internal clash but are presented as the essence of two separate characters, as in a medieval morality drama."[10]

Terry and Ruth consent to being added to Elliott's "collection" of twins for study, though Ruth shows some reluctance because she seems to believe that Terry might be guilty of the crime. The series of tests that Elliott administers is standard psychological stuff, but the findings again point more to a moral judgment than psychiatric one. When Elliott shows them inkblots, for instance, Terry's answers reveal conflict and even violence, as she imagines one to be a lamb doing harm to two people, and she comments, "The lamb looks so innocent, but it has two men under its paws." But her answers sound quite preconceived, as if she is trying to communicate a power to Elliott that reaches beyond her seemingly powerlessness appearance. Elliott assigns particular meaning to the contrast in Ruth's answers, which show less negativity, less threat (dancers around a maypole and skaters in an ice show for instance). Her manner is more timid, her hands folded in her lap, and she seems more willing to please, all of which for Elliott add up to his assessment that Ruth must be normal and Terry must fall into the mentally disturbed "20 percent" of people who see things in the inkblots that expose the "true secret patterns of their own minds." The results begin to prove, for Elliott, that "one of our young ladies is insane." By contrast, the free association test yields less information than Elliott hopes, mainly because the only unusual reaction that either gives is first Ruth's to the word "mirror," to which she responds, "death." Though he does not comment, he clearly looks forward to Terry's response to the same prompt. We never know what she might have said, however, because she gives the same response as Ruth—only because Ruth tells her what she had said. Terry becomes visibly upset upon hearing Ruth's answer, revealing that she understands some of "that mumbo-jumbo" and does not care about Elliott's "kindergarten games," she is clearly trying to cast doubt on Elliott's authority and reduce his tests to childish experiments. However, when Elliott administers the polygraph to Terry, it seems as though she cannot successfully manipulate it; the needle visibly jumps wildly at any mention of Ruth, especially when she is describing a boy that used to take an interest in Ruth. The final conclusion for Elliott is that Ruth is sane and innocent, but that Terry is "a paranoiac—a paranoiac has no more sense of right and wrong than a two year old—a paranoiac is capable of anything." Elliott recognizes Terry's intentions to manipulate the psychological tests, believing they were "another challenge to her, another opportunity to show the world what contempt she has for it. That was the tip-off." A marker for insanity, or at least "abnormality," for women, then, is the transgression of typical patriarchal authority. The "tip-off" to Elliott that Terry is the "wrong" twin is her effort to thwart the masculine power and rules that are being applied to explain her motives, psyche, and very existence.

Meanwhile, regardless of Terry's belief that she triumphing over Elliott's psychological "analysis," she is clearly threatened by the fact that he has developed romantic feelings toward Ruth. Terry has an obsessive attachment to Ruth and this, coupled with a mania to be the "superior" twin, causes her to take drastic steps to thwart this romantic relationship, as she has evidently sabotaged all of Ruth's other romantic relationships in the past. Terry's approach is to make her own play for Elliott, at the same time that she tries to make Ruth believe that she is losing her mind. She tells Ruth that she has been repeatedly talking in her sleep and waking up crying and terrified, apparently experiencing terrible dreams. Encouraging Ruth to take more sleeping pills than she normally would, Terry also surreptitiously uses a flashbulb to light up their bedroom in the middle of the night, causing Ruth to awaken in a panic, and she begins to believe that she is going crazy. In a shot in which Ruth suddenly grips both sides of her head, she exclaims, "Something's happening to me, and I don't know what it is. I don't understand it. I'm so scared; I don't know what to do." Terry's reassurance takes the form of complete possessiveness of Ruth: "Just remember that I'm with you and I'm always going to be with you . . . no matter what." Lutz Koepnick astutely points out that with this strategy, "Terry converts feelings of loss and fragmentation into fantasies of total power and god-like control; she projects lack onto her own sister in the form of psychological disorder."[11] Later, as Ruth becomes more and more uncertain of her own sanity, Terry similarly assures her not to worry because "no matter what happens, they can't do a thing without [her] consent"—implying that even if Ruth is mad, she needs Terry to keep her out of trouble. After all, she adds, "we'll be together as long as we live." Then, with true sisterly affection, she secretly turns on a music box so it will begin playing after she leaves their apartment, causing Ruth to think she is hearing music inside her head.

Throughout the film, Terry is constantly ego-driven and hungry for affirmation, probing Elliott about why he prefers Ruth to her. In the climactic scene of the film, Terry actually pretends to be Ruth with Elliott, and when she kisses him, she asks him if he thinks he can tell the difference. Even playing Ruth, Terry cannot resist lauding herself, as she tells him that "Terry is the smart one," the one men usually go for. Elliott, however, is not able to be fooled, as in an effort to make Terry confront her illness, he tells her as "Ruth" that "Terry" is "sick inside and needs help"; he lays blame on some incident that must have occurred when they were babies that has long been forgotten, but that ever since then, it has grown "more and more bitter and is now abnormal." This pseudo-Freudian explanation of an infantile slight being responsible for adult psychosis, as we have seen in *The Snake Pit*, rings hollow when compared to the myriad social factors that might have affected the psyches of the adult women. When "Ruth" tries to convince him that she and her sister have never been rivals, Elliott provides this "psychiatric" explanation: "All women are rivals fundamentally, but it never bothers them because they automatically discount the successes of others and alibi their own failures on the grounds of circumstances—luck, they say. But between sisters it's a little more serious. Circumstances are generally the same, so they have fewer excuses with which to comfort themselves. . . . That's why sisters can hate each other with such terrifying intensity. And with twins, it's worse." Elliott is trying to antagonize "Ruth" to the point that she reveals herself as Terry, by reminding her about past failures, such as a family that wanted to adopt Ruth but not Terry, and boyfriends who preferred Ruth to Terry. Terry's possessiveness may be interpreted as a desire to absorb Ruth, to eliminate the "difference" between them that haunts her and frustrates her desires. While Terry is rambling hysterically, Ruth suddenly appears, and as Terry sees her reflected in a mirror behind her,

Terry throws an object into the mirror and breaks it, trying to destroy symbolically the sister who has been a continual reminder of her shortcomings. Stevenson quips, "Even a nut can figure out that it's simpler to get rid of a rival than to go on knocking off her boyfriends all the rest of her life." His sarcastic humor seems ill-timed and it is after the sequence of events we have just witnessed—a humor that seems to undermine the impact of psychiatry in both its mystery-solving and curative efforts.

Kleptomaniac Nancy (Laraine Day) from John Brahm's *The Locket* (1946) also leaves several men in her wake, though not by directly murdering all of them. Nancy is only known by her first name in many cast lists of the film, likely because she accumulates so many names from various marriages; she collects these names in much the same way that she compulsively accumulates jewelry throughout the film. *The Locket* employs one of the most ambitious flashback structures in *noir*, utilizing three intertwined flashbacks, layered one inside the other. Though these intertwined flashbacks naturally call into question the nature of the "truth" (or "truths") presented in the film (especially since much of the information is a second or third-hand retelling), the entire premise of the film—that Nancy is a rabid kleptomaniac who is willing to kill to get what she wants—rests solely with this potentially inaccurate transfer of information. For this reason, the film itself seems to suffer from a kind of madness, as it appears unable to convey a consistent reality. As a result, the only first-hand knowledge of Nancy that the viewer experiences are scant minutes at the very beginning and very end of the film, her entire story (and psyche) entirely framed by the accounts of the men in her life. The immediate occasion for the action of the film is Nancy's impending marriage to John Willis (Gene Raymond), on the eve of which he is visited by her former husband, psychiatrist Dr. Harry Blair (Brian Aherne), who has come to warn him about Nancy. Blair calls her a "hopelessly twisted personality" before launching into the first and main flashback of the film. He tells Willis that he had only been married to Nancy for a short while when artist Norman Clyde (Robert Mitchum) accused Nancy of murder and asked for Blair's help to save a wrongly convicted man from execution. At this point, the second flashback ensues, as Clyde relates the details of his stormy relationship with Nancy, who was his fiancée. Clyde, like Blair, is struck by Nancy almost immediately when they meet, thinking her to be "perfect," and as Clyde says, the girl that you "never expected to meet and suddenly materialized." Both Blair and Clyde set aside doubts about her perfection and pursue her energetically. Nancy also benefits Clyde because her boss, Drew Bonner (Ricardo Cortez) is a wealthy patron of the arts and begins to sponsor his work.

One of the first paintings of Clyde's that Bonner sees is *Cassandra*, a painting of the ancient prophetess featuring blank eyes, a work for which Nancy sat as model. Bonner says he is not sure if he likes it, because when he thinks of Cassandra, he sees "a madwoman . . . a woman with prophetic eyes, wonderful eyes." The link between Cassandra and Nancy is compelling, since Cassandra's madness, according to Greek mythology, was a socially manufactured judgment, rather than an inherent quality; though her prophecies were true, no one would believe them and therefore deemed her insane. For Nancy, this phenomenon is somewhat reversed: there is a resistance to believe that Nancy is mentally ill, regardless of her suspicious behavior. For Clyde, this behavior begins at a party at the Bonner house where a guest's necklace is stolen, and Clyde finds the necklace in Nancy's purse. Nancy's initial reaction to his discovery is downright sociopathic in its nonchalance; when he asks her why she stole it, she says, "Because I wanted it . . . I don't really like diamonds. I always wondered what it would feel like to own some." Clyde's frustrated reaction ("People just don't take things because they see them!") causes her explanation of a childhood trauma involving jewelry, the third flashback of the film. It is important to remember that in the "present" of the film, Willis is hearing this story from Blair, who heard it from Clyde, who heard it from Nancy, who is drawing on childhood recollection. The viewer is being asked to accept foundational knowledge about Nancy's character though this diluted translation of information. Nancy relates that she was the daughter of a housekeeper to a rich family and was befriended by the family's young daughter, Karen. "When you are a housekeeper's daughter," says Nancy, "you see the world through half-open doors." Though Karen generously gives Nancy her locket, since she is not permitted to come to her birthday party, Karen's mother makes her give it back. Since Nancy had developed a fitful attachment to the locket, probably because of the significance it meant in terms of her friendship with Karen, she cries hysterically when she has to relinquish it, saying that if Karen had given it to any of the other children, then they would have gotten to keep it. Her mother tells her that if she is patient, she will get the things she wants. The ordeal regarding the locket is not over, however, since when the locket goes missing the next day, Karen's mother immediately accuses Nancy of stealing it, and even after Nancy's mother finds it caught in the hem of one of Karen's dresses, Karen's mother angrily shakes Nancy, accusing her of stealing it and hiding it. The scene ends with Karen knocking over a music box after being shaken, and her mother losing her job because of the incident. It is clear that wrapped up in the childhood trauma of the event are also particular class issues that follow Nancy throughout her life. She becomes a poised and self-confident woman, who seems particularly adept at placing herself with people and situations that can benefit her and better her prospects.

After Nancy assures Clyde that she would never steal again, Clyde feel sympathy with her because of her story, and agrees to mail the necklace back anonymously. However, the spectre of Nancy's stealing surfaces again at another of Bonner's parties at which Mrs. Bonner's prized diamond necklace goes missing, and Mr. Bonner winds up dead. Clyde cannot deny that he saw Nancy emerging from the Bonner bedroom suite just after the gunshot was heard, and though he wants to support Nancy and believe her story, he finds it increasingly difficult to do so. Though Nancy is cleared because of the alibi for her that Clyde affirms, their relationship becomes poisoned by his doubts, with Nancy calling Clyde "arrogant, neurotic, jealous" before leaving him. Clyde has come to Blair in part to ease his guilty conscience that an innocent man is about to be executed for the crime that he is sure Nancy committed. Though Clyde's story does plant some seeds of doubt in Blair's mind, he generally believes that Clyde is "obsessive," especially when he sees Nancy's self-assured reaction to Clyde when Blair invites him over to the house. Clyde, according to Nancy, is the "erratic" one, giving a different story about the Bonner death than Clyde shared and even denying that the childhood bracelet incident occurred. When Blair pronounced Clyde to be a "paranoiac with guilt fantasies," Clyde counters, "You're no psychiatrist—you don't know truth from lies. You're just a lovesick quack," adding that he will "make the same mistakes" as Clyde did. Clyde's shocking punctuation on the end of their brief relationship is to give Blair the "Cassandra" painting as his "fee," just before he commits suicide by jumping through Blair's waiting room window.

Frank Krutnik argues that in films such as *The Dark Mirror* and *The Locket*, the male psychiatrist is posited as an antidote to the mad female by being "established as a detective-figure whose principal function is to investigate and ultimately to eradicate 'deviance' (represented in these instances by excessive female desire)."[12] While this may be true to a certain extent, an odd side effect of being in proximity to Nancy's love and kleptomania is to be infected with the suspicion of madness yourself, even if you are a psychiatrist. Blair realizes that the obsession and paranoia of which he accused Clyde is becoming his own, after he and Nancy are enlisted in military service with the advent of World War II. Nancy arranges for them to spend a few days in the company of a lord and lady who have devoted their estate to "nerve-shattered" war workers. Blair wonders, because of the rough country and bad weather, why Nancy even chose this as a place to relax, until he hears the lord talk about his jewelry collection, which includes a locket belonging to Queen Anne worn at her christening. As they leave, the chauffeur tells them that the locket is missing, and on the train home, Blair clearly wants to look in her purse, but fails—a parallel to Clyde's discovery of the original necklace from the Bonner party. It is only when a bomb hits their building that night does he finds the missing jewels in the rubble. When Nancy shows up, a questioning close-up of her face reveals her eyes to resemble those of the *Cassandra* painting: blank and expressionless, as she reflects, much like Terry Collins, her madness onto the nearest and dearest recipient in order to deflect it from herself. She and the fellow military medics try to make Blair believe that he is delusional, and she finally divorces him after committing him to a psychiatric hospital. Now, as Blair is trying to calmly relate his story as a warning to Willis, he is seen as just as much of a lunatic as Clyde seemed to Blair. When Nancy, with her typical calm and reasonable demeanor is unshaken by the confrontation, Willis resumes his plans to marry Nancy, who reassures a somewhat nervous Willis by saying that Blair knew so much about her because he psychoanalyzed her, adding that Blair "wasn't the only one to crack up" in the war. As many maladjusted veterans as we have seen in *noir*, by contrast, here is one that has not in reality "cracked," but is being victimized by the imposition of this identity.

Few *films noir* can offer the kind of irony supplied by *The Locket* in its final scenes. Willis turns out to be the son of Nancy's mother's old employer; her future mother-in-law, Mrs. Willis (Katherine Emery) is the one who tormented her as a child and was evidently instrumental in her adult psychotic fixations. Her identity is unknown to Mrs. Willis, who offers her, in the moments before her marriage ceremony, the very locket that she coveted as a child. Mrs. Willis reveals that the necklace, a family heirloom worn by three generations of family brides, would have belonged to her Karen, but she had died. This revelation, combined with the bewildered Nancy knocking over the same music box she had as a child, sends her into a whirlpool of disorientation. She cannot reconcile the reality of obtaining the long-lost locket with this new reality of her soon-to-be mother-in-law who accepts her only because she does not know her origins. Added to this is the fact that Mrs. Willis' reactions so long ago are now contextualized by being perhaps more those of a distraught mother who believed she had lost a precious family heirloom than those of a monster. As Nancy proceeds to the wedding ceremony, the music box tune is superimposed by the wedding march, producing a dissonant, musical effect that becomes more pronounced with each step. She hears all the voices from her past in her mind, before screaming and having a complete breakdown just as she reaches Willis at the altar. "Mentally she's a child now," says Blair, who Willis calls for help later that evening. According to Blair, "Nancy never got her locket as a child and because it meant so much to her, she paid a terrible price. But lockets are only symbols—it was love she needed. It's love she needs now." The idea that mental illness can be caused by lack of love or frustration of desire is one that surfaces repeatedly in *film noir*. The existential importance placed on basic human emotion—and the consequences of their denial—in the *noir* cycle may account for this theme, as well as coincide with the socially progressive backdrop tied to the popularization of psychiatry. The plights of characters like Nancy, Terry Collins, and even *Possessed's* Louise Howell argues a general quality to neurosis and psychosis that can cause them to arise anywhere to anyone.

The long reach of trauma-causing psychosis is also seen in Roy Ward Baker's *Don't Bother to Knock* (1952). In what Durgnat calls a twist of "anti-expressionism," veteran-of-film-psychopath-roles Richard Widmark is cast as the voice of reason, while the sweet-faced Marilyn Monroe is cast as a psychopathic babysitter.[13] Both Jed Towers (Widmark) and Nell Forbes (Monroe) are having difficulty working out their individual problems and their coming together proves to have disastrous effects. Jed, a pilot, has received a "Dear John" letter from his girlfriend Lyn (Anne Bancroft) and has come to the hotel where she is employed as a lounge singer to try to work things out. Meanwhile, Nell has been hired by a couple, Peter and Ruth Jones (Jim Backus and Lurene Tuttle), staying at the hotel through her bellhop uncle, Eddie (Elisha Cook, Jr.), to babysit their daughter for the evening. Nell seems reserved and perhaps even depressed, but it is only gradually that the depths of her mental disturbance become clear. After she puts the daughter, Bunny (Donna Corcoran) to bed, Nell drifts around the room, eating chocolates, turning the radio on and off, and finally donning the earrings, makeup, perfume ("Liaison"), and negligee of Ruth Jones. Even these actions and her wistful looking out the window when she hears an airplane fly by do not seem more significant than the behavior of a poor and lonely girl; however, later they assume more serious proportions when Nell is shown to be dangerously and possessively disturbed. Jed enters her life because he sees her dancing through the window of the Jones' room from his own room across the alley and is so taken with her that he later appears at her door with a bottle. Jed is also restless and licking his wounds; earlier that evening, his attempt at reconciliation with Lyn fell flat. She insists that she can no longer be with him because he is lacking in feeling; she tells him that he lacks an "understanding heart," only focusing on "the cold outside of things, the simple facts." Ironically, what Ted hopes for with Nell—a simple escape from his troubles—will demand more "feeling" from him than his failed relationship with Lyn.

The source of Nell's melancholy is a dead boyfriend, and a close-up of her hands reveals scars on her wrists that point to a suicide attempt. Nell deludedly believes that Jed is her dead lover, who was also a pilot, miraculously found to be alive. She calls him "Billy" and talks to him as if in a dream, as if she is talking to the lost sweetheart. Enough of the details of the two men's lives are similar that Jed does not realize at first what she is doing, until she mentions that he had crashed in 1946 on the way to Hawaii, marveling at the fact that he did not actually die. Nell talks to Jed facing a mirror and looking at him in her reflection, an accurate representation of her state of mind in the conversation, one that only reflects Jed through her broken-hearted delusion. Before Jed can protest the inaccuracies of what she is saying, she kisses him passionately, which he cannot resist. Reality interferes, however, in the form of Bunny, who comes out and wants to know what is going on. She shatters the lies that Nell had told Jed about her circumstances by accusing them of trying to steal her mother's things and telling Nell to take them off. For Nell, Bunny now takes on the form of an evil harbinger of fate who is trying to thwart, once again, her wishes for happiness. She directs upon Bunny all the frustration she feels and is determined to take control of any force that is trying to control her. She coldly tells Jed, "If you don't pay attention to them, they stop," perhaps alluding to her own childhood neglect. When Bunny continues to cry from the other room, Nell tries to appear solicitous, offering Bunny water, a story, music, finally bringing her to the window for some air when she says she is too warm. As Bunny chatters, looking at people across the way in their hotel rooms, Nell looks dazed and says to Bunny, "You won't cry anymore, will you?" as she places her hand firmly on Bunny's back as she leans farther and farther out of the window. The scream of a woman across the way at Bunny leaning out of the window causes Jed to come over and pull her away; though Bunny says she was not going to fall and does not look scared, Jed seems to think that Nell is a genuine threat to her at that moment. Bunny's innocent voyeurism parallels Nell's arrested emotional development, as she too spends her time looking into the lives of other people, in an effort to forget the emptiness of her own life. When Nell puts Bunny to bed after the window incident, she ominously tells her, "It's wicked to come between people": "If your doll at home cried and spied on you, you'd want to get rid of it wouldn't you? You'd have to." Circumstances have been tragic enough in Nell's life that she believes that happiness can only be achieved through elements that she herself can control, even if this means manipulation of other people in her life, arranging them like paws, to achieve these ends. The blows of "natural" life have become too chaotic for her to bear. Hence, her assurance to Bunny that if she is quiet and goes to sleep, they will "all live happily ever after."

Nell's efforts to maintain possession of Jed throughout the evening causes him to grow by turns impatient and sympathetic toward her. He says he cannot figure her out: "silk on one side and sandpaper on the other." The "sandpaper" is the roughened aspects of her psychological suffering that she tries to hide, but that cannot be disguised by her "silky" desires. In fact, Nell has more baggage than simply a dead boyfriend; she evidently came from a household of repression and abuse, impoverished parents that whipped her and viewed her going to the movies with a boy to be a "sin." She appears to have put all her hopes in Phillip, her pilot sweetheart, and when he was taken away by the plane crash, her life must have seemed to end. Many of these details are revealed in a conversation she has with Eddie, when he comes by to check on her and forces her to take off the makeup and accoutrements of Mrs. Jones. When she resists, Eddie disappointedly says, "I knew it—you aren't cured," referring to the fact that she had just been released from a three-year stay in a mental institution after her suicide attempt. As is often the case in *noir*, mental illness is not only seen as pervasive and inevitable, but also fundamentally irrevocable, despite the best attempts at "cure." Eddie thought Nell had been "getting better"—after all, she "seemed okay until tonight." But the unpredictability of the effects of her damaged psyche—by extension, of the tragedies of the unstable post-war world—make relapse entirely likely. And when the child who has come to represent all the thwarted dreams she has had will not stay quiet, Nell must silence her more drastically: in a shocking pan of the camera in Bunny's darkened bedroom, we see that Nell has tied up Bunny in her bed face-down and gagged her. Though Nell never mentions a desire to have children, it may be assumed that another layer of her resentment toward Bunny is that she represents yet another aspect of normal life and marriage of which Nell has been robbed. When even silencing Bunny does not induce Jed to stay with her, Nell seems on the verge of murder, as she leans over Bunny's face and calls her a "devil," right before Bunny's mother bursts into the room.

In all the confusion that ensues after Bunny's rescue, Nell crawls away, confused and desperate. It is clear that Eddie's hope that if Nell could only "get out among people," then she would become well has not come to pass; the reverse has happened, in that Nell has brought her own instability among the ostensibly stable "people" in the outside world. She cannot accept the fact, as Jed tries to convince her, that there is a balance to the world, and that things "even up—good breaks, bad breaks." This platitude is likely a hard pill to swallow when there have been no "good breaks" in sight. For Jed, ironically, his brief relationship with Nell and the role he plays in stopping her from killing herself in the hotel lobby, works as a tonic in his relationship with Lyn. When she sees his patience and caring towards Nell and her predicament, as he admonishes the crowd for staring at her, Lyn realizes that he does have "an understanding heart" after all. As for Nell, Jed, almost like an emergency psychiatrist, talks her out of the suicide by getting her to recall that Philips's looks were nothing like his and to finally admit, "You're not Philip; you never were." As she is being taken away by the police, however, the uncertain look on her face and her coy shadow of a smile cast doubt about the substance of her admission. Perhaps she is meant to be seen as an aberration; as Ruth Jones says, "I guess we've never seen anybody like her." But the somewhat "everyday" nature of the circumstances surrounding Nell's madness make clear that this story is more about the proliferation of such disturbance rather than the rarity.

Another *noir* that probes the "public" implications of mental illness is Edward Dymytrk's *The Sniper* (1952). This aspect is made clear to the viewer even before the first credits, as the following "warning" flashes on the screen: "High among police problems is that of the sex criminal, responsible last year alone for offenses which victimized 31,175 women. Adequate and understanding laws do not exist. Law enforcement is helpless. Here, in terms of one case, is the story of a man whose enemy was womankind." The film immediately sets the tone for a world in which the acts of the "sex criminal" are not only rampant, but proliferate when law and even understanding are absent. The bleakness depicted extends even further when we meet the title character, ex-convict Eddie Miller (Arthur Franz), who is not only afflicted by murderous, misogynistic impulses, but also cannot find help for himself, regardless of his efforts. If a homicidal killer can ever seem sympathetic, one could very easily find Eddie so, as he lives a lonely and desperate life, devoid of love, fulfillment, or even companionship. We initially see life from his perspective as he sits in his apartment window with his sniper rifle sighting a woman on her steps across from his window, as she kisses a man. He pulls the trigger to an empty chamber, an act that only temporarily seems to relieve his discontent, as he gets angry and puts his gun away. Eddie is all too aware of his dangerous impulses and tries to mitigate them in various ways, such as going for a walk. However, every passing contact he has involving a woman leaves him visibly disillusioned or disgusted, whether it is two girlfriends talking about men, a man and a woman kissing in the park, or a mother slapping a child who is crying that he wants to go home. As he passes by this mother and child, Eddie holds his hand up to his own cheek as if he were the one wounded. Eddie is every bit this wounded child, as he too longs for domestic security, but has no real home to return to.

Eddie is desperate enough to call the state prison from a pay phone in a drugstore during his wanderings, in an effort to reach his former doctor there. Eddie is not exaggerating when he tells them that "it's a matter of life or . . ." when he tries to convey the urgency of the call, but he is still unsuccessful. It is impossible to know whether or not connecting with the doctor would have prevented any of the ensuing events, but Eddie is so tortured at the point when he returns to his apartment that, in an effort to prevent himself from shooting, he first beats hand against a dresser, and then puts it on a hot burner. A worm's eye view of his contorted face punctuates the level of his agony. The hospital emergency room provides immediate treatment for his severe burn, but little else. The inattention to Eddie's mental instability seems shocking, as the doctors clearly not only know that the burns were self-inflicted, but also are told by Eddie that he used to be in the "psycho ward" in prison. Eddie further reveals that he was imprisoned because he "hit a girl" and that now he does not "feel right." Despite this, the two doctors agree that it is "useless" to send him upstairs to the psychiatric ward because "they'll only wrap him in a cold sheet and send him home after three days." It is bizarrely sad how badly Eddie actually wants to be sent there; as they try to send him on his way, he resists their release of him, saying, "Don't you think this a funny way to get hurt?"

After all this, it is no surprise, that Eddie has no defense left against his own murderous impulses, and a series of shootings ensue, the first of which seems to define the nature of Eddie's resentments toward women. Eddie's job is to deliver for a dry cleaning service, and one of the cleaner's clients is Jean Darr (Marie Windsor), a nightclub piano player, and a woman to whom Eddie is clearly attracted. When he delivers her order, she asks him to bring it into her bedroom—not in a particularly seductive way, but with the kind of benign flirtation that signals that she feels as though he is not even a "man" in the sense that she would have to be guarded with modesty or convention. When she realizes that she has a stain on her dress, she asks him to wait while she takes it off so that she can give it to him as a "rush job" and tells him he should have a beer while he waits. He seems to feel relaxed and happy at the prospect that she seems to like him—until her trumpet-player boyfriend rings her doorbell and she tells him to finish his beer on the back porch, like the servant that he actually is. She becomes the perfect victim for him, as he follows her to her club that evening, fatally shooting her from a rooftop as she stands right in front of her publicity photo, the bullet shattering its glass case. The duality of this shooting—of both Jean herself and her glass-encased photo—signifies the symbolic meaning that this act has for Eddie; he is shooting less Jean than the sexual frustration and humiliation that she represents. He seems somewhat exhilarated and liberated after this act, as he goes to a bar and feels confident enough to talk to a woman who shows him some interest. He gets into trouble, however, when he lies about his job to her and she, catching on that he is not really an engineer, rejects him. Eddie cannot sustain the powerful feeling that he has gotten from the killing because of what he perceives as his own failings; blaming them on the women around him sends him into a spiraling cycle of continuous murder.

Jean Darr's murder will be the first of several that Eddie commits and the police officers assigned to the cases are, fittingly in this chaotic world, named Lt. Frank Kafka (Adolphe Menjou) and Sgt. Joe Ferris (Gerald Mohr). At every turn in their investigation, Kafka and Ferris come up empty, and their impotence is striking, especially given Miller's desire to be caught. He sends a note, written on a piece of cardboard from an ammo box, reading, "To the Police—Stop Me—Find me and stop me—I'm going to do it again." Since they cannot, his next victim is the woman who rejected him in the bar after his first killing. The camera, like Miller's gun, follows the drunken woman back into her apartment as she gets partially undressed, pours herself a drink and then as her back is to the window, she is shot by Miller in the back of the head through the window, a scene of shocking impact. It is after this murder that the public hysteria begins, as the incidents are beginning to be covered in gruesome detail by newspapers; this elevated public consciousness spurs the police inspector, Anderson (Frank Faylen) to lean heavily on Kafka and Ferris, telling them that the killer has to be found, or else every other "loopy" in town is going to "jump on the bandwagon" and they'll find themselves "knee deep in a slaughterhouse . . . it's happened before and it can happen again." The idea of mental illness as a contagious disease surfaces here again, and in this film more than many others, the sense of psychosis as a public plague, something that is becoming more and more commonplace, is disturbingly obvious. And as is the case with other public health emergencies, the government officials charged with protecting the populace find themselves ill-equipped to do so. The police inspector's strategy is to round up all the known "rapists, defilers, and peeping toms" and place them in a lineup, more for ridicule than discovery. It seems only psychiatrist James Kent (Richard Kiley) can shed any light on the "sex offenders," like Miller, that the police find so elusive. He tells Kafka that criminal fetishes tend to be compartmentalized, such that "peeping toms don't kill women; they stick to peeping," adding that the violence in this particular case is the key factor. When Kafka asks how these criminals become the way they are, Dr. Kent provides this explanation:

> Maybe some woman did something mean to him when he was a kid—he may not even remember what it was, but something in here [tapping head] remembers. Perhaps it was his mother; it usually is in these cases. He's past the stage where he could have been talked out of it. . . . But whoever it is . . . he's killing her over and over again; he's been doing it in his mind for years. Now that he's doing it for real, he's going to keep on doing it.

Aside from the Freudian mother-blame that Kent assigns, he also ascribes a certain hopelessness to Miller's malady; having come to this point, Miller can only enact the same dysfunctional ritual over and over again, though it does nothing to alleviate his original pain. Miller's plight is an exaggerated manifestation of that of any human being in the *noir* world: the repetition of meaningless actions believed to have some substantive affect on one's existence, but in reality having no meaning at all.

After Miller's third murder, and as Kafka and Ferris come closer to discovering Miller's identity, the heightened public panic about the killings becomes even more obvious. Miller's fellow workers comment about the perverse connection that the sniper has brought to everyday strangers, as people who do not even know each other find something to talk about in the common menace of the killer on the loose. They also speculate on the seeming randomness of the advent of these crimes: "This week, it's dames; the next week it's guys with one leg or false teeth, or something—or maybe guys who work in cleaning plants." The link between private torment and public terror is evident here, as the effect of Miller's inner pathology cannot be understood or cured, only displayed as an outward danger to humanity. And still there is no solution in sight, as powerful political types pressure the mayor and police inspector to do something about the "maniac on the loose." There is clearly no public solution, as the police argue they do not have enough manpower, the councilmen bicker over taxes, and the newspaper owner crows that they want him "punished, punished!" No one really wants to hear from the only person who might have genuine insight, Dr. Kent, who challenges their notions of punishment as the solution to the overall problem. Kent advances the cause that mental illness is an overarching social problem that needs widespread and broad solutions, rather than simply perpetrators being "killed the same way a mad dog is killed . . . or put in an insane asylum," as the political bosses advocate. Kent argues that the legal definition of insanity—that the subject cannot tell the difference between right and wrong—is outdated, since he claims that only a minute percentage of all "sex offenders" fall into this category. This assessment casts doubt on this kind of historical assessment of all other kinds of mental illness as well; if the determination of insanity rests with the moral distinction between right and wrong, the implication is that the world is in more trouble than we might have imagined. By this definition, in fact, the majority of the general populace, as depicted in *noir* at least, would be classified as mentally ill.

Kent emphasizes that the key to ameliorating this social problem is early detection and treatment, putting the blame on the archaic approaches by social institutions for the threat that Miller poses today. Predictably, the political heavyweights dismiss Kent, from whom, they say, they knew all they could expect was "a lot of psychiatric mumbo-jumbo." Only Kafka seems to take Kent's advice to heart, as he sends an adolescent suspect of the sniper killings, whose rifle cannot even fire, to the hospital psychiatric ward; the would-be sniper tells Kafka, "You think there's only one guy in this town that doesn't like people?" Kafka has sent him to the hospital because he does not want "to be looking for him in a couple of years when he has a real gun or an axe." Predictably, though, it is less Kafka's or Ferris' efforts that lead to the capture of Miller, but rather his own desperate actions that deliver the deciding blow of discovery. After the fourth murder, Miller goes to an amusement park and after trying to work off some of his frustration at the shooting gallery, he moves to the dunk tank. As the swimsuit-clad target taunts the throwers, when Miller steps up, his hard-pitched balls dunk her four times in a row, after which he begins throwing baseballs savagely, directly at the cage itself. This incident, followed by his sighting his next victim in broad daylight, leads the police on his trail. The juxtaposition of the smallness of Miller's individuality and the magnitude of his impact are captured in a striking shot of Miller climbing down a long fire escape ladder on the side of a building, looking like an ant against the sky and the huge urban façade. Even Miller's kindly landlady is sucked into the inevitable public hysteria as he arrives home, and the radio broadcast in the background crows that anyone who knows of a man with a badly burned right hand should report him to the police: after all, "he may be the sniper!" Miller's end is compellingly without drama; the police break into his room to find him sitting on the bed in his room, clearly not resisting his capture, embracing his rifle, as a close-up reveals a tear rolling down his face. Few *noirs* portray this kind of deep pathos when portraying the haunting qualities of post-war mental illness.

A final manifestation of *noir* psychosis comes in the form of Bluebeard-ish "mad artists." Edgar Ulmer's *Bluebeard* (1944) is one such film, though it does not take place in the post-World War II *noir* environment. Peter Godfrey's *The Two Mrs. Carrolls* (1947) and Fritz Lang's *The Secret Beyond the Door* (1948) are two other notable examples, in which creativity and obsessiveness with past trauma are conjoined. In *The Two Mrs. Carrolls*, Sally Morton (Barbara Stanwyck) has a whirlwind romance with painter Geoffrey Carroll (Humphrey Bogart), only to discover that he is married to an "invalid" wife. Though Carroll is desperate to hold on to Sally because he says she has "saved" him—he can now work again, whereas before he met her, his art had grown cold—she rejects him. The opening of the film in which much of this action quickly takes place is pastoral, a lake setting in Scotland, much like the Edenic atmosphere that cannot be retained in *Out of the Past*. Carroll, we will discover, is a disturbed artist who has come to need fresh female inspiration; his art depends on it, and he is willing to kill to have it. A trip to a London chemist and several glasses of milk later, the first Mrs. Carroll has died, and Sally has taken her place as the second wife. But two years after Sally marries Carroll, he is beginning to experience painting frustrations again, as is evident in a confrontation he has with Sally when she invites friends to tea and he has no interest in being social. Carroll's daughter Beatrice (Ann Carter) figures prominently in the story as well; she is an extremely precocious child, acting almost like a conscience or a Greek chorus to the adults around her.

During the aforementioned tea, Bea comments that her father's eerie painting of her mother, titled *Angel of Death*. is "creepy," but says eventually "you get used to it." She also adds, matter-of-factly, "We all die, sooner or later." This no-nonsense approach to human mortality being expressed by a child contributes to the backdrop of fatalistic despair that pervaded the film. Clearly, for some wives of Carroll, death comes sooner rather than later, especially when their replacements are found. Sally learns from Bea that her mother was not actually an invalid, and was actually "quite strong and in perfect health," until she fell ill after he came back from fishing in Scotland. Sally's replacement, both as artistic inspiration and love object, is the wealthy and decadent Cecily Latham (Alexis Smith), who aggressively pursues him to paint her portrait and also to have an affair with her. "Beauty is worth any sacrifice," says Carroll of his work, and he is desperately afraid of losing his artistic ability; at first, he does not even seem attracted to Cecily, telling her that what she represents is nothing he would want to paint. But she quickly becomes both his subject and his lover, right about the time that Sally begins to feel weak and ill with "nerves." Though Sally would like to see a "nerve specialist," Carroll insists that all she needs is to get her "milk regularly." Carroll's cycle of creative vampirism seeks to drain the inspiration found in his female subjects through the vehicles of art and sex. And when he has extracted all there is to inspire him, they must die so that he may cultivate the next muse. Curiously, the method that Carroll uses to accomplish the final stage of this process, poisoned milk, symbolically suggests a reversal of the usual vampiric metaphor: here, the victim ingests liquid, rather than surrenders it, and the whiteness of the milk symbolizes the emptiness that they now represent to Carroll. The "blood" of their inspiration extinguished, there is nothing left for them but to drink a substance that signifies what has become their lack of significance. Carroll's psychosis parallels vampirism as well, as it is a "disease" (perhaps infectious) that seeks the most drastic of cures.

Just as in his affair with Sally, Carroll's affair with Cecily comes to a head when she declares that she is leaving for Brazil, implying that she will end their relationship if he does not take some action to end his marriage. Meanwhile, Bea is reading a book about Van Gogh and ominously tells her father about what a shame it is that such a brilliant artist as he went insane. Carroll gets upset and grabbing the book away from her, comments about the "startling" things she says. He is increasingly tense and irritable and decides to leave with Cecily, telling Sally he is traveling to pursue a new commission. It is during this absence that Sally will find the opportunity to discover the "secret rooms" that house her husband's mental illness. Up until this point, she has had several unanswered suspicions: she has not been allowed by Carroll to see the new painting on which he is working, and she suspects that he and Cecily are having an affair. When she discovers that unbeknownst to her, arrangements have been made to send Bea away to school—a gesture that the viewer knows is a signal that another wife is about to die—she becomes even more suspicious and discovers from Beatrice that the symptoms of her illness are the same as those of Bea's mother, to whom Carroll was so "devoted," since he brought her milk himself every night. These details are chilling to Sally, and she takes Bea up on her offer to find the mysterious painting, though she already seems to know what she will find. In a dramatic scene, Bea, the only person who has the key to her father's studio—and symbolically, the only one with true insight of her father's psyche—opens the door with Sally to find a new portrait of Sally as the angel of death. The torrential rain outside drips a tear-like reflection on the surface of the canvas, before Sally faints at the sight of the painting, of her own impending fate. When Sally tries to confront Carroll, he tries to turn the situation around, telling her that she does not understand: his painting of her is finished—by extension meaning that not only their relationship, but also her life is finished as well. Carroll is insistent, even to the police that arrive to rescue Sally, that he had to do what he did to "go on with [his] work." Meanwhile, Sally has been caught in a nightmare of love turned to death, as she has become the representation of the demise of Carroll's artistic inspiration. His mental illness took the form of a vampiric hunger, using his love objects as fuel for his creative pursuits, and discarding them when they became bloodless.

Probably the most overt Freudian depiction of *noir* psychosis is found in *Secret Beyond the Door*, a film that features various re-castings of fairy tale patterns bound up with psychoanalytic interpretations of childhood trauma and sexual relationships. From the start, the film makes no artistic attempt to submerge its psychoanalytic frame. A friend of the main character, Celia Lamphere (Joan Bennett) quips at a party that her incessant garrulousness allows her to purge herself of her "repressed poisons," to which Celia responds, "Paging Mr. Freud . . ." This frame at times becomes almost uncomfortably exaggerated, the entire film often suggesting a dream state, even as it depicts "real" time. The film's opening dream sets this tone early on, and the film never entirely awakens from it. A blurry scene of a paper boat floating on a pond dissolving into flowers accompanies Celia's voice-over: "If a girl dreams of a boat or a ship, she will reach a safe harbor, but if she dreams of daffodils, she is in great danger." The voice-over then launches into what seems to be a return to reality, as she tells the viewer that this is no time to be thinking of danger because it is her wedding day. However, the voice-over in "reality" seems to be just an extension of a dream, as her words seem to drift in an almost stream-of consciousness reverie, musing about "something old, something new, something borrowed, something blue," and then segueing into how old the church was, and then back to Mark Lamphere (Michael Redgrave) being the "something new" in her life. We see her in her bridal gown as the voice-over continues, telling us that the intense pounding of her heart makes her feel as though she is drowning—and that "when you are drowning, your whole life flashes before your eyes." Elizabeth Cowie argues that Celia's dreams and flashbacks are analogous to the distinction in psychoanalytic theory between what is latent and what is manifest, following "the same division Freud describes for two aspects of the dream-work whereby the latent meaning of the dream is discovered indirectly through the associated thoughts and memories of the analysand as he or she recounts the manifest text of the dream. The film's opening images of Celia's dream implicitly motivate our reading of the film in this way."[14] However, these lines are rather blurry in the film, almost putting the viewer in the position of viewing the entire film as a dream, rather than parts that might give clues to the meaning of the whole.

Although Celia is not the character who is posited as the one with the possible psychological illness, she seems just as troubled, as her inner torment is made very obvious to the viewer. Thus, her reactions to unusual, but not necessarily alarming, events make her appear neurotic and disturbed. But it is important to note that the inner workings of anyone's mind would seem disordered and troubled, if they were laid bare at a conscious and public level, which is the milieu of the film, thereby highlighting the idea in psychiatric *noir* of the normalizing of mental disturbance. All of Celia's secret fears and desires are open for scrutiny from the time that she first encounters Mark on a trip to Mexico, as she witnesses a street fight between two men over a woman. She is mesmerized by the power that the woman must feel, "how proud she must be" because "death was in that street" because of her. The mixture of the sexuality and violence in the scene before her clearly makes her excited, and she sees Mark watching her, his "eyes touching [her] like fingers." Afterward, her friend tells her she looked as though she had seen "death himself," and the danger that Celia associates with Mark is a strong component of her desire for him. Kelly Oliver and Benigno Trigo, in their extensive analysis of *Secret Beyond the Door*, discuss the Freudian implicates of the Eros/Thanatos link, arguing that, "according to the film's logic, death is love's uncanny double"[15]—a doubling all too often seen in *noir*. When Celia contemplates a future with Mark, she is afraid of closing the door on a safe room with "a fire burning on the hearth" in favor of Mark's alternative: "Wind was there and space and sun and storm. . .everything's beyond that door." Even as the wedding ceremony begins, she is afraid, feeling as though she is "marrying a stranger."

The link between desire and death becomes particularly clear as the newly-married Celia discovers her architect husband's unusual hobby, which is "collecting rooms": staging and outfitting rooms in his house that depict murder scenes, down to the minute details of authentic furniture, weapons, and accessories worn by the victims. All these rooms are missing are the dead bodies, and all depict men murdering either a lover/wife or a mother. When Mark takes party guests on a tour of the rooms, one of the guests, a college girl who is a "brain psych major," comments that murder of a wife or girlfriend has its psychological roots in an "unconscious hatred for the mother," a comment that Mark tries to brush off. However, he finds it less easy to dismiss another assessment she makes later, that it was a pity that in the day of the murderer, Don Ignacio, "they didn't know about psychoanalysis." She asserts that if something had happened in that room that drove him to murder, "if he had been able to tell someone, like a psychoanalyst, what happened to him there, no murder would have been necessary." There is an implicit comparison here to Mark, who we suspect may also have dangerous secrets.

As an architect, Mark gives particular credence to the influence of space on human lives; he repeatedly uses the word "felicitous" to describe his theory that elements of a particular space make certain human actions possible, and therefore "apt" for that locale. He applies this concept to the joy in the 400-year-old church in which he marries Celia and also to the rooms that he "collects." What the viewer does not know at this point, is that his psyche is tormented by events that occurred in a particular space, and instead of focusing on his own interior, he fixates blame on the room itself, making it the locus for his pathological hatred of women. Mark's demeanor toward Celia vacillates from warmly loving to coldly remote—but even in his most loving and playful moments, he displays a resentment and superiority towards women. On their honeymoon, he tells Celia, "No woman can think . . . no woman should even try" because women are "nearer to nature"—more instinctual and emotional—and as "intelligence improves, instinct withers away." Mark's sister, Caroline (Ann Revere), as we will learn, is a strong and dominant personality, having taken charge of Mark after their mother died; the other woman in his life is Miss Robey (Barbara O'Neil), his secretary, who saved his son in a fire, becoming scarred herself. The ghosts of two other women, however, also hover in Mark's life: his mother and his first wife, Eleanor, who is described as falling ill after Mark had returned from the war.

Eleanor evidently died of a "lack of will to live," ascribed to Mark's ignoring her and denying her love and affection. Mark's unpredictable displays of and retreats from emotion also take a toll on Celia from the very start of their marriage on their honeymoon. When she locks her bedroom door on a whim, in order to make him more desirous of her, he becomes cold, suddenly announcing that he has received a telegram and has to leave to attend to a business problem. After he leaves and Celia learns from the maid that no telegram arrived, his hasty departure and the withdrawal of his affections cause an almost frenzied response in Celia, as she tortures herself, pacing around her room. In voice-over, she repeats, "Why had he gone? Why had he lied? Why had he gone? Why had he lied?" This scene reveals the psychological disturbance of Celia herself; Oliver and Trigo also point out that this repetition "creates the effect of a stubborn psychological pain that will not let up . . . a turbulent interior psychic space."[16] Though she is inspired by her maid's playful comment that she should make Mark "wait," what prompts Celia to lock her bedroom door? It is characterized in the film as a honeymoon "prank," but there is a difference between keeping a man waiting and locking him out of the bedroom. The mixture of desire and fear in Celia's love for Mark sheds some light on her action, as she is not only somewhat afraid of Mark, but also her expression of love for him involves a sadistic removal of herself from his access to further increase his desire. Later in the film, when Celia tries to defend Mark's son David in a fight they are having, and Mark gets angry at her, Celia's interior monologue voice-over once again dominates the scene, as for no reason she says she keeps thinking about "red carnations and lilacs, somehow signifying pain that can no longer be borne." She seems to be connecting the lilacs that Mark's mother loved (but that Mark seems to hate) with Mark's anger toward her for interfering. Her mind wanders further, as she second guesses everything she just did when she tried to intervene, her thoughts then jumping to wondering how Eleanor had died. The way that Celia's insecurities about herself and fears about Mark manifest themselves in this stream-of-consciousness pseudo-advancement of the plot create an atmosphere of constant psychological chaos and instability.

This uncanny and unstable atmosphere is heightened by the numerous appearances of mirrors in the film, which parallel the various psychological doublings (Celia and Eleanor, Celia and Mrs. Lamphere, Mark and David, etc.). On the night that Mark leaves abruptly during their honeymoon, Celia is seen gazing into her dressing table mirror at length, as she brushes her hair. Though Mark characterizes her, when they first meet, as "a twentieth-century Sleeping Beauty," who "has lived her life in cotton wool, but who wants to wake up," Celia equally resembles the wicked queen of "Snow White" as she sits pensively in front of the mirror, entranced with her beauty and searching for answers to the mysteries surrounding her. Her room in Mark's estate home has a prominent mirror above a fireplace mantel; this mirror appears several times, including the many scenes involving an important pair of candlesticks. When Celia discovers that Mark has finished a "new" room, but will not let anyone see it, like Bluebeard's wife, she takes the opportunity to use the wax from one of her candles to make an impression of Mark's key so that she can have a copy made. When Mark notices that one of the candles is shorter, he does not seem suspicious, only disturbed by the lack of "symmetry." Every scene involving the candlesticks necessarily involves a shot of the mirror behind them, often catching the reflection also of Celia or Mark. The candlesticks represent Celia's inner doubt and fear of Mark, the reflection representing the reversal of her love and affection. When Celia finally enters the secret room (numbered the usual "lucky" 7, another reversal), she first believes that it is a replication of Eleanor's old room, except that it is absent any of the personal effects that Mark uses in his other rooms. Celia opens curtains only to see a brick wall, signifying her initial conclusion that Mark built the room because he felt guilty about Eleanor's death. But then in a chilling shot, she notices the two candles on the mantel, one of them shorter than the other, and realizes, "This is my room, waiting for me."

Celia's realization causes her to flee the house, unbeknownst to Mark, who, in a singularly odd and disorienting *noir* technique, begins his own voice-over. We see Mark in his room alone, his voice-over, declaring, "It will be a curious trial—Mark Lamphere for the murder of his wife, Celia." He wonders what he will he say when they ask if the murder were premeditated, as he holds a scarf, the murder weapon from Don Ignacio's room. Though this new voice-over is somewhat jarring, it not only confirms Mark's murderous impulses, but also reinforces the sense of creeping unconsciousnes invading waking reality that began with Celia's dream-like mental wanderings. Celia returns to the house, appearing like an apparition or a dream, telling him that she came back because she married him for better or for worse. Though Celia's return seems meant to be "real" to both Mark and the viewer, there is a certain surreal quality to her reappearance, both visually and substantively. Mark's subsequent voice-over declares that he is afraid of what he will do to Celia if he is alone with her. What we may not expect is Celia staging a scene that forces just this situation, as she brings lilacs to Room #7, then sits and waits for Mark to show up. The link between love and death surfaces again, as Celia prepares to sacrifice herself to Mark if she cannot save him. She is employing a kind of "shock" therapy by making him act out a situation that he is afraid to face. When he enters and his attention fixes on the lilacs, she says, "Yes, lilacs have something to do with it," asking him to search his mind for "something that he's locked up inside it, just like the room is locked up." The camera focuses on the scarf Mark holds in his hands, as he twists it as if preparing to strangle someone. Celia pushes him by telling him that she knows something happened to him when she locked her bedroom door on their honeymoon, and it is this catalyst that sends the entire story of Mark's childhood trauma pouring out.

Mark remembers gathering lilacs with his mother when he was ten years old, stating that though she and his father were separated, he did not care, since she was his "whole world." He became jealous when his mother told him that she was going out dancing, but she said he should come to her room, and she would read to him. When the young Mark tries to leave his room but finds himself locked in (a practical joke by Caroline), he says he pounded on the door until his hands were bloody, finally seeing his mother drive away with a man, and he cried, believing she was the one who had locked him in. He said he was enraged, and hated her, wanting to kill her, and instead, ripped up all the lilacs in the yard. This revelation alone does not "cure" Mark, as he still approaches Celia with his twisted scarf, until she tells him that it was Caroline who had locked him in his room that night so many years ago. Mark then drops the scarf abruptly, as if a spell has been broken. Though the viewer's immediate impulse may be to feel relieved, at both Celia's preservation as well as her ability to solve the mystery of Mark's odd behavior, the fact remains that Mark has nearly murdered Celia because one night as a child, he believes that his mother locked him in his room. This would be a fantastic level of psychosis in a child, let alone carried to the pinnacle of homicidal urge in Mark as an adult man. None of this is ever commented upon, though, as the narrative turns to focus instead on the house fire from which Mark saves Celia. Mark's selfless act is thus intended, though quite hollowly, to mitigate his near-murder of her moments before. Miss Robey who started the fire in order to remove Celia from the picture, presents an interesting counterpoint to Celia, as she too enacts the same kind of distance-desire dynamic in order to attract Mark. Ironically, neither of them consciously realizes that this was the same dynamic that caused his pathological hatred of his mother, and by extension, all women thereafter. Though Miss Robey took to wearing a scarf over the scarred side of her face, she had gotten plastic surgery to repair the scar, thinking that she could lure Mark into loving her. However, when this failed, she continued to wear the veil, to attract sympathy and thereby retain her job. Doane points out that "the veil in this instance functions to hide an absence, to conceal the fact that the woman has nothing to conceal, to maintain a debt, and thus to incite desire."[17] Once Miss Robey is fired by Mark earlier that day, as he is trying to purge the influence of all the women in his life, she has nothing more to conceal, and so tries to eliminate Celia as a final effort to hold on to Mark. Though she survives the fire, Robey still emerges as a Bertha-like "madwoman in the attic," nearly killing Celia and Mark as the house erupts in flames immediately after Mark's revelation in Room #7.

The final moments of the film cannot pass, then, without revealing yet another character with neurotic/psychotic impulses; as if the shock of Mark's near-murder of Celia is not enough, Miss Robey's setting the house ablaze lends an almost apocalyptic cast to the film's conclusion. The idea of the terrifying events of the film as a dream is reinforced by the pastoral return to Mexico at its close, as Mark and Celia appear to be journeying on a second honeymoon. Mark tells Celia that she "killed the root of the evil" in him, but then says he "has a long way to go." She responds by saying *they* "still have a long way to go." They might have been discussing a marital infidelity or alcoholism, rather than the fact that Mark nearly strangled Celia because of a seemingly insignificant childhood slight by his mother. The depths of these implications are never probed, however, which is an ironic shutting of the "door" of the film's exploration of psychoanalytic themes. For all the interior turmoil being brought to the surface, the most disturbing truth of all, once having peeked around the corner of the open door, cannot be coaxed out into the open. All, therefore, can never be resolved, as is usually the case in a psychiatric *noir*; the framework of discovery is introduced but can never be wholly successful.

The number and variety of neuroses and psychoses depicted in noir overwhelmingly paint the backdrop of the film cycle to be inherently dysfunctional. Whether murdering sadists, nihilistic kleptomaniacs, vampiric artists, or possessive avengers, the psychologically unstable characters in these films suggest a pervasive anxiety regarding the prospect of mental illness and cure in the post-war world—an anxiety that perhaps extends to the despair at finding any psychological satisfaction in this world. Psychiatry is present, but is found wanting. Its repeated presence suggests a need that requires fulfillment—perhaps a general psychological malaise arising from the difficulty of satisfactorily filling what appeared to be the void chaos of everyday life and lack of potential for human connection.

Notes

1. Raymond Durgnat, "Paint It Black: The Family Tree of *Film Noir*," in *Film Noir Reader*, ed. Alain Silver and James Ursini (New York: Limelight Editions, 1996), 49.
2. Nicholas Christopher, *Somewhere in the Night: Film Noir and the American City*, (New York: Free Press, 1997), 190-91.
3. Jack Shadoian, *Dreams & Dead Ends: The American Gangster Film*. 2nd Ed. (Oxford: Oxford University Press, 2003), 111.
4. R. Barton Palmer, *Hollywood's Dark Cinema: The American Film Noir*, (New York: Twayne, 1994), 145.
5. Palmer, 149.
6. According to Ingrid Bergman's 1983 autobiography, *My Story*, Robert Montgomery, angry that he was being asked to play this role against his will, told Bergman, his co-star in this film, that he did not intend to act at all, but merely say his lines. His "lack of emotion," as it turns out, was perfect for this role.
7. Mary Ann Doane, *Femmes Fatales: Feminism, Film Theory, Psychoanalysis*, (New York: Routledge, 1991), 27.
8. Jacques Siclier, "Misogyny in *Film Noir*" in *Perspectives on Film Noir*, ed. R. Barton Palmer (New York: G.K. Hall & Co., 1996), 74.
9. Richard Lippe, "At the Margins of *Film Noir*: Preminger's *Angel Face*" in *Film Noir Reader*, ed. Alain Silver and James Ursini (New York: Limelight Editions, 1996), 167.
10. Foster Hirsch, *The Dark Side of the Screen: Film Noir* (New York: Da Capo Press, 1983), 190.
11. Lutz Koepnick, "Doubling the Double: Robert Siodmak in Hollywood," *New German Critique* 89, (Spring-Summer 2003): 93.

12. Frank Krutnik, *In a Lonely Street: Film Noir, Genre, and Masculinity* (New York: Routledge, 1991), 52.
13. Durgnat, 50.
14. Elizabeth Cowie, "*Film Noir* and Women" in *Shades of Noir: A Reader*, ed. Joan Copjec. (London: Verso, 1993), 155.
15. Kelly Oliver and Benigno Trigo, *Film Noir Anxiety* (Minneapolis: University of Minnesota Press, 2003), 87.
16. Oliver and Trigo, 78.
17. Doane, 48.

Chapter Five

The "Gaslight" Phenomenon

Inducing Insanity in *Noir*

> "If I were not mad, I could have helped you. Whatever you had done, I could have pitied and protected you. But because I am mad, I hate you. Because I am mad, I have betrayed you."
>
> —Paula Anton, *Gaslight* (1944)

As we have seen in the previous chapters, mental instability in *noir* is so tightly woven into its fabric that its stories would likely unravel without it. Its pervasiveness in the post-war world is depicted as both a frightening epidemic and eerily commonplace. Perhaps the most frightening subgroup of these films are the ones in which insanity is being induced—in which one or a group of characters is trying to make another character believe that he or she is mentally ill. This phenomenon ups the ante on the typical theme of nightmarish persecution found in *noir*, similar to what we have seen in the amnesiac narratives previously discussed: the only thing that may be more terrifying than a loss of identity that was a product of the past is the loss of one's mind in the present. As characters are made to question their own mental faculties and confront their fears of loss of control, the very foundation of their own identities are called into question. The prototype of this film is George Cukor's *Gaslight* (1944) in which Paula Anton (Ingrid Bergman) is being slowly convinced that she is mad by her pianist husband Gregory Anton (Charles Boyer), who married her solely to get access to jewels that he believes are hidden in her late aunt's house. By making subtle changes to her everyday familiar environment, Gregory changes her secure surroundings into an uncanny nightmare, in which she can no longer trust her thoughts or her actions. Gregory removes objects from places that Paula puts them, and when they reappear in other places, he convinces her that she is forgetful and absent-minded. He slowly removes her from public contacts, strategically causing these "accidents" when she is in the society of others, so as to heighten her embarrassment. She is the only one who hears noises in the attic and a change in the level of the gas-powered lights in the house whenever Gregory is ostensibly away working in his music studio, but unbeknownst to Paula, is rooting around in the attic, looking for the jewels.

Paula's friendship with Scotland Yard detective Brian Cameron (Joseph Cotten) ultimately saves her, as Gregory seems on the verge of committing her to an asylum; Cameron discovers what Gregory is up to, including that he was actually her aunt's murderer. At the end of the film, in a chilling confrontation with Gregory, Paula makes Gregory believe momentarily that she will kill him because she is "mad," though she now realizes that she is completely sane. The audience likely appreciates this turning of the tables, and it highlights the fear that Paula has been facing by seeing it from another perspective. Gregory, like the other *noir* insanity-inducers we will see, was able to fix on a small glimmer of insecurity, trauma, or doubt, incrementally burrowing a hole of anxious uncertainty in the mind of his victim. The effects of the films in this group are almost hypnotic, showing the power of suggestion when it comes to human fear and doubt. In a comfortable and secure world, the probability of one's own environment and eventually mental faculties turning against oneself would seem unrealistic; however, in the *noir* universe, what is familiar can (and does) become unfamiliar in the blink of an eye, including one's own psyche.

The usual conditions for this kind of scenario to be possible necessarily involve those the protagonist is closest to (spouse or family members) because of the level of trust required. An additional level of irony is added when the family members depicted in these films are imposters, or "false" families. Such depictions are the most extreme example of the dysfunctional family in *noir*, noted by Sylvia Harvey: "It is the representation of the institution of the family, which in so many films serves as the mechanism whereby desire is fulfilled, or at least ideological equilibrium established, that in *film noir* serves as the vehicle for the expression of frustration."[1] Additionally, Andrew Dickos points out that family "often emerges in *noir* cinema as the vehicle for muted rage, long-bred resentments and jealousies, and the possessiveness that becomes a mother's (or father's) obsession with a child."[2] We have already seen how family dynamics are portrayed with often disastrous circumstances in other psychiatric *noirs*, but in the "gaslight" *noirs*, the depiction of domestic dysfunction is at its peak when the "family" is not really the family at all, but nefarious pretenders, taking advantage of traditionally sacred human bonds in order to cause harm. One example of this type is *My Name is Julia Ross* (1945), in which Julia Ross (Nina Foch) is an American in London who finds herself in need of a job as she is recovering from an appendix operation. Under these most innocuous of circumstances, she meets Mrs. Hughes (Dame May Whitty) and her son Ralph (George Macready), who are in search of a live-in secretary. As Foster Hirsch argues, the film "is a clever variation on the *noir* theme of unstable identity; who you are can be altered, or eradicated, by the simplest act—by something as mundane as a job interview."[3] What the Hugheses are searching for is a young woman with no family or boyfriend, who could stay at least a year, and Julia fits this description, all alone with no relations in a foreign city. What Julia does not know is that the job search is a cover, even the job agency being a front for what they are really seeking: a look-alike for Ralph's first (and murdered) wife. They are pleased that Julia seems like the right choice—"perfect," Ralph says, "even a small resemblance." Julia has become a doppelganger of a dead woman, as her relatives become their own doppelgangers to Julia's real, but absent, family. Upon Julia's arrival to the house, she is drugged, and her identity completely eradicated by the Hugheses, as they destroy all her clothing, bags, and identification. The level of danger Julia may be in is suggested by the way that Ralph disposes of her belongings, cutting them up with a knife, rather than just discarding them. His mother tells him to put away the knife, adding, "Remember that if it weren't for your temper, we wouldn't be in this awful trouble today." The "awful trouble" turns out to be the fact that the psychotic Ralph has murdered his wealthy wife and now the Hugheses must cover up the crime by creating her double in Julia, moving to a new town, and systematically planning a realistic scenario for her "suicide."

Meanwhile, Julia wakes up to realize that she is in a different bed than the one in which she first fell asleep, also noticing that she has lost time when she sees the calendar. As the camera pans around the room, emphasizing the unfamiliarity she has with her surroundings, she also notices that everything is monogrammed with "MH." When she tries to open the bedroom door, she discovers that she locked in, and opens the bedroom window to find that she is evidently in a house on a cliff overlooking the sea. Both her view from the window and the subsequent shot of the secluded large house on a jutting cliff over the water confirm her isolation. Her confusion is compounded when the maid, enters, calling her "Mrs. Hughes," and saying that she hopes she "feels better today" since she slept all day Friday. Moreover, the maid says this is her "new home" in Cornwall, and mentions how worried her husband has been about her. Julia seems about to argue, and then notices the wedding ring on her finger. The fact that the Hughes family has tried to create this transformation through sleep is particularly effective; her identity has been removed upon her awakening, as if her previous life had been a dream. The lack of certainty about reality one feels when dreaming is conveyed when Julia finds herself, when she opens her eyes, in another life, one that seems completely foreign to her. The instability of dream states, as we have seen in other psychiatric *noirs*, is reflected here, the idea of one's identity being removed or replaced through the act of sleep a terrifying prospect. The vulnerability of the self when surrendered to sleep is underscored as Julia awakens to find her old name and her old life obliterated.

The Hugheses plan is to attempt to convince the outside world that "Marion," Ralph's wife, is mentally disturbed, after which they can stage an "accident" in which she appears to have killed herself, an event no one would then question. Part of this plan then, involves treating Julia as thought she were Marion, so that her denials of her identity seem part of her psychosis. For instance, in the midst of Julia's initial confusion, Ralph enters with his mother and calls her "Marion." When Julia insists that she is Julia Ross, Mrs. Hughes says, "You haven't forgotten us again, Marion?" Mrs. Hughes admonishes her to be careful so that she does not have another "attack," and that they are doing everything in their power to make her "get well again." To her credit, Julia seems immediately aware that she is being tricked. She refuses to drink the tea offered to her, saying that it is probably drugged with "sleeping powders" like the other ones. Her strength of personality is also noticed by the maid, who muses that "if you didn't know she is like she is, you'd think she was telling the truth." However, this strength cannot protect her from her fear in the middle of the night, when she senses someone moving around in her room and coming toward her. Desperate, she screams and throws an object from her nightstand across the room, shattering the dressing table mirror. Julia's reaction to this shadowy threat is a symbolic rejection of the identity being projected onto her; there is no need for a mirror in the room to reflect the persona of "Marion Hughes" in the room in which Julia Ross is living a false life. The maid and the Hughes family, when they arrive in her room, try to convince her that she had a nightmare; they say it must have been her imagination or a dream, that there could not have been anyone in the room, since the door was locked. Julia agonizingly cries, "Why did you bring me here? Are you trying to drive me crazy, is that it? Tell me what you're planning to do with me!" They say, quite deliberately in the presence of the maid, a potential witness, that they only want to make her well.

Though the phenomenon of someone trying to make someone else believe that he or she is insane is similar to *Gaslight*, in *Julia Ross* the actions of Ralph and Mrs. Hughes are less about truly convincing Julia that she is actually insane and more about outside appearances. Oddly, even when he and his mother are alone, they both refer to Julia as "Marion," rather than "Julia" or even the neutral "she"; for instance, when Ralph sees Julia running from the house, he reports to his mother, "Marion is going toward the road." Though they may do this to stay in "character" for the benefit of the servants and outsiders, it seems that they in part truly see her as a reincarnated Marion and are perfectly comfortable with enacting the charade. Likewise, Julia is never truly in doubt about who she is and never stops trying to escape. She tries in vain to enlist the help of the maid, who does not believe her, saying she has "everything a woman would want" and tries to reassure her by saying, "You're letting yourself be took up by illusions . . . letting it gnaw at you and gnaw at you. It's all in the mind. People can think themselves into anything." The "illusion" is, of course, the reality—who Julia used to be—and despite Julia's determination to maintain her identity, the position she is in makes clear how easy it might be to convince someone that he or she is a different person.

As the film progresses, it becomes more and more clear that Ralph is not only a murderer, but has genuine psychotic tendencies. In a scene in which Mrs. Hughes tells him that he has to be more cautious about his temper, he is first whittling, then hacking away at a stick before she tells him to stop. In a chilling shot, he slowly puts the penknife down on the table and stares off into space; as his mother reaches out for the knife, he grabs her hand and struggles for it briefly, still staring straight ahead, before releasing it to her. Ralph is portrayed as a violent and destructive child, one who appears to remain under the thumb of his mother, but who we know is capable of losing control. Mrs. Hughes locks up the penknife in a drawer; we see it joins other sharp instruments that she has presumably confiscated. The mental instability that is being projected onto Julia is actually fully realized in Ralph, whose violent impulses are the cause of Julia's captivity. These tendencies are further evidenced as Ralph walks down to the gate, whipping hedges with a switch, as Julia is stopped from running any further by a huge gate. Her efforts to convince the gate keeper to open it fail, and predictably, the more she insists how sane she is, the crazier she sounds. Showing remarkable savvy, Julia decides to walk with the dangerous Ralph around the grounds, trying to get him to reveal information about "her," such as who she was before they met, relatives she might have, and so forth. She says that perhaps Ralph and his mother are really right about her, that maybe she really has been ill and asks for his help in remembering. The scene of this ensuing conversation on the cliff overlooking the crashing waves is one of the most illuminating and creative in the film. Ralph turns away from Julia, musing about the beauty of the sea. As he speaks, the camera shoots him from behind as he looks at the sea, while she faces the camera. Ralph tells her, "[The sea] doesn't say anything, does it? That's what I like about it. It never tells its secrets. But it has many. Many, many secrets . . .", and the shot moves into close-up on the upper part of Julia's face, so that only her eyes and nose are seen looking over his shoulder. She appears to be looking at his face and at the camera at the same time, but the viewer only sees his shoulder and her eyes over it. The effect is incongruously claustrophobic—though they are standing in the open air, she appears completely surrounded by his body and has become shrunken into a pair of eyes. His presence signifies the threat of her slow disappearance from the world as she fights to hang on to her reason, signified by her gaze. This kind of dynamic is explained by Mary Ann Doane, who argues that "what is particularly interesting about *film noir* for a feminist analysis is the way in which the issue of knowledge and its possibility or impossibility is articulated with questions concerning femininity and visibility. The woman confounds the relation between the visible and the knowable at the same time that she is made into an object for the gaze."[4] Ralph is looking intently at Julia, who may be looking at him or looking into space toward the camera. It is an incredibly disorienting moment for the viewer, who almost experiences a kind of vertigo on the cliff with Julia Ross and her entire identity at risk. The camera returns to a medium shot, after Ralphs tries to kiss her and she breaks free. This is only one of the many times that Ralph attempts to molest her; he sees no reason to resist the temptation of Julia, since she is only a tool to achieve his ends.

Though Ralph evidently did not initially intend to kill his wife, his instability suggests that this loss of control could have occurred at any time. He tells his mother, "It was Marion's fault—she shouldn't have cried." Marion's undoing apparently was that she had asked him whether or not he married her for her money after she found out that he lied about his income. When he said yes, and she started to cry and slapped him, his temper was ignited. Ralph almost begins to demonstrate for his mother, by saying, "I had my knife in my hand and I . . .", as he trails off and then starts violently slashing the couch on which he is sitting, its stuffing flying out. She tells him, as she must do so many times within the film,

"Stop it, stop it . . .," and tries to take the knife away from him. Similar to the earlier scene with the whittling penknife, Ralph resists, his face setting into an intense grimace, and through gritted teeth, tells his mother, "Don't . . . do . . . that." She, equally grimly, stares him down, and says, "Put . . . that . . . away." As before, he relents, and the intensity of the mother-son dynamic is striking; though Ralph is clearly a violent psychopath, his mother still maintains control of him when he is with her. When Ralph says they should have called the police and said a prowler broke in and killed Marion, Mrs. Hughes, implying Marion was too mangled, responds that they could not let anyone see "the marks of [his] fingers on her or see the scratches on [his] face."

Julia actually overhears this conversation, and some suspense is generated by the fact that the vivid description of what Ralph had done to the real Marion clearly unnerves her, appearing to break her resolve to escape. The camera follows her, as with a despairing expression, she finds a bottle of poison and tearfully clutches it. When found by the maid in the next scene, everyone thinks she has taken poison; however, this was yet another ploy by Julia to find a route to escape, hoping that a doctor would be called. The Hugheses call a "doctor" all right—yet another imposter—but a second and "real" doctor arrives, called by the nervous maid. Because Julia actually seems insane, this doctor says that he will pick her up in the morning to take her to a hospital. Ralph ominously replies, "She'll be ready." Because their plan depends on Julia's death, not commitment, the false family has to act fast. That night, Julia hears a whispering voice call "Julia . . . Julia Ross . . . Hurry." Since the voice uses her "real" name, she believes it may be a rescuer, and so she follows it. It is actually Ralph trying to lure her, and she catches on when she recognizes the voice as unfamiliar: "Who are you? Why are you calling me Julia?" In her confusion, she nearly slips on the stairs, aided by Ralph's prior removal of some of the steps. It is not long after she recovers and returns to her room that Ralph and Mrs. Hughes hear a scream; they arrive in her room to find the bars opened on her window and a white-clad body on the cliff below.

This turn of events, of course, appears to be good news for the Hughes family; she saved them a lot of trouble, they say. But Ralph cannot resist going down to the cliff to make sure Julia is dead—to the point of picking up a rock to hit her for extra insurance. In fact, Julia had thrown her robe down on the cliff and crawled out through a secret passage in her bedroom—a test to see what Ralph would do, with the end goal not only Julia's freedom, but Ralph's prosecution. Dickos argues that "women in the *film noir* are created and seen through the eyes of men, and the perception of them stems, as has often been written, though the power they wield in disorienting the male object."[5] Julia succeeds in making Ralph Hughes relive the murderous scene of power and frustration that he experienced with his real wife Marion, and his making of Julia into a surrogate Marion only leads to his downfall, as he must confirm Julia's actual death—and perhaps gain some final satisfaction in potentially finishing the job himself. The real Marion haunts him, and he cannot believe that the death of the faux Marion will put his mind at ease without him actually performing the final violent deed of killing her. Though he killed her before, she did not "publicly" die and free him, and truth be told, he seems as though he would not forego the by-product satisfaction of actually bashing in Julia's skull as repayment for her rebuffs of his sexual advances. But unlike the real Marion, the faux Marion is not truly alone; the promised appearance and intervention of the doctor prevents Ralph's freedom, but insures Julia's. The reiteration of the film's title holds true, as Julia can re-assert her own identity; she has in fact finally orchestrated her own freedom from the imposter "family" and the false identity of insanity that they tried to impose on her.

The impersonating family scenario in André de Toth's *Dark Waters* (1944) is even more existentially terrifying than that of *Julie Ross* in that the protagonist, Leslie Calvin (Merle Oberon), is in true fear of losing her mind, surrounded by those who were supposed to be her protectors. Unlike Julia Ross, Leslie is primed for psychological victimization, having been traumatized by a boat accident that killed her wealthy parents, but left her alive. She and her parents are fleeing wartime fascism in Europe and are on the last leg of their difficult journey to America when their ship is struck by enemy fire. One of the opening shots of the film shows Leslie's stricken face, recounting to an unseen listener how the other passengers died while she was yearning for water to drink; in addition to her physical injuries, she is psychologically haunted by the grief and survival guilt she endures after the outward injuries are healed. She is recuperating in a New Orleans hospital when the film begins, and is encouraged by her doctor to contact her only living relatives, Aunt Emily Lamont, her mother's sister, and her husband, Uncle Norbert. She is apprehensive, because, she tells the doctor, "I don't know them." Leslie is all alone in the world and hesitates to reach out for distant familial connection. However, she takes the doctor's advice and receives a warm letter of invitation in return, asking her to come to their sugar plantation in Belleville, Louisiana. Leslie's uncanny experience begins when she arrives at the train station in Belleville, and no one is there to meet her, even though she had sent a telegram with her arrival information. Moreover, the train conductor says that though he knows the name of the plantation, he never heard of the Lamonts; no listing for them is found in the phone book either. The next thing we know, Leslie has fainted and is being aided by the kindly Dr. George Grover (Franchot Tone). Distraught, she says she now wants to go back, afraid that her relatives do not want her because they do not know her, adding that it was "the fear of being alone" that made her faint. Feeling completely isolated in the world after the accident, Leslie is particularly conscious of what is "known" and "unknown." Her relatives have an automatically societally recognized relationship to her even though she has never seen them and does not "know" them. Likewise, she imagines that her anxiety about the prospect of connecting with them is also felt by them too, and the thought of being abandoned by them as well, her last family in the world, is overwhelmingly hard to absorb.

If her "family" seems surreal in the abstract, it is even more surreal in reality. She meets an odd array of characters at the sugar plantation, a southern gothic venue of swampland and mystery. In addition to her "Aunt Emily" (Fay Bainter) and "Uncle Norbert" (John Qualen), the other denizens of the house include their overbearing friend, Mr. Sydney (Thomas Mitchell), who acts as though he is the real owner of the place, and the sleazy overseer, Cleeve (Elisha Cook, Jr.). Confusion abounds upon her arrival as they say that they did not receive her telegram, and maintain that they do have a phone listing. The more information Leslie tries to gain, the more she is stymied, as if she is in a funhouse in which nothing seems as it appears. Grover, who drives Leslie to the plantation, tells Sydney that Leslie has "been through a terrible time"; she is exhausted physically and emotionally, she has nightmares, and she is afraid that she is "turning into a mental case." The smooth Sydney assures the doctor that they will not "question her too much" about her ordeal, and when the doctor leaves, he proceeds to throw Leslie's telegram, which he had hidden in his pocket, into the garbage. In fact, Sydney is a criminal con man, who, along with his henchman Cleeve, has murdered Leslie's real aunt and uncle and installed imposters to act in their place until he can get rid of Leslie, thereby completing his theft of the plantation. Ironically, Leslie has begun to be calm enough to enjoy the fact that she seems to have a home with her "own people" now, but her happiness will be transformed into a nightmarish search for her own sanity.

Once Sydney learns of Leslie's fragile state, he does everything possible to provoke her anxiety. At dinner, he asks about the family's escape and the accident at sea in detail, causing her to cry and run away. The next day, he and Cleeve take her on a tour of the sugar plantation, describing in details the dangers of the place, like quicksand. They walk her along the bayou water on a perilous ledge, and though she is clearly nervous being that close to the water, they do not relent. Cleeve is sexually attracted to her, and tries to take her on a boat ride by force. Finally, they both take her to see a movie, which is preceded by a newsreel involving submarines sinking boats "perhaps carrying refugees." What she sees on the screen is not seen, only the audio and her stricken expression before she runs out of the theater. Later, she hears strange sounds in her bedroom, her lights go off and on mysteriously without her touching them, and she hears noise from a radio that is not plugged in. With each incident, she becomes more and more unnerved. Even the attentions of Dr. Grover, which are a pleasant distraction, cannot be a complete antidote; when he asks her to marry him, she is paralyzed with fear at the prospect, telling him that she cannot tell him what is wrong, but can never see him again. She confesses to her "aunt" that she "can't marry him or anyone else," because she is going out of her mind, convinced that she is truly seeing and hearing things that are not there. She says she belongs "under the water" like her mother and father, her mental faculties called into such question that it has become a burden for her to keep on living. She cannot understand why she was spared the fate of the others in the accident if this was to be her future.

Just as in *Gaslight*, it is the corroboration of another person that breaks the spell of suspected insanity in the victim. Leslie thinks she hears a voice calling her name in the middle of the night and follows it out to the swamp; as she fights her way through the darkness and brambles, it is as though she is searching for the truth of her own identity and sanity amid a treacherous psychic landscape. What she discovers is not the source of the voice, but something almost as reassuring: Pearson Jackson (Rex Ingram), the former caretaker of the plantation, who hears the voice too. She is shocked and relieved that the voices are not coming from inside her head, but still anxious that they cannot be explained. Pearson thinks the place is haunted, and in a way it is, by the ghosts of both her real aunt and uncle and her parents too—everyone who has abandoned her and left her in a position to be victimized. Not knowing yet that Emily is not her real aunt, Leslie turns to her for comfort and insight, believing that Sydney and Cleeve must be behind the strange occurrences. This conversation brings about a revelation that Leslie did not expect, however; after Emily reassures her about Sydney, Leslie asks her about what her mother was like when they were younger, and Emily talks at length about what a good dancer her mother was. But Leslie's mother had been an invalid, unable to walk since childhood. It is at this chilling moment that Leslie realizes that she is completely alone and friendless in the household, an alien in an alien environment. From every avenue where she has sought reassurance and solace, she has only found darkness and suspicion. Her experience parallels that of many war-scarred individuals: they have survived the threats of war only to find new threats at "home" afterward, in a world that becomes increasingly difficult to navigate.

Leslie now realizes how intently she is watched by everyone and though desperate to escape, like Julia Ross, she is trapped. She believes the assistance of Grover is her last possible salvation, and when he sees Sydney eavesdropping on their conversation about her theory, he believes her. However, he pretends to humor her by suggesting that she only needs a "few hours sleep" and writes her a prescription for a sedative. Meanwhile, he tells Sydney that she is getting dangerously ill and might be developing a "persecution complex," adding that he will get a "good psychiatrist" in New Orleans to come out to the house. The film is mirroring Leslie's anxiety here, implying that all hope is lost, until she reads Grover's "prescription," which is really a note to her saying that he believes her, but that she needs to hold on because it is too dangerous to leave now. This is the best medicine that Leslie could get, an affirmation that not only is she sane but also that she has secured assistance outside the toxic "family." Meanwhile, as Sydney's scheme is beginning to disintegrate, he and Cleeve decide to take Grover and Leslie out on a boat—Leslie's biggest fear—to dispose of them in the bayou. For a non-psychiatrist doctor, Grover does a good job of playing head games with both Cleeve and Sydney that undermine their efforts. Grover successfully weakens Cleeve's resolve by suggesting that he does all of Sydney's "dirty work" and when it comes time for Sydney to order him to kill Leslie and Grover, he resists, now distrustful of Sydney's motives. Their fight allows Leslie and Grove to escape into the waterlily-choked bayou. Leslie has overcome her fear of the water, and when Grover asks her to take the wheel of the boat to steer them out of the dark morass, though she initially hesitates, she knows that she no longer has anything to fear, confidently asserting to Grover and to the audience, "I'm all right."

A more distant, but equally twisted, familial situation is depicted in James Kern's *The Second Woman* (1951), in which architect Jeff Cohalan (Robert Young) is slowly being made to think he is insane by his vengeful boss and near father-in-law Ben Sheppard (Henry O'Neill). Though the film has *Rebecca* and *Suspicion*-like undertones, the main female protagonist, insurance accountant Ellen Foster (Betsey Drake), ostensibly at risk from the mysterious and potentially dangerous Cohalan, acts as the strong "male" savior of the male victim, who is portrayed as superstitiously "female." Because of the traditional male/female dynamic of reason vs. emotion, it is generally a woman who is the victim in a *Gaslight*-type film, as she would seem to be more likely to be susceptible to subjective suggestion from other parties. However, *The Second Woman* turns this idea on its head, making creative use of the idea of a woman saving a man from the same kind of fate. Cohalan's penchant for attributing life events to luck is seen early on in the film, from the moment he meets Ellen on a train. When he knocks over a salt shaker, he throws a pinch of salt over his shoulder to "show proper respect for the powers of darkness," and pretends to read Ellen's tea leaves, telling her his grandmother, who learned it from an old witch in Ireland, taught him the trick. By contrast, Ellen is a "disbeliever," motivated by facts and reason. However, she is not without emotion, as she feels more sympathy than fear towards Cohalan when she learns that his fiancée was killed in a car accident with him the night before their wedding. Despite rumors of Cohalan's odd reclusive behavior and inability to make mention of Vivian, his dead fiancée, Ellen makes no secret of her feelings toward him, feelings that turn from pity to romance.

Meanwhile, odd circumstances and events surround Cohalan at home and at work. A figurine is found broken, a painting fades overnight, and a rosebush dies, all suddenly and without explanation. He finds his horse's leg inexplicably shattered, though it was confined to a stall, and his beloved dog goes missing, only to be discovered dead near his house. As these incidents begin to take a toll on Cohalan, everyone notices his distracted and even hostile behavior, as his blueprints go missing at the office and he publicly accuses one of Ben's servants of prowling around his house the night his dog was killed. His lecherous and opportunistic co-worker Keith Ferris (John Sutton) comments to Ben that Cohalan is getting "rather absent-minded lately." This information is no surprise to Ben; though he vocally and publicly defended Cohalan, he is behind all these incidents. He even plants the suspicion of Cohalan's insanity in the mind of general practitioner Dr. Hartley, who is all too willing to run with the idea. Hartley latches onto the concept of paranoia, calling it the "delusion of persecution . . . it starts with inability to withstand stresses . . . but if a person is psychotic to begin with, he may start to imagine things. He might even begin to imagine that there's a conspiracy against him. That's when he gets dangerous." But what of the dangers of real persecutions, real conspiracies? These lines are blurred in *noir*, and Cohalan's predicament is a frightening trap—the more he fights against the stresses and accusations he faces, the more suspicious he seems.

And the more Ellen learns about Cohalan and what is happening to him, the more she becomes convinced that he is not insane or paranoid, but rather that someone is truly out to harm him. She tries to reason with him, pointing out that all of his accidents are unusual, commenting that his "bad luck is too bad to be true . . . the impossible can happen, but not over and over again." Ever reasonable and mathematical, she says mathematical odds are too great for him to have undergone six separate accidents, all of them killing something he loved, beginning with Vivian. But Cohalan refuses her help, wanting to chalk it all up to "typical Cohalan" bad luck; he seems afraid to delve too deeply into what might be going on, preferring to assign the blame to a mysterious force that is punishing him for no reason. Even when his house inexplicably burns down, he does not want help from Ellen, who wants to investigate the circumstances of each accident scientifically. And she does, without Cohalan's consent, taking charge of his situation, like a man would protect a woman. She discovers that his painting could have been faded with a sunlamp and that the soil of his dead rosebush was laced with arsenic. Even faced with this evidence, Cohalan will not accept her conjectures or her further investigation, becoming more and more depressed, especially after a second set of blueprints for an important commission disappears.

He begins to internalize the suspicions of others, urging Ellen to protect herself, and not to trust anyone, even him. Having come to believe that someone may indeed trying to hurt him, he stages a suicide attempt in an effort to make himself seem more vulnerable, and he hopes to draw the culprit out into the open, especially so the person does not take a further step to harm Ellen. And shockingly, seemingly kindly mentor and boss, Ben admits that he has been torturing him to avenge the death of his daughter. Ben, turns out to be his nemesis, underscoring the vulnerability of the human psyche when it opens itself up to any kind of trust. In the climactic scene, Ben asks him how he likes his own medicine: "How do you like waking up every morning wishing you were dead?" In a plot pattern common to the "*Gaslight*" *noirs*, Ben freely confesses, believing that no one would believe Jeff even if he told, since he is thought to be insane. This kind of Cassandra-like *noir* torment thereby causes a helpless paralysis in the victim, to be unable to communicate one's own pain, suffering, and danger in a world that would only turn a deaf ear or a dismissive glance.

Though the largest mystery of the film is solved, Ellen provides a final piece of evidence that adds a level of depth to the nightmarish situation. It turns out that it was Keith Ferris, Vivian's lover, and not Jeff who was driving the car on the night that Vivian was killed; therefore, Ben's persecutions were aimed at a man even more innocent than he could have imagined. In an almost "feminine" impulse of self-sacrifice, Jeff never revealed that Vivian had been with Keith in an effort to spare Ben the indignity of Vivian's memory, especially given the fact that Vivian's mother, Ben's former wife had evidently left him years earlier under scandalous circumstances. The enormity of this revelation is reflected in an extreme close-up of Ben's eyes, the camera then pulling back to a close-up of his astonished face. Dazed, he begins to repeat Vivian's name, and starts to talking to her, imagining, as Vivian's face is superimposed on Ellen's, that she is really there. When Ellen tries to run away, Ben says he will kill her first, and Jeff, finally being able to take control of his own destiny and protect the woman he loves, steps in front of her, taking the bullet that Ben fires in his shoulder. Though no psychiatrist emerges to explain Ben's condition any further, Hartley, the substitute psychiatrist, proclaims Ben as "the psychopath from the beginning" but now that he has had "what the psychiatrists call a catharsis—he's brought his troubles out into the open—he'll be all right now . . . in time." As it turns out, Jeff was not insane, and not even unlucky, but rather the victim of the person he perhaps trusted most in the world; only a dogged persistence to uncover buried details can save his life and his sanity, and it is painfully ironic that such a fate befalls one who is fundamentally and altruistically moral and good, qualities that in *noir* are never enough to save one alone.

As we have seen, family members in *film noir* have a unique vantage point from which to victimize others using inducements of insanity. But one has an equally good chance of being victimized in this way by a stranger, if one is unfortunate enough to be in the wrong place and the wrong time, as the only eyewitness to a crime. Roy Rowland's *Witness to Murder* (1954) and Alfred Werker's *Shock* (1946) are prime examples of this phenomenon. In *Witness to Murder*, Cheryl Draper (Barbara Stanwyck) has the unfortunate luck to awaken during a stormy night, only to witness ex-Nazi historian/author Albert Richter (George Sanders) strangling a woman in a building across the street. In a similar scenario to that of *Rear Window* (released that same year), Cheryl sees the murder take place, but cannot get anyone to believe her, and puts herself in danger because of her refusal to believe that she is mistaken. Unlike *Rear Window*, however, the viewer sees the murder committed, so the only mystery is how long Cheryl will be able to survive before being silenced for good. Richter is a powerful adversary—intelligent, genteel, and well-spoken. He effortlessly convinces police lieutenant Larry Mathews (Gary Merrill) and sergeant Eddie Vincent (Jessie White) that no murder took place in his apartment, even taking pains in their presence to "accidentally" tear the curtain that was already torn during his struggle with the young dead woman, whose body he has already hidden in a vacant apartment next door. When Mathews reports back to Cheryl that there is no evidence of a murder, there ensues the first of many scenes in which Cheryl protests her feminine "subjective" eyewitness account against the lack of "objective" evidence able to be procured by the male police authorities.

Instead of merely accepting Mathews' suggestion that she dreamed the whole episode, Cheryl, asserts, "But I saw it!" Mathews counters, "You mean you dreamt you saw it. . . . You had a nightmare and thought you were awake but you weren't. So you saw a murder that didn't take place. It's not uncommon to be fooled by a dream." She tells him that she can tell the difference "between dreaming a thing and seeing it," asserting indignantly, "I'm not a mental case, if you please." However, as might be expected, the more she asserts her sanity and her version of events as true, the more like a "mental case" she sounds. In an effort to reinforce her own convictions, she plays detective, like Ellen Foster, discovering, by pretending to be interested in the vacant apartment next door to Richter, drag marks on the floor and earrings on his desk, which she steals in the hopes they will be evidence that will be believed by the police. But this effort, like almost all of Cheryl's attempts to prove she is correct, will backfire on her, as Richter reports the earrings stolen and Cheryl is nearly arrested for theft. Now Richter knows who his accuser is and begins to systematically rob her of credibility by suggesting that she was not only dreaming, but is actually insane. To Mathews, he comments that Cheryl is a "victim of a compulsion she's not responsible for," adding, "looking at her, it's hard to believe . . . it's obvious she's not well." Richter then begins writing threatening letters to himself, breaking into Cheryl's apartment to use her typewriter, and claiming they were written by her. Richter seems to want extra insurance that the possible eyewitness will be completely discredited, but ironically, his own efforts end up leading to his discovery.

To his credit, and also because he is attracted to Cheryl, Mathews does check up on Richter, almost hoping to find that there is some tangible evidence for her story. When he comes to her apartment early in the case, and she shares with him some of the "peculiar ideas" in Richter's book (such as the quasi-Nietzschean "violence is in the nature of progress. . . . Man is born in pain to give pain or die"), he informs her that Richter was "a minor bigwig in Hitler's army," but that this alone is not enough to make him a murderer. He is worried about her, saying, "I don't like the desperate way you're running after this thing, turning fantasy into reality. It's unhealthy; you're too nice a girl." What Mathews thinks is non-evidence is what makes Cheryl so sure: her own eyes and conviction, as well as the fact that she "feels it." She says that Richter's smile and his eyes "don't go together"—his eyes are calculating—and that since he thinks killing is all right, she's "next in line." Though Cheryl asks about different ways that the scientific evidence might be followed up, Mathews scoffs at her "woman's intuition" because he thinks she is obsessed. Cheryl will not let her own mind be undermined: "You mean you think I'm mentally ill; if you think it, why don't you just say it?" Mathews says he does not mean any such thing, but says, "You could be if you don't face up to the truth"—as if mental illness occurs by letting one's mind wander just a little too much or a little too long. This characterization of mental illness as inherently unpredictable follows the same pattern as any misfortune in *noir*: the most mundane and everyday thoughts or activities can send one spiraling with no warning into destruction. When Cheryl asks Mathews what she should do, he says "Just try to lick this thing . . . lick it before it licks you." But just as one's sheer will can fail when trying to surmount overwhelming obstacles in other aspects of life, Cheryl says she has tried to tell herself that the thing did not happen, only to hear from him that she should try just as hard to prove that it did not happen as she has that it did. Telling Mathews about the letters with which Richter has confronted her only creates more doubt, as she asks whether or not they "could have been written unconsciously." When he says, "It's possible," for the first time, she appears truly doubtful and troubled, as if she could have written the letters but not known it. The seeds of doubt sprouting now, she tells him that Richter told her she should see a doctor and maybe she should.

At the same time that Mathews is skeptical of Cheryl's beliefs, he does everything to try to defend her to his captain who succeeds in getting her committed to the city hospital to undergo "a preliminary medical examination to establish her responsibility." As she fiercely resists, saying they are all against her, once again she seems hysterical. A whirlpool dissolve ends with her in a *Snake Pit*-like observation ward, where her condition is set in contrast to the other occupants: an attempted suicide, an elderly delusional, and an exhibitionist, who advises her, "Don't say anything, especially to the doc. Just agree with him—otherwise, you'll be in the loony bin before you know it." The staff psychiatrist queries her about how often she cries and whether or not she is afraid of the dark, asking her if she "often translates dream images into reality." At this point, Cheryl seems at least outwardly resigned to the fact that she must have written the letters to Richer, although she admits to the doctor that she does not remember writing them. When she asks him if she is "all right" at the end of her interview, he replies noncommittally, "We'll see." The more those outside her tell her that she must be losing her mind, the more Cheryl begins to believe it; she begins to be worn down by forces that will not acknowledge the reality of her perceptions. She asks Mathews if she could really be out of her mind: "There must be something wrong if I wrote those letters. . . . I did write them didn't I?" He responds, "The evidence does point to them, Cheryl. . . . You can go to a doctor and get cured, just like any other kind of sickness." But as much as the *noir* atmosphere tends to the idea of mental illness being the norm, even Cheryl discerns that "it's not like any other kind of sickness." It is worth noting that still, even in the darkest doubt of her own sanity, Cheryl confesses that she still believes she saw the murder and that she did not write the letters, asserting, "It's as if I were two different people, both strangers to each other." Cheryl's fear captures the core existential anxiety found in *film noir*: the ability to consciously exist and yet be a stranger to oneself.

As we have already seen in other "*Gaslight*" *noirs*, the victimizer cannot help but reveal himself to the victim, believing that the specter of insanity will cloak any attempt to incriminate him. When Cheryl sees Richter buying copies of all the newspapers once his victim has been identified, she buys these papers as well and goes to his apartment to confront him. When she is surprised to hear that he admits the murder, he says, "I have nothing to fear from you; you're insane," pointing out that anything she says now would just corroborate the charges of insanity: "They'd put you in an asylum most likely." The undertone of Richter's Nazism comes roaring to the surface, as Cheryl asks him what right he had to kill the young woman: "She had less right to live, and what was she? A creature with whom I amused myself. An insignificant little nobody." Richter is engaged to a wealthy heiress and believes that this newfound wealth will bring him the power to disseminate his poisonous philosophy: "the key for which history awaits, the gospel which may well be the religion of centuries to come . . . on the bones of ranting house-painters, Italian clowns, and Georgian peasants." Full of the impending glory of being greater than Hitler, Mussolini, and Stain combined, Richter starts shouting in German, an act shockingly symbolic of the most villainous tyranny—though we know that he is literally the most immediate and direct threat to Cheryl, the idea of the even greater threat of mental instability or the inability to communicate one's own sanity is ever present.

Cheryl has tried to do everything that a law-abiding, upstanding citizen faced with heinous crime should do: report all incidents and suspicious evidence to the police. But each attempt at such has brought her further and further toward her own peril as each piece of evidence she provides is deemed "circumstantial" and a product of her own "obsession." Such is the case when she arrives one final time at the police station to report Richter's confession, only to be told by Mathews that there is still no proof, and all he wants is "one single thing to go on" besides her guesses to corroborate her story, since he still wants to believe her. At this, Cheryl can only say, "we're lost . . ." in such a resigned manner that she may mean the fate of their love relationship, the fate of the murder case, her own fate, or the fate of the world at large. Devastated, she drives home, hearing Richter's words that there is "nothing to do but end it" echoing in her mind, as she rounds dangerous curves in the dark. Like her worst nightmare, she find Richter waiting for her in her apartment, ready to read her the suicide note that he has composed for her (on her own typewriter, of course) and proceeds to try to orchestrate her suicide. She is able to escape, but her flight seems akin to a bad dream in which one believes she has escaped from a shadowy threat, but keeps ending up in the same treacherous place. Meanwhile, Mathews, bothered by Richter's previous offer to pay for Cheryl's commitment to a sanatorium, ratchets up his investigation for one last try, as he and Vincent comb the dead woman's apartment. They find Richter's book, a title out of place with the apparent pulp and romance novels that the victim had on her bookshelves. This piece of the puzzle, though equally as circumstantial as the numerous pieces that Cheryl uncovered, is suddenly deemed the missing link to the mystery and sends the detectives in hot pursuit of Richter. All end up in the chase for Cheryl, who runs up the stairs of a hollow building under construction and nearly falls to her death before Mathews, in a struggle with Richter, pushes him down into the empty interior of the building. It is fitting that Cheryl's near end and Richter's destruction occur inside the skeleton of an urban high-rise—an outward symbol of modern science and progress, much like psychoanalysis, but an inward shell of danger and destruction.

In *Shock* there is an added layer of psychiatric intrigue as the witness to a murder, Janet Stewart (Anabel Shaw), not only suffers psychological trauma upon watching psychiatrist Dr. Richard Cross (Vincent Price) murder his wife, but also becomes subject to his "treatment" following the incident. The circumstances surrounding Janet being at the wrong place at the wrong time also set the tone as one of post-war anxiety, as Janet is to meet her husband, returning army lieutenant Paul Stewart (Frank Latimore) at a hotel. This would normally be a cause for celebration, except that she "thought he was dead for two years," and even now still does not know "if he's hurt or what." The fact that it gets later and later and Stewart still does not show up only increases her anxiety. The film runs only a few minutes before framing itself in the psychoanalytic world, as Janet falls asleep waiting and has a dream with typical symbols of anxiety: in a swirling smoke, she hears someone banging on a door and her husband calling her name, asking to be let in. She runs toward the door, but not only does it just get farther and farther away, when she finally gets to it, the door has also become enormous, with a huge doorknob. After struggling to open it, she emerges into a hallway to find nothing but the echo of her husband's voice saying he cannot find her. It is in this distraught state, perhaps believing that her husband will never return to her, that she awakens to discover neighbor Cross arguing with his wife about a divorce, and then bludgeoning her to death with a candlestick when she threatens the public exposé of his infidelities. Janet's long-awaited reunion with her husband becomes instead an occasion of panic, as he finds her in the hotel room the next morning in shock, wide-eyed and catatonic. Doane argues that the shocking effect of this sight "suggests itself as a microcosm of the cinema-spectator relation"[6]; as we have seen, the experience of the viewer often mirrors that of the mentally unstable character in *noir*, drawing the audience into the psychosis.

Though there are numerous mental health professionals and psychiatric treatments depicted in the film, the view of insanity is still seen as a mysterious enigma. The hotel house doctor cannot provide much insight into Janet's condition, believing it to be due to "some sort of shock," but noting: "The mind's a strange instrument. What affects me may not bother you in the slightest. The workings of the mind depend on so many things inside, as well as outside. You can't make hard and fast rules." One would think that the kind of doctor needed for her case, a "nerve specialist, a psychiatrist," such as Dr. Cross, who happens to live right next door, would help shed some light on the subject, but even Cross tells Stewart that "the mind is a delicate fragile thing . . . it's almost as intangible as faith"—which is what Cross says the lieutenant needs now. Once again, the introduction of psychiatric framework in *noir* simultaneously undercuts its efficacy, as faith seems just as important here in the ultimate health of the patient. When Cross tells Stewart that he can no longer think of Janet "as she was," the ex-POW veteran husband thus is depicted as returning, not to face the struggle of the memories of his own mental trauma, but rather his wife's subhuman state, as if she is an uncanny doppelganger of the wife he left behind. The post-ward situation of the Stewarts highlights the many subtle anxieties faced by war's after-effects—the temporary "mental illness" of Janet symbolizes the loss of human connection caused by war separation and the changes in identity that occur, making the most secure relationships foreign and unfamiliar. Furthermore, the ministrations of the type of doctor who is supposed to be uniquely qualified to treat such cases cannot be trusted, as he is a criminal himself. When Cross learns Janet's proximity to his own room and the estimated time of her collapse, he realizes that she could have seen him, and quickly repairs her to the constant supervision at his sanatorium in the country, where he will do everything he can to exacerbate, rather than cure, her mental trauma.

Cross, in contrast to some of the other nefarious *noir* psychiatrists, is portrayed as a complex character rather than a one-dimensional villain. He seems to kill his wife on impulse, rather than premeditation, and is periodically wracked with guilt about both the murder and what he is doing to Janet. His nurse and lover, Elaine (Lynn Bari), is an amoral femme fatale who spurs him along on this avalanche of misdeeds. Elaine tells him that Janet will only "talk if you let her," and this encourages him to use a variety of psychiatric treatments meant to break down mental barriers for healing, first to find out what she knows and then as an avenue to attempt to plant false memories in her mind. The initial treatments involve scopolamine, an anesthetic similar to sodium pentothal, which encourages free thinking and talking. In a series of disturbing sessions, Cross tries to unhinge Janet further by making her imagine that the killer she saw is trying to kill her and tries to suggest that she wants to keep these upsetting images hidden and forgotten. Cross and Elaine are also unexpectedly aided by the frightening near-attack of another patient on Janet one stormy night, and to their delight, she seems to confuse him with the actual killer she saw before. Elaine is jubilant, telling Cross how fortunate it is that the episode happened, because "now she can talk her head off, and no one will believe her," and they can have her committed for good. As we have seen in previous *noirs*, Janet, the only witness to the truth, is ironically the one least believed. Unfortunately for Cross, there are others watching him and watching out for Janet—for instance, his previous mentor, Dr. Hartley (Charles Trowbridge), who advises him to reduce Janet's sedation, and who thinks there was something else besides her wifely anxiety that brought on the attack. Stewart had called Hartley in for a second opinion, and he continually questions the treatment she is getting with Cross. When Stewart queries Stevens (Michael Dunne), Cross' innocent associate, Stevens reassures him by saying that the sanitarium is the best and that Dr. Cross is "tops." He adds that there are numerous other treatments that may be tried on Janet, such as "electric therapy, insulin shock." Stewart acts surprised at this suggestion, telling Stevens "they use that in the Army on guys who . . . well, they're 'tops.'" Stevens replies, "Well, sure they do. That's because it often helps." As we have seen, the psychiatric treatments pioneered in the military began to filter into civilian life, and serve in this scene to give credibility to Stewart's doubts. But the play on the slang use of "tops" reinforces the unpredictable nature of mental disturbance—not only is Cross thought to be "tops" in his field as a psychiatrist, but he is also a little "tops" and perhaps in need of his own medicine.

Compared to the other "*Gaslight*" *noirs*, Janet is not a character at the forefront of the film's action, almost serving more as an instrument or pawn to the more active character of Cross. She is sedated or catatonic much of the time, and it is Cross' reactions to her various mental states on which the film focuses. She is in the same kind of danger as the other victims, facing either asylum commitment or death, however, and when she does regain consciousness, she is not hesitant to forcefully maintain that Cross is the man that she saw kill his wife. Typically, the more she tries to escape and assert her sanity, the more she is seen as insane. When Cross tries a different tack, trying to convince her that she is insane, rather than simply mistaken, he shows her a newspaper that reports his wife's death as occurring only a week ago, and tries to convince her that she has been confined for three weeks. He tells her that she is beginning to lose her mind, that her "delusion" has been a "vivid dream and [she] must fight these dreams" or else they will become worse. Like Cheryl Draper, she stubbornly resists, and it becomes clear to Cross that, especially now with the district attorney sniffing around the case, he will have to take more drastic measures. He begins to lay the groundwork by communicating the "worsening" of Janet's condition to Stewart and requesting permission to administer insulin shock therapy. As explained earlier, this early psychiatric treatment involved administration of high doses of insulin to induce coma-like states, designed to jolt the mind into normalcy. Cross' real intention is to administer the course of injections, giving her a fatal overdose for the last one. Janet Walker points out that Cross' intentions, objected to by numerous psychiatrists when *Shock* was released, imply that "psychiatry can rewrite truth itself and, moreover, that psychiatric treatments may be invasive and inappropriate."[7] When Stewart queries him about the certainty of effectiveness, Cross once again undermines the credibility of his own profession in order to protect himself: "I'm neither a miracle man nor a prophet, Lieutenant. If medicine were an exact science and not an art, I might be able to tell you." And again psychiatry itself, though meant to be a realization of progress in the study of the mind, here is reduced to the subjective characterization of aesthetic sensibility. As noted above, because Stewart has seen this technique work in the army, he consents. However, also because he has seen it work in the army, he is highly suspicious after three injections do not bring about any change in her condition. Janet is still insisting that she saw Cross murder his wife with a candlestick and is unwilling, in her rare lucid moments, to accept any other alternative.

Even in the final moments of his impending murder of Janet, Cross is tormented by guilt, and despite the diabolical Elaine's urging that "they can hint or guess all they want, but without her they have nothing," Cross, upon giving Janet the final and fatal injection, decides that he wants to save her by giving her dextrose. Elaine's frantic struggle to stop him ("it's her life or ours," she says) ends up with Cross strangling her too—in effect, a perverse act of righteousness, as he destroys the force that encouraged him to kill in the first place. Though Dr. Harvey and Stewart arrive in what would have been the nick of time to save Janet, Cross is about to save her anyway. This is an unusual redemptive turn of events for a "*Gaslight*" *noir*, but one that emphasizes the pervasive psychological torment of all characters, not just the victim. A resigned Cross, like *Double Indemnity*'s mortally wounded Walter Neff, records in his Dictaphone that in the case of Janet Stewart, "Dr. Harvey completed the treatment successfully and the case is closed." His slow and deliberate removal of his white coat for his coat and hat before being led away by the D.A. underscores his temptation and fall, his psychiatric power gone horribly wrong as it nearly sent an innocent women into a spiralling threat of mental illness and death.

Perhaps the most similar *noir* to *Gaslight* is Douglas Sirk's *Sleep My Love* (1948), in which wealthy heiress, Allison Courtland (Claudette Colbert), is systematically drugged in order to convince her that she is going insane, and ultimately, to lead to her own suicide. The mastermind of the scheme is her husband, architect Richard Courtland (Don Ameche). The opening sequence of the film appears to be chilling evidence that Allison is losing her mind, as she awakens on a train, startled to find herself there and asserting that she had fallen asleep that night in her own bed. Like George Steele in *Crack-Up*, Allison finds herself on a vehicle speeding into the unknown, with a blank future and an unstable past. When a doctor on board asks her how many sleeping pills she had taken, she proclaims that she never takes sleeping pills, only "hot chocolate" every night to help her sleep. The fact that the porter and another passenger corroborate that they saw her get on the train at the station is unnerving to her, and she is particularly shaken to discover that she has a gun in her purse. Similar to the experience of Paula Anton in *Gaslight*, Allison's husband is beginning to construct an alternate universe in which she will reside, one in which she has no control over her impulses or actions. Diane Waldman argues that these kinds of films "dramatize the attempts of a patriarchal order to achieve hegemony over feminine perception and interpretation. In these films the husbands are systematically attempting to drive their wives insane. . .and in general, attempting to negate their experience."[8] Allison, subjected to drugs and powerful suggestion, will soon no longer be able to own her own psyche, as she becomes continually in doubt of what she sees, hears, and feels. On her way back to New York City from Boston, where the train finally ended up, Allison converses with the policeman sent to escort her, asking him if he thinks she is "daffy." Though he says no, he admits, "Some of the nicest people you ever took a gander at suddenly go daffy and make chop suey out of their best friends with a meat ax." Soon enough the viewer will have no doubt that Allison's delusions are externally manufactured, but the mood of the film—indeed, what makes it a *noir*—suggests that mental instability can be as ordinary and impossible to avoid as the common cold.

"Dick" Courtland, like many of the predatory, insanity-inducing *noir* figures we have seen, is intelligent and smooth, able to convince outsiders of the version of reality he is trying to construct. When Allison goes "missing" on the train, he calls the police and reports her absence, only "reluctantly" admitting to them that "this has happened before." In reality, Dick has a seductive and demanding mistress, Daphne (Hazel Brooks), for whom he is trying not only to break free from his marriage, but also to secure his wife's fortune. Thus, he has formulated a plan with an accomplice photographer, Charles Vernay (George Coulouris), to destroy Allison's sanity. After the incident on the train, the time is ripe for Dick to suggest a visit from a psychiatrist, especially after he leads Allison to believe that she shot him as she left the house that night. However, even given all of these strange circumstances, Allison protests, saying she is "not neurotic or maladjusted or unbalanced," and that if there is anything wrong with her, unless she can work it out by herself, she is not going to get better. This independent mindset may undermine the potentiality of psychoanalysis, but it makes a powerful statement about the self-determination of a modern woman, who, in contrast to the turn-of-the-century Paula Anton does not rely entirely on the will of her husband. Nevertheless, Allison consents to see the eminent Dr. Rhinehart, but what she does not know is that Dick has asked Vernay to impersonate the doctor for their initial meeting. Allison explains to the false psychiatrist that though she started walking in her sleep two months ago, she has "always been perfectly healthy and happy, in fact almost monotonously so." When she tells him about the train and "admits" she shot her husband, he plants further anxiety in her mind by suggesting, "Who knows what you may do the next time?" When she says there would not be a next time, he says, "How can you be sure? How can you be sure of anything?" This dilemma is, of course, the ultimate existential crisis depicted in *film noir*—the absolute uncertainty of anything previously deemed certain: government, society, family, one's own mind. He further heightens her anxiety by not telling her what her diagnosis is, only pretending to phone her husband and reporting that he must see him right away, and that "it's very serious." When the "doctor" then seems to disappear without a trace, Allison phones her husband's office only to discover that he had left a half an hour ago, and once again must question everything that she thought has occurred, especially when Dick appears moments later with the "real" Dr. Rhinehart (Ralph Morgan) and "cannot understand" her stories about another doctor coming to the house.

Allison's savior does not come in the form of a Scotland Yard detective, but in Bruce Elcott (Robert Cummings), the boyfriend of one of her childhood friends. He takes an immediate liking to Allison and is all too happy to be her escort when Dick begs out of a social engagement the night after she is traumatized by the psychiatrist incidents. Like other *Gaslight* victimizers, Dick tries to keep Allison as isolated as possible from public scrutiny, except when it might help his scheme. But Allison rejoices in attending the wedding of Elcott's Chinese brother Jimmie (Keye Luke), getting tipsy on melonskin wine, and confessing to Elcott that people like Dick are "all tightened up inside—can't talk, can't even feel. They don't have a happy time." Unbeknownst to Allison, Dick is indeed having a "happy time" with Daphne, as he gifts her with an expensive emerald bracelet and assures her that "everything has to be very carefully worked out," but she will get everything she wants if she is patient. Meanwhile, Allison comes to feel very safe with Elcott, which is why, upon returning home and finding the fake psychiatrist Vernay in the living room again, she screams and runs out to get Elcott before he drives away. Of course, when they go back in, there is no one there, only Dick, who, at his reasonable best, sends Allison into a frenzy by asserting that no one could have been there either time. He then endeavors to gain Bruce's sympathy by telling him about how sometimes Allison seems so normal, and then has "hallucinations." For no particular reason, except that he is attracted to her, Bruce distrusts this explanation and returns to the house, only to find Allison about to jump from her balcony and saves her at the last second.

We discover that Dick is drugging Allison's nightly hot chocolate and then stealing into her bedroom once the drug has taken effect to hypnotically suggest to her that she is being pursued, in an effort to get her to commit suicide. Once the character of Rhinehart—both real and fake—has been introduced, this provides an increased ability for Dick to plant frightening ideas in her receptive mind. In her waking state, Allison still protests that there was a real impersonator in the house, and Dick humors her by letting her report to the police, knowing that they will doubt her too, as police detective Strake (Raymond Burr) agrees with Dick that there is no point in swearing out an arrest because "she is delusional." However, Allison believes that not only is Dick on her side, but also that she is taking steps to alleviate her condition, and so she resists when Elcott, based on his own amateur detective work, suggests that she not "take anything to drink in the evening for a while." Like the comfortable and secure relationship she has come to know with her husband, her nightly ritual of hot chocolate is something that Allison cannot accept as a sudden threat. Still, she has become suspicious enough to refuse her chocolate that night, then seeming to herself to be a heartless doubter when Dick drinks a cup himself. What Allison does not see is Dick stumbling around his own room after leaving hers, clearly drugged to the point of unconscious collapse. This charade makes it much easier for him to get Allison to accept a drugged glass of brandy the next night, and thus orchestrate the final push for his plan. He has arranged for Vernay to appear again, but this time, leads Allison to kill him in her stupor, thereby freeing himself from everyone associated with his plot. As before, while Allison is sleeping, he begins to whisper to her, "You must get up now . . . that man . . . he's come to kill you . . . he's waiting downstairs," as he gives her a gun and follows her downstairs, going so far as to grab her trigger hand and shooting the gun at Vernay himself. What Dick does not count on is Vernay surviving and coming after him, exposing all the details of their scheme to Allison. Like Cheryl Draper, Allison flees to the highest point she can reach, up the stairs of her house, as Vernay falls to his death through the greenhouse skylight through the hollow interior in the main staircase. The Courtland home, once perhaps a place of security and refuge, has become a terrifying death trap of suspicion and murder. At the center is Allison, who only narrowly escapes destruction at the hands of a familiar, and therefore particularly insidious influence—one that can only be broken by a chance connection with a savior stranger. The film itself, like other "*Gaslight*" *noirs*—indeed, *noirs* in general—becomes a nightmare from which it is difficult if not impossible to awaken.

The *Gaslight noirs* encapsulate what is most telling and terrifying about the influence of psychiatry on *noir*. *Noir* paints a picture of a world where normalcy, as we might have known it, or hoped to imagine it, ceases to exist—where the things we most depend on as human beings fail to have any comfort or power. Even in the most horrifying crisis, one's own mind should be a firmament on which to depend; however, *noir* shows this to be a crumbling illusion, fraught with unexpected inconsistency and danger, from loss of memory to loss of control. The structure of these *noirs* themselves are unstable, drawing the viewer into the same kinds of doubt and uncertainty depicted on the screen and showing only enough of possible scientific ameliorations to prove that such efforts are largely ineffective and meaningless at best, and only a new way to inflict psychic pain and torture at worst. The unique influence of psychiatry on the films in the *noir* series made them able to depict the painful realities of post-war existence, the devastating turning point and loss of innocence in the consciousness of American society from which it could not retreat.

Notes

1. Sylvia Harvey, "Woman's Place: The Absent Family of *Film Noir*," in *Women in Film Noir*, ed. E. Ann Kaplan (London: BFI Publishing, 1998), 36.
2. Andrew Dickos, *Street With No Name: A History of the Classic American Film Noir*. Lexington: U of Kentucky P, 2002. 146.
3. Foster Hirsch, *The Dark Side of the Screen: Film Noir* (New York: Da Capo Press, 1983), 182.
4. Mary Ann Doane, *Femmes Fatales: Feminism, Film Theory, Psychoanalysis*, (New York: Routledge, 1991), 103.
5. Dickos, 156.
6. Mary Ann Doane, "The Clinical Eye: Medical Discourses in the 'Woman's Film' of the 1940's," *Poetics Today* 6, no.1/2 (1985): 221.
7. Janet Walker, *Couching Resistance: Women, Film, and Psychoanalytic Psychiatry*, (Minneapolis: University of Minnesota Press, 1993), 141-42.
8. Diane Waldman, "'At Last I Can Tell It to Someone!': Feminine Point of View and Subjectivity in the Gothic Romance Film of the 1940s" *Cinema Journal* 23, no. 2 (Winter 1984): 34.

Bibliography

Biesen, Sheri Chinen. *Blackout: World War II and the Origins of Film Noir*. Baltimore: Johns Hopkins University Press, 2005.

Bogdanovich, Peter. *Who the Devil Made It*. New York: Knopf, 1977.

Borde, Raymond, and Etienne Chaumeton. *A Panorama of American Film Noir: 1941-1953*. Translated by Paul Hammond. San Francisco: City Lights Books, 2002.

Boucher, Arline Britton. "They Learn to Live Again." *Saturday Evening Post* May 27, 1944, 20; 105-106.

Boyd, David. "The Parted Eye: *Spellbound* and Psychoanalysis." *Senses of Cinema*, May 2000. http://www.sensesofcinema.com/contents/00/6/spellbound.html.

Brandell, Jerrold R. "Eighty Years of Dream Sequences: A Cinematic Journey Down Freud's 'Royal Road." *American Imago* 61, no. 1 (2004): 59-76.

Brill, Lesley. *The Hitchcock Romance: Love and Irony in Hitchcock's Films*. Princeton: Princeton University Press, 1988.

Britton, Andrew. "Hitchcock's *Spellbound*: Text and Counter-Text." *Cineaction!* 3/4 (Winter 1986): 72-83.

Brown, Royal S. "Hitchcock's *Spellbound*: Jung Versus Freud." *Film/Psychology Review* 4 (Winter-Spring 1980): 35-58.

Burnham, John C. "The Influence of Psychoanalysis Upon American Culture." In *American Psychoanalysis: Origins and Development*, edited by Jacques M. Quen and Eric T. Carlson, New York: Brunner/Mazel, 1978.

Christopher, Nicholas. *Somewhere in the Night: Film Noir and the American City*. New York: Free Press, 1997.

Crichton, Kyle. "Repairing War-Cracked Minds." *Colliers*, Sept. 23, 1944, 22-23; 54.

Cowie, Elizabeth. "*Film Noir* and Women." In *Shades of Noir: A Reader*, edited by Joan Copjec, 121-165. London: Verso, 1993.

Deutsch, Albert. "Dramatic Effects of 'Truth Serum.'" *Science Digest*, October 1946.

Dickos, Andrew. *Street With No Name: A History of the Classic American Film Noir*. Lexington: University of Kentucky Press, 2002.

Dimendberg, Edward. *Film Noir and the Spaces of Modernity*. Cambridge: Harvard University Press, 2004.

Doane, Mary Ann. *Femmes Fatales: Feminism, Film Theory, Psychoanalysis*, New York: Routledge, 1991.

———. "The Clinical Eye: Medical Discourses in the 'Woman's Film' of the 1940's." *Poetics Today* 6, no. 1/2 (1985): 205-227.

Douglass, Wayne J. "The Criminal Psychopath as Hollywood Hero." *Journal of Popular Film and Television* 8, no. 4 (1981): 30-39.

Durgnat, Raymond. "Paint It Black: The Family Tree of *Film Noir*." In *Film Noir Reader*, edited by Alain Silver and James Ursini, 37-51. New York: Limelight Editions, 1996.

Fearing, Franklin. "The Screen Discovers Psychiatry." *Hollywood Quarterly* 1, no. 1 (Jan. 1946): 154-58.

Fine, Reuben. *A History of Psychoanalysis*. New York: Columbia University Press, 1979.

Fishbein, Leslie. "*The Snake Pit* (1948): The Sexist Nature of Sanity." *American Quarterly* 31, no.5 (Winter 1979): 641-55.

Fleming, Michael, and Roger Marvell. *Images of Madness: The Portrayal of Insanity in the Feature Film*. Rutherford, NJ: Fairleigh Dickinson University Press, 1985.

Freedman, Jonathan. "From *Spellbound* to *Vertigo*: Alfred Hitchcock and Therapeutic Culture in America." In *Hitchcock's America*, edited by Jonathan Freedman and Richard Millington, 77-95. New York: Oxford University Press, 1999.

Freud, Sigmund. "The Uncanny." In *The Standard Edition of the Complete Psychological Works of Sigmund Freud*. Translated by James Strachey. Vol. 17. London: Hogarth, 1957. 218-252.

Fuery, Patrick. *Madness and Cinema: Psychoanalysis, Spectatorship, and Culture*. New York: Palgrave Macmillan, 2004.

Gabbard, Glen O. "The Cinematic Psychiatrist." *Psychiatric Times* 16, no. 7 (1999), http://www.psychiatrictimes.com/p990714.html.

Gabbard, Glen O., and Krin Gabbard. *Psychiatry and the Cinema*. 2nd Edition. Washington, D.C.: American Psychiatric Press, 1999.

Grinker, Roy Richard, and John P. Spiegel. *Men Under Stress*. New York: McGraw-Hill 1963.

Grob, Gerald N. *The Mad Among Us: A History of the Care of America's Mentally Ill*. New York: Free Press, 1994.

Hale, Nathan G. Jr. *The Rise and Crisis of Psychoanalysis in the United States: Freud and the Americans, 1917-1985*. New York: Oxford University Press, 1995.

Harvey, Sylvia "Woman's Place: The Absent Family of *Film Noir*." In *Women in Film Noir*, edited by E. Ann Kaplan, 35-46. London: BFI Publishing, 1998.

Hirsch, Foster. *The Dark Side of the Screen: Film Noir*. New York: Da Capo Press, 1983.

Holland, Norman N. "Psychiatry in Pselluloid." *The Atlantic Monthly* 203 (1959): 105-107.

House, Rebecca R. "Night of the Soul: American Film Noir." *Studies in Popular Culture* 9, no. 1 (1986): 61-83.

Koepnick, Lutz. "Doubling the Double: Robert Siodmak in Hollywood," *New German Critique* 89. (Spring-Summer 2003): 81-104.

Krutnik, Frank. *In a Lonely Street: Film Noir, Genre, and Masculinity*. New York: Routledge, 1991.

Kubie, Lawrence S. "Psychiatry and the Films." *Hollywood Quarterly* 2, no. 2 (Jan. 1947): 113-117.

Lippe, Richard. "At the Margins of *Film Noir*: Preminger's *Angel Face*." In *Film Noir Reader*, edited by Alain Silver and James Ursini, 161-175. New York: Limelight Editions, 1996.

Lyons, Arthur. *Death on the Cheap: The Lost B Movies of Film Noir*. New York: Da Capo Press, 2000.

Maltby, Richard. "The Politics of the Maladjusted Text." In *The Movie Book of Film Noir*, edited by Ian Cameron, 39-48. London: Studio Vista, 1992.

Manon, Hugh. "X-Ray Visions: Radiography, Chiaroscuro, and the Fantasy of Unsuspicion in *Film Noir*," *Film Criticism* 32, no. 2 (Winter 2007/2008): 2-29.

Maxfield, James F. *The Fatal Woman: Sources of Male Anxiety in American Film Noir, 1941-1991*. Madison: Fairleigh Dickinson University Press, 1996.

Morris, Christopher D. *The Hanging Figure: On Suspense and the Films of Alfred Hitchcock*. Westport, CT: Praeger, 2002.

Mulvey, Laura. "Visual Pleasure and Narrative Cinema." *Screen* 16, no. 3 (Autumn 1975): 6-18.

Oliver, Kelly, and Benigno Trigo. *Noir Anxiety*. Minneapolis: University of Minnesota Press, 2003.

Palmer, R. Barton. *Hollywood's Dark Cinema: The American Film Noir*. New York: Twayne, 1994.

Pelizzon, Penelope, and Nancy West. "'A Perfect Double Down to the Last Detail': Photography and the Identity of *Film Noir*." *Post Script* 22, no. 3 (Summer 2003): 34-35.

Polan, Dana. *Power and Paranoia: History, Narrative, and the American Cinema, 1940-1950*. New York: Columbia University Press, 1986.

Pomerance, Murray. *An Eye for Hitchcock*. New Brunswick: Rutgers University Press, 2004.

Pratt, Ray. *Projecting Paranoia: Conspiratorial Visions in American Film*. Lawrence: University of Kansas Press, 2001.

Rabkin, Lesley. "The Celluloid Couch: Psychiatrists in American Films." *Psychocultural Review* 3 (Spring 1979): 73-89.

Reid, David, and Jayne L. Walker. "Strange Pursuit: Cornell Woolrich and the Abandoned City of the Forties." In *Shades of Noir: A Reader*, edited by Joan Copjec, 57-96. London: Verso, 1993.

Renov, Michael. *Hollywood's Wartime Woman: Representation and Ideology*. Ann Arbor: UMI Research Press, 1988.

Schneider, Irving. "The Psychiatrist in the Movies: The First Fifty Years." In *The Psychoanalytic Study of Literature*, edited by Joseph Reppen and Maurice Charney, 53-67. Hillsdale, NJ: The Analytic Press, 1985.

Semarne, Veda. "*The Snake Pit*: A Woman's Serpentine Journey Toward (W) holeness." *Literature/Film Quarterly* 22, no.3 (1994): 144-50.

Shadoian, Jack. *Dreams & Dead Ends: The American Gangster Film*. Second Edition. Oxford: Oxford University Press, 2003.

Siclier, Jacques. "Misogyny in *Film Noir*." In *Perspectives on Film Noir*, edited by R. Barton Palmer, 66-75. New York: G.K. Hall & Co., 1996.

Sward, Keith. "Boy and Girl Meet Neurosis." *The Screen Writer* 4, no. 3 (Sept. 1948): 8-10, 24-26.

Telotte, J.P. "Siodmak's Phantom Women and *Noir* Narrative." *Film Criticism* 11, no. 3 (Spring 1987): 1-10.

———. *Voices in the Dark: The Narrative Patterns of* Film Noir. Urbana: University of Illinois Press, 1989.

———. "Voices from the Deep: Film Noir as Psychodrama." In *Film Noir Reader 4*, edited by Alain Silver and James Ursini, 145-159. New York: Limelight Editions, 2004.

Thomas, Deborah. "How Hollywood Deals with the Deviant Male." In *The Movie Book of Film Noir*, edited by Ian Cameron, 59-70. London: Studio Vista, 1992.

Time. "Spit it Out, Soldier." Sept. 13, 1943.

Truffaut, François. *Hitchcock*. Revised Edition. Translated by Helen G. Scott. New York: Simon and Schuster, 1984.

Tuska, Jon. *Dark Cinema: American* Film Noir *in Cultural Perspective*. Westport: Greenwood Press, 1984.

Waldman, Diane. "'At Last I Can Tell It to Someone!': Feminine Point of View and Subjectivity in the Gothic Romance Film of the 1940s" *Cinema Journal* 23, no. 2 (Winter 1984): 29-40.

Walker, Janet. *Couching Resistance: Women, Film, and Psychoanalytic Psychiatry* Minneapolis: University of Minnesota Press, 1993.

———. "Hollywood, Freud and the Representation of Women." in *Home is Where the Heart Is: Studies in Melodrama and the Woman's Film*, edited by Christine Gledhill, 197-214. London: BFI, 1987.

Walker, Michael. "*Film Noir*: Introduction." *The Movie Book of Film Noir*, edited by Ian Cameron, 8-38. London: Studio Vista, 1992.

Watson, Robert. "Crack-Up." *Film Monthly* 3, no. 6 August 12, 2001. http://www.filmmonthly.com/Noir/Articles/CrackUp/CrackUp.html.

Wickware, Francis Sill. "Psychoanalysis." *Life*, February 1947.

Williams, Tony. "The Naturalist Horizons of *Nightmare Alley* (1947)." *Excavatio* 22, no. 1-2 (2007): 121-37.

Index

About the Author

Marlisa Santos is an associate professor and director of the Division of Humanities in the Farquhar College of Arts and Sciences at Nova Southeastern University in Fort Lauderdale, Florida. She has published essays on film in numerous anthologies, and her areas of research and teaching include *film noir*, classic film studies, and food and film.